"LIBERALS" AND THE CONSTITUTION

*An inquiry as to how far our
political philosophy has moved to the left.*

"Liberals"
and the Constitution

By HENRY PLOWDEEPER [pseud.]
(Spitsbergen, Henry Essing)

**Published by Liberty and
Freedom Press**

Suite 404
1311 G Street N.W.
Washington, D.C.

Copyright 1955

By H. E. Spitsbergen, LL.M.

No part of this book may be reproduced in any
manner whatsoever without written permission, except in the case of brief quotations embodied in
critical articles and reviews. For information address
Liberty and Freedom Press.

JC
251
.S7

DEDICATED

TO

MY FATHER AND MOTHER,

God-fearing, Hard-working, Humble, Honest, Honest
enough to recognize that economic security disappears
when too many voters become dependent upon government for food, shelter and jobs.

Alma College Library
Alma, Michigan

CONTENTS

CONTENTS

SUMMARY

"It's Later than you Think."

SUMMARY

THIS outline of government was undertaken because
citizens have again been misled into supporting economic
structures which, if the past has any significance, will
bring them poverty, oppression and distress, instead of
the hoped for economic security. Those who do the
misleading, following an ancient practice, call themselves
Liberals, although they are advocating more and more
governmental authority.

Citizens are easily misled in these matters because
they do not give sufficient weight to the fact that political
leaders are *human beings* and, therefore, naturally, enthusiastic about situations which increase their power.
It should be expected, therefore, that they will recommend government controls, as such a course increases
their power, their security! But it also creates a Frankenstein of political machinery which no human being can
manage. However, the urge for power (self-interest)
makes the "liberal" feel, although it has never been done
before, that he can make such machinery produce abundance and freedom instead of the terrorizing fear and
want that it engenders in Europe.

But the reverse is bound to occur as that kind of
government forces too many improper relationships between the citizen and his government. This is so because
it requires that sovereign power be used in too many instances or circumstances. As sovereign power is not financially responsible for its conduct, it must, to avoid these
relationships, be substantially restricted in its authority.
That is especially true with respect to ownership of property and the distribution of jobs, food and shelter, at
home or abroad—an elementary principle of government,
but a most important one. It is the basis of the Constitution.

Nevertheless, the "Liberals" insist that the citizen give to them more power over jobs, food, shelter and property than any potentate ever exercised. In view of the distrust of business men, one must wonder how a "Liberal" can repose so much confidence in a human being who is to exercise sovereign power—a power under which he is not financially liable for mistakes, may avoid investigation under cover of public necessity, and may order the last man to the altar? The underlying objective of free enterprise, as conceived by the Forefathers, was to avoid such a dangerous situation. It, therefore, is LIBERAL with authority for those *who have to pay in money for their mistakes.*

The confidence of the "Liberal" in his form of government is based on these premises: human nature has changed so much that political leaders may be trusted with any amount of power; American leaders will not react to power in the unfortunate manner that the Russian leaders do; the ballot will keep them from going too far to the left; Americans are too smart to be fooled like the Germans or the Russians; so many other nations have accepted government control that it is necessary for the United States to do so; that a government official may be trusted with power because he is not spurred by a profit motive; that a businessman's profit motive makes him untrustworthy.

On such fallacies and premises the "Liberal" assures the citizens that his way, notwithstanding its similarity to the Russian form of government, will bring abundance to all with the minimum of effort.

They present their fallacies so effectively that even leading industrialists, prominent clergymen and well-informed statesmen openly push for "planned" economy. They are ready to abandon the constitutional protections for private property and accept in the "name of freedom" government control of the means of production only a little short of what the Russians practice. It is probable that the fallacy which deceives most people is the one that points to the sixty-million jobs, the wide authority of labor unions and the thriving corporations as evidence that all is well.

The citizen would not be led astray so often if every day he repeated: a government official is not to be trusted too much because he is driven by a *political power motive* (urge); is not financially responsible for his conduct; does not have to pay in money for his mistakes, and is in a position to say to the citizen, "go to war, work *or* starve, work *and* starve." And the citizen should repeat with particular emphasis: when government is tied into business as it is today, an economic collapse results in collapse of the government, which means that government bonds will be worthless, and that the hate of the disappointed and distressed citizen will be directed toward his government instead of toward a private citizen or corporation as is the case in free enterprise; that government of that character *cannot avoid creating concentration camps, restricting religion, and stimulating blood purges and war;* and that so long as war is frequently occurring, poverty and distress, fear and want, will prevail *and make a cruel jest of all promises of* the "Liberals" regarding security, freedom of speech, short terms of office, recognition of religion, and independent courts and legislators.

It should be obvious that the greatest danger to democracy (public welfare) does not arise from the communists who are advocating equalitarianism—everybody the same amount of food, shelter, wages and comforts. The foes of public welfare are the "under-cover communists" who claim that free enterprise, private ownership of the means of production, can be properly protected under the political management of business as proposed by the "Liberals".

The situation can be summed up by saying that two ideologies are contending for supremacy: one, the Russian or European way, well represented in the United States, which teaches that man will find freedom from want when he submits to full government control—surrenders most of his rights to own property and bestows upon government the control or ownership of the means of production; the other, the American way which emphasizes the right of the citizen to own property, especially the means of production. It is the confusion about these two divergent conceptions of government which disturbs the world under threat of the sword. It raises the question of how far can government regulations be utilized before they defeat their purpose—public welfare; or how much freedom can there be in private ownership of property or business?

It may be assumed that all are sincere in the quest for the structure which will produce the maximum of the desirable with the minimum of hardships. However, it is not private ownership of property (profit) which causes the sweat, tears and blood of the innocent and weak in maintaining a civilization. It is the swift, unrelenting, heart-breaking, nerve-rending, never-ending tasks involved in creating a structure with ships, railroads, farms, highways, cities, homes, children, preachers, doctors, lawyers, musicians, philosophers and statesmen—all of which to maintain under any kind of government, demands the uttermost, during peacetime or wartime.

Worthwhile adjustments can be made when leaders become honest enough to admit that civilizations are maintained with blood, sweat and tears: the tears of the weak, the inadequate, the ignorant and the frightened. There is no way to eliminate much of their terror, distress and agony. Economic structures which emphasize the right of individuals to own property, especially the means of production—free enterprise—constitutional government—have afforded them the greatest measure of benefits and protection against misery and want.

Out of the confusion and welter of the present days three schools of thought have developed. One is that by *government planning* an economic structure can be kept in high gear and avoid depressions. Of the other two, one teaches that a collapse is unavoidable, and that when it comes the thrifty should be prepared to invest. The other teaches that when a collapse overtakes the government planning programs, absolute government control must be the result and, consequently, free enterprise destroyed; or, no sudden collapse, but a slower movement of drifting into permanent economic distress for two-thirds of the people.

"LIBERALS" and the RUSSIAN CONSTITUTION

KEY PROPOSITIONS
FOR THE FIRST CHAPTER

THE glamour of the Russian idea of government is its promises of relief to the under-privileged, and it opportunities for the strong to exercise authority. Its deception is its promise that government control of the means of production will lead to economic security. Its terrorism and tyranny arises because it gives to human beings too much governmental authority. Its viciousness is in its appeal to envy, hate, jealousy and spite.

The "Liberals" and the Russians have the same objective—elimination of poverty by governmental mandate. The Russians propose to do it by *abolition* of private property; the "Liberals" by *taxation* of private property. Both systems compel citizens to supply food and shelter to persons not entitled to it. (Tyranny)

The "Liberals" claim to be Free Enterprise advocates, notwithstanding their business-paralyzing and money-wasting political Frankenstein. They are the beneficiaries of this Frankenstein. One, therefore, should not expect them to admit that it has liquidated Free Enterprise. Under sovereign prerogative, *as government officials,* they can by legislation and decree waste public funds with impunity. *That is why the Constitution limits government officials in spending tax money.*

The Russians condemn as a crime against society the food destroying programs of the United States. They hold capitalism (free enterprise) responsible for the crime! However, in both countries ,the officials "deem" their course necessary to "protect" security—themselves.

(1) The following definitions represent the faulty but popular political and religious conceptions of communism:

[1] A communist is a bleary-eyed, ignorant, vicious and dumb agitator who believes in having everything in common.

A communist is a person who is in favor of the brutal and vicious conduct of the Russian leaders.

A communist is a person with a fairly good government ownership program, but who foolishly tries to introduce it by violence.

A communist is a person with a fairly good social plan, but who is hostile to the religion of the Christian, or any belief in God.

A communist is a person who is in favor of higher wages, shorter hours and more government control than the dominant labor leaders recommend at the present time.

A communist is a Russian spy or traitor who wants to destroy the United States regardless of whether it has a good or bad government.

[1a] Henry George used the same line of reasoning to abolish ownership in land. The theory forces the citizen to substitute for the *profit motive* a *political-favor* motive—security depending on political relationships, the most vicious and destructive of all motives.

The "Liberals" ignore that fact. They, therefore, do not complain about the "planning" in the Russian constitution. It appears that they are totalitarians —believe that such "planning" is the remedy for economic distress—the Russian theory—so-called communism. They would avoid criticism by stating how much planning they want beyond what the Constitution provides.

They resent being called communists because they restrict the meaning of that word to spies, traitors and card-carrying members. If a person is not in such category, in their judgment, no matter how far he is to the Left, he is eligible for the most sensitive spot in the government. (Many of the leading nations freely admit communists to high office.)

There are about 10 million voters so tinged with their philosophy, and so placed, that the major parties dance to the tune these voters play. Consequently there is no easy way to change the present leftward trend, or to determine who is a Communist, Totalitarian, Socialist, Liberal or defender of the Constitution.

"Come, and let us reason together."

"LIBERALS" AND THE CONSTITUTION
OF THE U.S.S.R.

CHAPTER I

FAR beyond what most people realize, the Russians' theory of government (as set forth in their constitution) has been accepted throughout the world, including the United States. It is repudiation of the Constitution and, consequently, destructive of economic security. This discussion therefore relates to that *theory,* and not to the popular spy and traitor concepts of communism,[1] or the abusiveness of their administrators. The theory is:

Abundance will prevail when government owns the resources (business) of a nation—eliminates the private industry profit motive; that the results of that motive are such that government is justified in abolishing private industry. When it does so, it is not immoral, nor using unwarranted force, but is fulfilling a duty.[1a]

The quarrel is with the theory. There is no way to determine how many persons subscribe to it. Even "Liberals", no matter how far they are to the Left, declare they are opposed to it. To do otherwise, *at present,* would subject one to political, economic, social and religious disadvantages. Wholesale denials of belief in this theory should therefore be expected. The Test is: To what extent do they propose to tax property to eliminate economic distress; or, what limitations do they propose for the ballot, the judges, legislators and the executive.

Why does this theory have so many fanatical and intelligent cohorts, disclosed and hidden? The main reasons are:

(1) It offers *unlimited* political power. Political leaders therefore, in *every* country by hook and crook, undertake to get this power. (The *smart* ones loudly proclaim their loyalty to the Constitution).

3

(2) The promise of abundance has an irresistible appeal to the indigent.

(3) These groups develop fifth columns that over-ride constitutional protection for protesting minorities. The inducements account for the lying, cheating, spying, murdering, and revolution that the followers indulge in to destroy opposition.

(4) The desire to appear to be extra honest and intelligent traps persons of prominence into becoming tools of this Heaven-promising theory. Self-righteousness blinds them so that they cannot see a development which will prevent citizens from acquiring enough property to be independent of political favor—BE FREE.

A disturbing feature is that this theory of government, artfully disguised and called democratic, now has a world-wide sweep and a rapidly growing Fifth column in the very countries that *boast* of its containment. This is so because of the preachments of the "Liberals" that economic distress may be eliminated by taxation of property, as distinguished from abolition thereof.

The "Liberals" have advanced six propositions (fallacies) to bolster their theories. They are:

(1) Industrialists are under too much of a profit urge to be trustworthy.

(2) American political leaders can be given authority without danger of them becoming arbitrary or tyrannical.

(3) The ballot will keep them from going too far to the left.

(4) Human nature has changed for the better.

(5) Their proposed form of government does not impair the Constitution, the Bill of Rights, the courts, parliaments, free speech, title to property, local government, the franchise nor religion.

(6) The circumstances confronting the nation require the recommended changes in government, *even though they are unconstitutional*.

Another disturbing feature is that these propositions have acceptance in the academic institutions and by leaders in the professions and business, although the Constitution is based upon opposite premises. Self-interest precludes them from being factual. It is, therefore realized that this assignment is difficult. Nevertheless it will be undertaken to refute the arguments and also show:

(1) That a government official is given a narrow field of authority because of his immunities.

(2) That Constitutions are futile under "planned" economy, and that a collapse thereof forces complete government control.

(3) That the primary threat to security is the world-wide acceptance of the Russian theory of government.

The best way to drive these points home is to proceed in this manner:

THE present Russian Constitution, formulated in 1936, reflects the philosophy of the "great liberal" Karl Marx. That philosophy may be stated as being that poverty and distress will disappear when government has charge of the means of production—owns the farms, factories, etc. (It should not be forgotten that Marx, Trotsky, Mussolini, Hitler, Lenin and Stalin proclaimed themselves as Liberals and Humanitarians, and that the beneficiaries of their teachings are satisfied, beyond the reach of logic or reason, that they may rightfully claim such titles.)

However, neither the teachings of Marx, nor the preachments of the present-day "liberals", emphasize that under such an economic structure the citizen is not allowed to own or acquire property to any extent, that money degenerates into token or script, that government officials, generally, are the employers, that the incentive to work (produce) has to be created by an appeal to patriotism or a governmental threat of punishment, and that in lieu of the *profit motive* there is substituted the *motives to obtain* government favors and unlimited political power, the most destructive of all influences with respect to economic security. (The free enterprise incentive is the promise to the worker of enough income, wages or ownership of property to make him free from the necessity of accepting the bankrupting-tax-created government "help" and the accompanying snoopers.) Neither is it emphasized that under such a structure courts and parliaments must occupy a sub-subservient or very subordinate position, elections cannot be more than gestures, free speech is destroyed and religion, so far as individual convictions are concerned, out of the question. In addition, before long, it will convert elections, courts and parliaments into instruments of oppression, and make the employers (government officials) just like the Russian leaders. The officials become that way because of lack of checks on their authority and because of their onerous duties—prevent citizens from owning property, especially the means of production, business. Moreover, government of that character can have little respect for religion. The employer, therefore, generally, will be one who is extremely hostile to religious ideology.

Unfortunately many of the Conservatives are smug in their conviction that the present welfare laws, regulations and controls will not force additional steps, and eventually usher in government ownership of the means of production—totalitarianism—the Russian form of government.

This chapter will compare the philosophy, spirit and text of the 1936 Russian constitution (the Stalinists' constitution) with the Constitution of the United States and general world trends. The objective will be to show that the Russian form of government (not silly communism as conceived by the Red Dean of the British Isles) is being introduced into the United States much faster than is realized; indeed, quite generally with the *consent* of most of the people. This is so because of the delusion that the Chase-Laski-Atlee-Wallace kind of government controls are not the fore-runners of the Mussolini-Hitler-Stalin types of government, and the acceptance of the fallacy that *such kinds of government can be managed without the leaders becoming tyrannical and eventually destroying their country through political favoritism, oppression, unjust taxation and useless wars.* Because it is so important, it will be frequently emphasized that people are misled in these matters because of the misuse of such terms as democracy, liberalism, humanitarianism, security, full employment, equality, liberty, banishment of poverty, a world without hardships—one world. Most of the misleading is brought about by the repeated statements that industrialists are concerned only with "bags of gold", and government officials (although of the same kind of clay) *only with public welfare.*

The provisions of the 1936 constitution are called "fundamentals", which at least is paper recognition of the first principles of constitution building. And on paper that constitution appears to reflect the basic propositions of democracy, namely, local administration, free elections, short term of office, free speech, and three branches of government on equal footing. *But the pretension of democracy is a vicious subterfuge for that constitution prohibits private citizens from owning the means of production,* and consequently obliges or compels them to be dependent upon government (political relations) for their food and shelter. Under such circumstances the propositions referred to as constituting democracy have no significance.

It is dishonest to call that kind of government democratic. The Russians were honest enough, at first, to call it dictatorship.

The Constitution of the United States, with respect to property, does the exact opposite of what the Russian Constitution does. It encourages people to acquire property and to own the means of production in order that they may be independent of government (political relations) for their food and shelter —be free; that is, free from the necessity of doles and pen-

[2] Even Miss Thompson's keen and analytical mind seems to overlook that fact when she says "in a Communistic state * * * the only way to survive is to become a Communist—if allowed—and a docile and obedient servant of communism, in any case. Dec. 8, 1948. Wash. Even. Star.

[2a] **"My general conclusion is that persons of * * * un-American viewpoint have no place in representative or sensitive positions." Senator Lehman of New York.**

The Senator evidently does not realize that his "welfare" state has many "sensitive positions". He would therefore, like the Russians, only employ those who "toe the mark." Where the others could be employed would be a problem, for the "welfare state" has charge of most everything.

The self-righteousness of a politician, the desire to appear to be extra kind, and the lure of unlimited political power, keeps him from realizing that important fact.

sions which barely provide for an existence, and, besides are dependent upon the whims of an arbitrary master. *The primary distinction between these two constitutions, therefore, is the the position taken regarding how much property the citizen may own*—real estate, money, banks, factories, farms, or business of any character.

We must *assume* that the builders of these two constitutions had the same objectives, namely, more production and better distribution—abundance, security for all. The same *presumption*, generally, must be indulged in with respect to the leaders. The matter for consideration, therefore, relates to *methods of procedure (form of government), not motive.* Economists as well as statesmen and labor leaders, especially the Russians, have refused to recognize that simple but vital truth.[2] Consequently the disagreements are expressed with disastrous results for all by calling each other harsh names. The Russian leaders have been the most effective in the art of name calling. That raises a presumption that their motives are really improper and that, therefore, they are not entitled to much, if any, confidence. However, the name-calling makes it appear that the quarrel is about *who shall exercise the power* that the Russian leaders enjoy (abuse), instead of being *about form of government which will help the downtrodden!*

We digress here to say that every citizen is under an obligation to overthrow corrupt and oppressive government. Overthrow it, if necessary, by force and violence, in the same manner as the Forefathers did the British colonial rule. A "violence" test to determine whether a person is "loyal" is therefore not academically sound. The need for such a test, generally, arises because of political expediency.[2a] If it does, it comes within governmental perogative to apply it. It should be kept in mind that the Russians *claim* that capitalism is so

[3] A most graphic description of that spirit is found on page 89 of "The Real Soviet Russia" by Dallin:

"Everything that stood in the way of equality was to be abolished at once, completely; that was the spiritual crux of the November revolution and of the ideology of the early period of the Soviet Regime. Equality in consumption and strict rationing were to eliminate inequality in the distribution of food supplies. The floor space of houses and apartments was carefully measured and the available space equally distributed among the population. The peasants divided landlords' estates, and the workers seized the factories and drove the old owners into the street. Expeditions from the cities requisitioned grain * * * from the peasants. Soldiers tore shoulder straps from officers' uniforms. All ranks were abolished to make sure that not a vestige of the old inequality would be left. * * * worker and peasants were to rule * * * all were to be equal * * *. The selfishness of the landlords and capitalists (as well as the religious and political leaders) stood in the way of the coming millennium. It was necessary, therefore, to destroy them, and no sacrifices were too great. Every sacrifice was considered justified, and every cruelty, however great, was believed endowed with high human purpose. * * * thousands died for those ideas and thousands of enemies to them were maimed, tortured and killed. * * * Money lost almost all value * * * state employees lived not better than workers * * *. Equality was attained—on the basis of the lowest minimum subsistence. * * * the enthusiasm of equalitarianism soon ebbed * * * equality in hunger led to disappointments. * * * The Soviet Government found that it could not take a single step forward without breaching the surface cover of equalitarianism in a thousand places. * * * The new period began * * * sweeping industrialization and collectivization. * * * Instructions from above were, 'Down with equalitarianism'. Those who attempted to resist were eliminated. * * * Stalin denounced * * * the 'nonsense that money was unnecessary' and 'trade a dead letter'. * * * Tomsky (no doubt supported by Trotsky) objected to the differentiation in wage scales. * * * He was removed * * * committed suicide. 'More inequality' was now the cry. * * * The idea was adopted of 'Distinguished men in the Soviet land'."

"vicious" that any method for its destruction is justified, and that their "humanitarian" form of government will be ineffective until all forms of capitalism are destroyed.

The 1936 Russian constitution provides for a very nominal amount of ownership in property and for paying workers what they *earn*—not what they *need*—capitalistic tendencies. Here, therefore, is a good place to state that the true communists look forward to a classless society—no captains of industry, no extra pay, no powerful political or military leaders, script instead of money, everybody the same amount of food, clothes and shelter—equalitarianism.[3] The Russian constitution, however, does not provide for that kind of government. That even is too silly for most of the Russians. One, therefore, need not be concerned too greatly in that field. But what is disturbing is the hosts of people in the United States and throughout the world who are fascinated by the Russian ideas that government should own the means of production, and that it is private ownership of them which creates poverty and misery.

Many leaders do not care to, and often do not dare to (it would destroy their political chances or prestige), express their convictions. But what else could be the import of their recommendations? Is there any activity of significance which they have not suggested should be under complete government control? They are not in obvious accord because each one wants to protect his own particular private interest. But what is the significance of their agitation that government officials yet must have more power over wages, hours of work, property, farms, corporations or business of any kind, before there can be justice for the downtrodden? Does it not mean that like the Russian political leaders, they are dedicated to the philosophy that it is private ownership of the means of production

‍ The recommendations by orthodox Republicans and Democrats are startling enough. They want to head off communism by introducing the same kind of government. They worry about profits as though profit is always used for an unholy purpose—never to create more business, and are sure, absolutely sure, that government officials use tax funds only for public welfare, notwithstanding the fact that the records show that the converse, generally, is true. They all pretend, especially when they call themselves Liberals, that they do not want to go as far to the left as the Russians, the Stalinists or Trotkyities. Their good faith may be challenged because they never draw the line as to how far they can go before they will be forced to go all the way.

⁵ See PM of Oct. 7, 1945, under caption "Debunking Attack on Full Employment Bill." The article implies that there is no intention of following the Russian idea of full employment, but it offers no solution for putting the big square plug in the small circle. After all, what are compulsory insurance acts, minimum wage and hour laws, rent controls, wage tax, OPA, FEPC, NLRA, ceiling prices, bottom price, heavy inheritance taxes, etc., but laws which carry an implication that a private individual is too abusive when allowed too much control over his property and business. Accordingly he has been reduced to a silent partner. Government and labor unions tell him how to run his business. His private ownership title has been destroyed. He has, in fact, only a paper title.

which constitutes the stumblingblock to security. The "Liberals" and Leftwing group leaders, and 20 million others, should take time out to ascertain just how much government control they want. However, our Forefathers believed that private ownership of property (freedom from dependence upon government for food and shelter, jobs) provided the incentive which would cause persons to work hard enough to create security for all—abundance. They, therefore, tried to establish a form of government which would encourage and make it possible for the citizen to acquire enough property to be independent of governmental dole or favor. In a free enterprise structure that is called the "ownership of property incentive." (Incidentally, the forefathers did not believe that a "patriotic incentive" would be adequate.) But that idea has been repudiated, and not only by the Russians. The full-employment (share or divide employment) theory is an implied repudiation of it because of the governmental regulations it requires to be successful.[5] In lieu of the free enterprise incentive (the right to own property) the citizen has been forced to accept the incentive of governmental favoritism—an arrangement with the poorest reputation for production. Bearing the foregoing in mind, Stalin was not so wrong in his assumption that our economic structure was ripe for a Czechoslovakian coup. However, any Russian administration that insists on paying subjects what they *earn* will be overthrown or resisted by the group that wants to pay according to *need*. That predicament is not understood by our leaders, it appears.

But to get down to particulars. The first three articles of Chap. I of the Russian constitution deliberately exclude from participation in government affairs and government protection persons who own property. But regardless of the fact that such a proposition completely reverses the Fathers, including Jefferson, it is not without sponsors in the United States.

Articles 5, 6, 7, and 8 amplify that doctrine. For instance, article 6 states that all natural resources, means of transportation, communication, manufacturing and production, including the bulk of all dwelling houses, belong to the State, that is, "belong to the people." Of course, not the original owners.

Article 7 allows the farmer to have for his personal use "a small plot of land" and a limited amount of poultry, livestock and working implements."

Article 9 and 10 modify the foregoing, particularly Article 6, by providing that private enterprise that does not involve employing others may be practiced and that citizens have private ownership in their personal incomes, household property and inherited personal property. (That capitalistic flare is not in the earlier constitutions.) Apparently fearing that the concessions in Article 9 and 10 might be too great, Article 11 practically nullifies them by specifying that the economic life of the nation shall be directed by the State. The Constitution of the United States turned upside down! Yet the "liberals" call the Russian constitution democratic! It should be repeated that the "liberals" find no real fault with the Russian form of government. Their complaint is directed at the leaders. *Obviously they feel they should exercise such power—could be trusted with the power the Russian leaders enjoy* (abuse). Let us repeat, that is the most dangerous fallacy of all!

The United States Constitution is predicated on the theory that protecting ownership of private property, particularly private ownership of the means of production (free enterprise), is the government's first obligation, because protection of that furnishes more opportunity for comfort and advancement for the citizen than any other way, notwithstanding its misfits, hardships and injustice. It should never be overlooked that the theory of free enterprise presupposes judges, legislators, and an executive branch, and that they shall be on equal footing; that is, the judges supreme in interpreting law, the legislators supreme in making the law, and the executive branch in the enforcement thereof. If that rule is observed, the other aspects of democratic government naturally follow, and with them the maximum opportunity to earn a decent living, and maintaining a strong and independent country. If that is the result under free enterprise, it is less brutal, more humane, than the other systems, no matter how glamorous they appear to be, which promise the abundant life by restricting citizens to the minimum ownership of private property. The minimum, of course, may be reduced to nothing anytime the government finds it convenient to do so, and which it generally does because courts, elections and parliaments become mere gestures under that kind of government—a point that the "liberals" and "humanitarians" conceal, soft-pedal, or fail to understand. Moreover, that kind of government creates war hazards, obviously so, and war distributes destitution instead of abundance. How false and idle are their promises?

As already suggested, the alarming features of the doctrine of the "abundant life" by precluding or curtailing ownership in private property, especially in the means of production, are the preachments in its favor by responsible persons in every country. Their endorsement is evidenced by their constitutions and legislation and proposed constitutions and legislation, and by their statements that governmental debt has no significance,[6] that corporations always abuse profits, that industrialists are not trustworthy, that there should be no restrictions on the right to strike, etc. Their propositions are rooted in the theory that

[6] Imagine what would happen if wages dropped back to the 1932 level. Relatively, that would make the national debt about 900,000,000,000 dollars. The interest rate, relatively, would also treble! Such a situation would force complete government control.

⁷ Stuart Chase in discussing profit in "Government and Bussiness", p 261, states: "Clearly there are other motives than bags of gold." The general implication of that phrase is: the urge for profit cancels all regard for mercy, justice and progress. In a sense that is true. But the profit urge is merely an offshoot of the *security urge.* The latter, in a much broader sense, has no regard for the things mentioned.

The indictment of gold (profit) is recognition that human beings are prone to abuse power to obtain an advantage. If they are smart, they do it in the name of humanity by way of governmental authority—sovereign power—an irresponsible agency. Professors and economists, under the present set-up, cannot emphasize that fact because it would offend too much the self-righteous politician whose success depends on denying it. Obviously protection for security requires that sovereign power be substantially restricted. At least that is what Locke and the Forefathers believed.

⁸ Sir John Boydon stated that one-half of the population in England is undernourished. The British Welfare State has increased the proportions and practically dissolved the Empire and made it a nation unable to pay its debts

⁹ Chase, expressing majority sentiment, no doubt, on p 208, "Economy of Abundance" calls for a government created unhampered flow of goods as the method to sustain a minimum (adequate) standard of living. It appears he does not expect that lack of production opportunity (*work*) will occur under the new concept of government. A mandate is sought which will guarantee every worthy person what he needs. That is now accepted as the objective of nearly every government and is the alleged objective in the early Russian constitutions. (Stalin, as shown in the text, repudiated that approach.) Its accomplishment requires abandonment of our Constitution. However, the "Liberals", generally, insist that such extension of government authority will not impair, *unjustly,* property rights, nor *interfere* with the normal democratic functions of courts, elections, checks and balances, religion and free speech.

Incidentally, the Russian government was indisposed to accept security responsibility for those who were unreasonable about increasing the family circle. It, accordingly, encouraged "safe" sex relations. Economy in child production is not a unique government practice when it undertakes to guarantee subjects what they need.

¹⁰ "My definition of communism is * * * to each according to his "needs." Dean of Canterbury. The Dean is at odds with Stalinism.

"The study of scientific socialism side by side with the study of Christian theology convinces me that Christianity is the high road to socialism and communism. p 20, "The Soviet Power." *Many Christian leaders, although disclaiming against communism, accept that premise.*

the "profit" motive of the private owner forces him to become too brutal and too unreasonable to be entitled to a position of authority, or much authority, over an industry that vitally affects a community—public welfare.[7] Marx, Lenin, Trotsky and Stalin theories summed up in one sentence.

It is true, and probably always will be, that under free enterprise many people, say one-third [8] will never enjoy property possession much beyond that authorized by the Russian constitution, but, of course, not provided. *But there is this difference:* The government has not said that they cannot have more. In countries where the government has said that, the result has been as in Russia, three-fourths of the people, instead of one-third, are permanently consigned to destitution. (The territory of the Old Russian Empire was not conducive to production. There was therefore ample excuse for poverty under the Czars.)

Article 12 contains the proposition that work is a duty and will be required of every able-bodied citizen, including women and children. It represents in the extreme the capitalistic doctrine that only those who work shall eat. It is more brutal than the present attitude in the United States which is dedicated to the proposition that women should not be subjected to manual labor and that people shall not starve whether they work or not.[9]

Article 12 contains also the declaration "From each according to his ability: to each according to his *work*." The last word of that phrase in the former constitutions was "needs", and "needs" according to Marx, Trotsky, Lenin, Browder, Wallace and many other prominent leaders, including clergymen,[10] is the proper word. Stalin's practical mind caused the change of that word in the Russian constitution. But if citizens are going to be paid according to what they accomplish, what they

[11] " * * * The average earnings of intellectuals are about twice the average of workers; particularly high are the earnings of engineers, who * * * earn several thousand rubles a month as compared with the average monthly wage of from three to four hundred rubles for workers * * * picked groups * * * in addition to their salaries * * * receive all sorts of special grants, are given the use of automobiles * * * occasionally exempted from paying taxes, etc. * * * The higher aristocracy of Soviet society * * * comprising no more than twenty or thirty thousand persons. Dallin, in "The Real Soviet Russia."

[12] "In the years which have intervened since the Adkins Case we have had opportunity to learn that a wage is not always the resultant of free bargaining between employers and employees; that it may be forced upon employees by the most ruthless of their competitors. * * * a wage insufficient to support the worker * * * casts * * * on government * * * the burden of solving the problems of poverty, subsistence, health and morals * * * A generation ago they were for individuals to solve; today they are the burden of the nation. I * * * perceive no * * * objection ** * to * * * requiring * * * industry to bear the subsistence cost of * * * labor * * *. (From dissenting opinion of Justice Stone in Morehead v. State ex rel Tipaldo, 298 US 587, concurred in by Brandeis and Cardozo.

It is not clear from the dissenting opinion whether the judges wanted industry to guarantee the employees subsistence of whether that was the duty of the taxpayers in general. But it carries the implication *that employees must be paid what they need regardless of what they earn.* The Communists thought they had solved that problem. But it appears Russia has about 12 million people condemned by the government to the maximum of labor *without* pay. It is also to be observed that the relationship of the soldier and the government does not contemplate collective bargaining, or equal footing, or consent, and may require 18-year-old boys and girls to meet death on the battlefield. It would seem, therefore, that the dissenting judges are not in a position to fulfill their Utopian conceptions of building a civilization. They take death for teenagers on the battlefield for granted, but balk at it in the field of production.

are worth, instead of according to their "needs", it will not be long before some of the workers will have much more than others,[11] unless the principle of restricting ownership of property to the minimum is adhered to. But if that principle is invoked, Article 12, with respect to paying people what they are worth, is futile. One of them is a joker. Trotsky's stubborn defense of the principle that subjects should be paid according to their "needs" cost him his life. Discarding it amounts to repudiation of communism. The abandonment of it accounts for the progress Russia made under the Great Discarder. The latter theory is the basis of private property and leads to concentration of wealth—capitalism in the full sense of the word. The first seven articles of the Russian constitution were introduced to prevent that from happening in Russia. They concentrate political power; Article 12 concentrates commercial power. One of them has to be concentrated in order to make it possible to create abundance—security. *Under free enterprise it is assumed that political power is the most dangerous and detrimental to public welfare. It, therefore, is curbed as much as possible.*

It should be observed that while Russia, on paper at least, has gone back to the proposition that only those who work shall eat, members of the United States Supreme Court, on paper, subscribe more to Trotsky's proposition.[12]

Article 12 states the basis for all progressive civilization, namely, that all able-bodied citizens must work if they expect to eat, and that workers must be paid according to their ability. But in its implications it is more brutal than anything a capitalist in a free enterprise country ever openly dared to suggest. It does not strain its language to give it a meaning that no one can work hard enough, or long enough, or save enough to become financially independent, to escape work. (One bright gleam in free enterprise is that possibility.) It destroys all

[13] The Full Employment program is perhaps the best example. It is being introduced as a most innocent piece of legislation, but obviously if the government is going to assure every person a job, it will have to take over complete control of business. It is absurd to expect the theory of free enterprise to work so long as government has so many restrictions on business in the field of price controls, including wage and hour controls. The NLRA, even as amended, can be readily administered in such a way that private industry cannot function.

"The Act does not interfere with the normal exercise of the right of the employer to select its employes or to discharge them." Chief Justice Hughes in Labor Board v. Jones & Laughlin.

The Chief Justice apparently recognized that interference with the right to hire and fire could cripple industry. Apparently, he was not satisfied with the Act, but could not rule against it, much as he would like to do so, because of the inadequate evidence submitted by the corporation lawyers.

[14] In Russia the rule was, do as much as you can for as little as possible, whereas in the United States the labor union rule is, do as little as possible—but get the maximum in pay. Russia at the present time seems to have about 10,000,000 government slaves that it can compel to do as much as possible for as little as possible. Dallin names about 50 labor camps in Russia. P 205 "The Real Soviet Russia." If they are intelligent workers, Russia is certainly in a position to make the "capitalists" governments with their tenderness toward strikes and labor union pay tribute or go out of business.

[15] What could be more subtlely tinted with the philosophy of "pay according to need instead of according to merit" than the proposition that business men have to be compelled to utilize efficient help—that they use inefficient help because of race prejudice. This is the basic theory of FEPC.

opportunity to be financially independent at any age. It brings about a situation where few will be free from the inquisitorial inspections and investigations that accompany governmental "protection", political relationships with respect to food, shelter and jobs.[13]

And it is not a private citizen who says "work is a duty; that he who does not work shall not eat; the worker shall be paid according to his ability", as in the case of capitalism. It is the all-embracing, ever-present, inescapable, all-powerful, merciless, arbitrary government that is saying it and saying it in its constitution—the fundamental law of the land, by way of a human being.

Moreover, if the rule of paying according to ability is to be applied, there will be created so-called employment discrmini-nations in Russia, for like other countries, perhaps more so, particularly in its old boundaries, Russia has many persons who are not apt at any kind of work, especially the academic or the mechanical.

The former wording of the phrase "to each according to his needs" is more in accordance with the philosophies of the American "humanitarians" than its present form which bases pay on the value of the work.[14] In its former dress it is rockbottom communism. The substitution of the word "work", better expressed as "merit", makes it the rockbottom philosophy or principle of capitalism, unless we give that word a silly meaning.[15]

To pay according to merit is a cruel and hard obligation of private industry to enforce, as mercifully as possible by the use of independent judges and elected legislators. Under the constitution conceived by the Russians that obligation is a mandate of unlimited government from which there is no appeal.

That capitalism, or free enterprise (the means of production

[16] "A few miles outside of Kuibyshev we passed one of the big concentration camps reserved for political prisoners. Beyond that we saw a long line of them working on a new road. * * * We winced, I think, because these prisoners were women." From "Only the Stars are Neutral."

"We drove into Yakutsky in a heavy black Soviet limousine. Between the airfield and the town we looked for the usual concentration camp we have seen in other cities—half-barbed wire fences, with sentry boxes at the corners." From "One World" by Willkie.

"More than 200,000 prisoners were employed on the project. More than 50,000 died during a period of a year and a half. The work day was eleven hours. There were no Sundays. * * * Despite the terrible Karelian cold, prisoners were forbidden to build camp fires * * * I myself saw dead people who had been frozen while at work. * * * Responsibility for discipline was placed collectively * * * if a prisoner escaped the rest were punished * * * Those caught escaping were shot." P 198 "The Real Soviet Russia" Dallin.

owned by private citizens), results in many individuals living in near slavery (destitution) may be conceded, or not denied. But that government when conducting business will offend ten times more, *and without any relief to the down-trodden,* must be expected, if the past has any significance.[16] The *Russians apparently by-passed the 13th Amendment's prohibition on involuntary servitude by introducing forced labor (slavery) as a penalty for political offenses.* The hard-boiled truth is that civilizations cannot be built or maintained without terrible hardships, at least so long as war is used as an arbitrator! The tempo must vary according to the resources of each country and it must be also borne in mind that no economic structure can avoid all the hardships which arise because of inventions, natural catastrophes, and the miscalculations, in war or peace, of the leaders.

Article 12, no doubt, shows the cunning, practical and fact-facing spirit of Stalin. The other articles and the word "need" probably represent the dreams and fantasies of Marx, Lenin and Trotsky, as well as their vicious readiness to achieve popularity and power by deceiving the downtrodden. That Article alone should help anyone to appreciate the rule that only well established and recognized principles, not untried economic theories, should be accepted for a constitution. Bitter experience taught the Forefathers that truth. Only bitter and disillusioning experience born of oppression and distress will teach men to respect it again.

These twelve articles represent the political philosophy or goal of the Russian leaders. The capitalistic idea of paying only those who work, and paying them according to what they *earn,* is bitterly opposed by the true communists. They comfort themselves by believing that what is being done is a step toward their goal. That point is overlooked by the critics who

" "The continued coexistence of private economy and state economy is an impossibility * * * and demands that the Socialist economy of the State "devour" the private section. Stalin. p 44 of Dallin's "The Real Soviet Russia."

Belgrade, Nov. 7, 1951. Marshal Tito of Yugoslavia today chided the West for campaigning against "communism" rather than Russian aggression and said that Russia is not a true Communist state. * * * Reactionary circles in the West are promoting a crusade against communism, but this propaganda is very dangerous because Russia is not communist. It is not even truly Socialist. * * *

I believe that Communist and capitalist countries can live peacefully side by side and that the internal political systems should be left to each country to decide for itself. Marshal Tito.

A radical departure from prior positions, and false so far as communism and capitalism not being hostile to each other. No doubt, he is sincere. It is his fear of Russia that is coloring his judgment. But it also serves his purpose in making it appear that he is in harmony with the philosophy of the "liberals" in the United States.

describe the Russian Government as communism instead of communistic. Every orthodox communist understands that as long as a part of the world is capitalistic, i.e., allows citizens to own property and the means of production, communism cannot achieve its goal. It therefore is *dependent.* government— cannot succeed unless all other countries follow the same course. Consequently, appear the strenuous efforts for world conquest, dominance and control, in season and out of season, by bold and open declarations, by fraud and deception, by hook and crook, or by *war* or any other means which might make it possible to maintain their position.[17] The present Russian government is under the same necessity. The Marshall plan suggests that the United States is being driven in the same direction. The communists have achieved much more than people realize. Practically all recent constitutions are based upon the proposition that capitalism, the right of a private citizen to own property or enterprises (the means of production) under a three-branch government as contemplated by the Forefathers, is horse-and-buggy stuff, and that the world has come to a place where government must take full charge of the economic structure as expressed in the Russian constitution. The most dangerous aspect of the situation arises from those who are fascinated by that kind of government, but deny, or do not realize, that they are working to establish it. For instance, in the United States politicians make their bid for office on the ground that the industrialists, the owners of business (private property), have still too much authority, and that more government regulation is the remedy. Their motive may be challenged because they adroitly avoid stating how far they wish to go. Also their motive may be challenged because they claim that it can be accomplished without the complete government control adopted by the Russians or the tyranny that prevails in Russia.

[18] Both believe in free institutions, in two or more political parties, in a free ballot and in private enterprise. But they differ about the ends for which these shall be used. The difference simmers down to one question—which comes first, men or dollars. p 92 "An Uncommon Man" Kingdon.

The difference between them is that the conservative considers that the first duty of these institutions is to preserve the rights of property, while the liberal considers that the first duty of these institutions is to conserve the rights of human beings." Kingdon "An Uncommon Man" p 94.

One would gather from that statement that the conservative is mentally and morally depraved, inhuman—brutal. A paralyzing thought, for there are a great many of them! The truth is, and everybody knows it, that there is no security anywhere outside of granting the individual an "unqualified" title to property. Brother Kingdon is playing with words. It's a profitable occupation.

---

[19] "I am convinced that governmental bureaucracy, from the standpoint of honesty, efficiency and fairness compares very favorably with corporation bureaucracy. There is less nepotism, less of arbitrary and unfair action, and a more continuous consideration of the general welfare. This is not because human beings in government bureaus are so much finer as individuals than human beings in corporation bureaucracies, but because continuous public scrutiny requires a higher standard." Wallace "The American Choice."

Kingdon on page 90 of "An Uncommon Man" sums this up by saying that no matter how much power the government official has it will be properly restrained as such power will be in "the hands of the people."

The Constitution, however, tried to keep business out of the hands of governmental bureaucracy and put government into the hands of experts and persons financially responsible for their conduct. The government of Russia was in the hands of the people from 1917 to about 1923. That period represents the reign of terror for Russia as 1793 represents the reign of terror for France when its government was in the hands of the "people."

All these government control programs are introduced under open declarations or innuendos that industrialists, business men, have no respect for human beings—consider only the dollar.[18] It is freely taught that labor and government officials are the only persons concerned about the downtrodden and, therefore, should have management authority to a much greater degree than is the practice.[19]

The National Labor Relations Act is certainly watered with that philosophy. However, it leaves responsible labor leaders absolutely helpless with respect to furthering public welfare because it affords them no protection against the unscrupulous leaders. (The Act assumes that their are no unscrupulous labor leaders.) Leaders of labor make out-cry against communism, but they dare not, except on paper, turn away from a destructive and paralyzing course of more and more pay and less and less work. If they do, the undercover communist will grab their power. They, therefore, are captives of the forces that they want to repudiate. They are well aware of the fact that the program spells disaster and leads to complete government control. They need the Taft-Hartley Act for protection, but dare not defend it; are obliged to repudiate it against their own judgment.

Prolonged abundance, scarcity, or war, can readily mold the Agricultural Act into collective farming, a cornerstone of Russian so-called communism. Much of the agricultural products as well as heavy industrials are already being used as Stalin used them—taken away from the land of origin for political purposes. However, he was not ever obliged to give away his material to foreigners to stop a political movement! Coupled with all the other so-called social laws and labor union policies (sponsored often by the big corporations, at least indirectly), another straw can easily make the excuse for going all the

[20] Wallace is sure, and he is not alone, that when the next economic collapse develops that government will have to take over. The "humanitarians" apparently feel that the time is not ripe for the destruction of the "Kulak." They have not been made soft enough by benefits, etc.

David Lawrence on Nov. 8, 1948, Wash. Even. Star, states part of the issue: "Investors are too scared and if they make any gains they are taxed away. No more certain way exists to bring on state socialism than to deprive business of the means of raising risk capital. For then the government (the taxpayer) has to provide capital and this means government personnel in the management and finally a totalitarian regime * * *"

[21] According to Senator Butler in the 1943 December issue of "Readers Digest" the practice has been introduced into South America. It is nearer the truth to say that "Newdealism" was introduced in the United States from abroad.

[22] Russia's sin, no doubt, was her refusal to follow the destructive and restrictive programs of her neighbors. Her refusal to follow put her in a position to become the leading producer, the strongest nation, and would make the restrictive programs of her neighbors futile.

However, in "The Real Soviet Russia" Dallin states on page 120 "there were 154,000 combines in Russia, but this colossal apparatus turns out no greater volume or production than the peasants formerly produced before the 'supermechanization'."

"The Soviet Journal Problems of Economy gives a comparison between two electric stations, one in the United States and the other in the Soviet Union, each producing the same amount of electricity. The American station had 51 employees whereas the Soviet station had 480." p 132 "The Real Soviet Russia."

* * * What was worse, the majority of the peasants, fearing a new anti-peasant maneuver, refrained from expanding their economy * * *. To have gone beyond that would have meant rising from the status of middle peasant * * * and exposing themselves to * * * reprisals. * * * peasants feared to sow too much, or to increase the number of their cattle * * *. Dallin "The Real Soviet Russia" p 167.

It would seem that the "capitalistic" nations were needlessly frightened.

[23] What better propaganda could Stalin have to spread his form of government, to ridicule free enterprise (capitalism)? If he couples it with our strike procedure, it seems he could not help but win. It is highly improbable that he is concerned about our "race prejudice problems."

way.[20] Does not the whole set-up carry an implication that it is believed that in the future almost everyone, at least the great majority, will be dependent upon government for food, clothes, shelter, pensions, doles, etc., from the cradle to the grave? And that cannot be accomplished without accepting the form of government that Russia has. Many people believe that government of that kind, if properly directed, will bring in a paradise, notwithstanding the fact that the Declaration of Independence gives government officials a most unfortunate reputation for abuse and injustice, except toward the usual amount of favorites. Can any honest mind fail to perceive that these so-called social laws are born in the underlying philosophy of the first twelve articles in the Russian Constitution? We are kidding ourselves about the whole matter, and especially about the assumption that our economic structure can stand the strain. The cry that there are no more frontiers implies the same philosophy—more government control. Russia used the cry of *too* many frontiers to introduce government control. Mussolini and Hitler used the "no frontier" cry for their programs!

To many persons much of the foregoing will be considered as ridiculous. However, the ridiculous is not unusual. We passed through a phase where workers were told to do as little as possible and machinery was discarded because it did the work too fast. And right now, the government is destroying food to keep prices high, or at least from coming down.[21] Such procedure to the Russian must be more fantastic than anything Marx ever dreamed of or Stalin ever suggested. Indeed Russia ridiculed, and intelligently, the "capitalists" engaged in their production retarding and crop destroying programs.[22] Perhaps her starving millions would have justified her in sending over "missionaries", armed ones, in the name of humanity to stop the waste and destruction of desperately needed food.[23]

[24] The real situation is not grasped because of the piece-meal approach. The tenant is satisfied to accept confiscatory rental laws; the employee accepts wages and hours that force business into bankruptcy; the farmer accepts subsidies that will overtax the treasury; business and professional men also are human beings! The citizen is against government control only when it interferes with his property or profits. Management of big industry should not be expected to realize that laws which benefit big industry have a tendency to eliminate smaller ones. Labor leaders must follow the policies of the big industries. It is not recognized that when government invades one area of this character circumstances soon arise which compel further invasions. Wage and hour laws must be followed by price and production controls. When the economic structure has accepted such controls situations develop that force complete government control. Logic and reason cannot be used to combat the programs because they start with direct money benefits. Self-interest precludes the victim from realizing before it is too late that he is in the spider's web.

The presumption or conviction in the minds of the beneficiaries that government can pay unemployment benefits and maintain short hours of work and high wages, prevent child labor, and grant pensions and old-age security, no matter what happens, could be the greatest and most dangerous delusion of all.

[25] However, it has much in common with the model constitution proposed in 1938 by the New York State Constitutional Convention. (See Chapter VII for an analysis of that Constitution.)

The similarity of the present philosophies of government in the United States to those of Russia are not obvious because the United States, through labor unions and channels not so obvious, uses them to *retard* production, while Russia has to use them to *stimulate* production. The next upheaval will disclose that the difference is not so great as many complacent citizens imagine, and that they are strikingly parallel to the twelve articles referred to. That is not going too far, for many responsible spokesmen are advocating plans of government control which in no way fall short of the objectives, policies and practices advocated in the U.S.S.R. constitution.[24]

Chapter II with sixteen articles, 13 to 29, deals with the powers that may be called the Federal Government. In style and approach it follows Article I of Sec. 8 of the American Constitution, and suggests that American training influenced its formulation. The style and approach, however, are the only similarities.[25] It provides that the Federation is "voluntary" and reaffirms that policy in Article 17 by providing that every Republic is given the right to freely secede. However, the powers given the central or federal government in Article 14 are so great and so comprehensive that seceding would amount to commercial suicide. Its present weakness is that it has to call upon well-resourced provinces to support the poor ones. (Tito is complaining about that and is acting on the presumption that the other rich provinces will follow his course.)

This chapter contains stipulations about the jurisdiction of the central government over the constitutions and laws of the different States (political divisions), which is truly constitutional matter. However, instead of clearly specifying the jurisdiction of the three branches of government, it dumps their

[26] The secret of efficiency of the English Constitution is the close union, the nearly complete fusion, of the executive power and the legislative power.(paraphrased) p 18 "A new Constitution Now" Hazlitt.

Morris Ernst is fascinated by the English form of government because of the "relatively unimportance" of the courts. See p 223 of "The Ultimate Power."

But the "nearly complete fusion" makes Parliament supreme. It was because Parliament had become too oppressive that the forefathers tried to avoid such an arrangement. However, Great Britain notwithstanding her great empire has not been able to meet her foes, nor her debts since 1914, which would indicate her government is not so effective as her admirers suggest. Moreover, the United States with far less resources than the British Empire, and often with that Empire as an enemy, made more headway in a century than Great Britain did in three centuries. It is only in the last decades that the United States took a course that retarded her commercial progress. For instance, during the depression years Russia made better commercial progress than the United States. Under such circumstances, one should hardly expect Russia to be enthusiastic about our government. But it is startling to note how similar the fusing idea is to that in the Russian constitution.

[27] "The English revolution of 1688 had established the principle that legislation could be enacted only by Parliament, and the Act of 1701 had removed judges from the king's exclusive control by providing Parliament with the power of removal in cases of bad behavior. After 1748 the colleges in the Colonies received outlines of the novel ideas of one Montesquieu, a French politicalist, who had urged the division of the State into three powers—executive, legislative and judicial." p 160 "The Ultimate Power" Ernst.

"Turning then to the New Deal, what attitude may it be said to represent regarding dictatorship. I think it may fairly be assessed as an effort to attain some of the results of dictatorship by a mergence of legislative power with presidential leadership." "The Twilight of the Supreme Court" p. 140. Corwin.

sovereign powers into Article 14 under the caption "Organs of the State." Under that heading it lists foreign relations, the war-declaring power, admission to the Union, interpretation of the Constitution, control of the military forces, state boundaries, economic policies, budgets, taxation, administration of banks, transportation, communications, control of the monetary system, insurance, loans, control of natural resources, education and health, national economic statistics, principles of labor legislation and legislation with respect to judicial procedure, criminal and civil codes, citizenship and acts of amnesty.

(Under Articles 15 to 22, the individual political divisions are given jurisdiction over what is left, which includes making their own constitutions. Articles 23 to 29 describe the territorial limitations of the States of the Union, a proper function of a constitution, generally.)

The commingling of powers without specifying which branch shall have jurisdiction over the different powers is an outright repudiation of the ancient doctrine of well-defined powers endorsed by the American Constitution.

But the Russian idea is not unique. All the recent constitutions point in that direction. Responsible leaders in the United States are advocating the same idea.[26] It is now generally taught that the Forefathers completely misinterpreted the form of the British government in operation at the time the Constitution was made, and fell for the "far-fetched" doctrines of Locke and Montesquieu with respect to separation of powers.[27] But is it not more than far-fetched to assume that so many active and independent thinkers and students of those days should be all wrong with regard to the form of government which they had just repudiated at the risk of their lives?

Chapter III, Articles 30 to 56, concerns itself with the branches or political organs of the Union. The *highest* organ (abandonment of the equal footing doctrine of the three branches) is described as the Supreme Soviet (legislature). It is given authority over the general powers mentioned in Section 14, except for the powers exercised by the Presidium, the Council of Peoples Commissars and the Peoples Commissariats.

The exceptions are ambiguous enough to leave the responsibility for legislative authority a mystery. This mystery aspect is hardly a democratic principle and is entirely out of harmony with the American Constitution, but not out of harmony with the trend of political philosophy.

The legislative assembly (the Soviet) has two elected chambers. One is called the Soviet Union and the other the Soviet of Nationalities. The set-up is complex, perhaps, unavoidably so, because Russia's area is enormous and there are within her borders about 170 different languages. Members of the legislatures are elected for four years. Laws are enacted under majority rule. The Soviet or legislature is directed to convene twice a year.

These provisions, of course, are democratic in character. However, they have no significance in the Russian constitution because it is easily amended or side-stepped. It affords, consequently, only the minimum of protection for its alleged fundamental principles. It converts them into mere statutory law. *It is, indeed, a subtle, arbitrary and undemocratic denial of the right of the Russians to have a constitution—the fundamentals under effective protection.*

The position of the legislative body is made precarious by the provision that if it cannot agree on matters before it, the Presidium dissolves it and orders a new election. Its independence is further curtailed by the Presidium (a committee of about 33 members chosen from the legislative body) which has power to interpret the laws, issue decrees, convene the assemblies and order new elections. The Presidium can also conduct referendums, annul decisions and orders of the commissars, confer titles of honor, grant pardons, declare war, and ratify treaties. It, therefore, is in charge of practically everything—a committee with extraordinary judicial, legislative and executive authority.

There is, to be sure, the so-called safeguard that the legislature must meet twice a year and upon the termination of its four year term a new Presidium is created. (Article 49 sets forth the powers of the Presidium.) [28]

All in all, the procedure appears to be a roundabout way to abolish legislatures and courts of the type the American Constitution tried to perpetuate. In practice, it has worked out that one person heads the committees, holds office for life, and is a dictator in the real sense of the word—one person in charge of the political, commercial and religious life of a nation. But should one complain about that kind of government for Russia? Could that country under the circumstances for the territory it embraced before the war, function effectively under any other kind of government?

But the Anglo-Saxon and the Teuton, the people representing middle Europe, are not responsive to so much regimentation. A pertinent question therefore is, how much further can Great Britain and the United States, or the people of Middle Europe, drift toward that kind of government without inviting serious consequences?

Due to the turmoil that has torn Russia apart and her backwardness, it is more than probable that she must function, so

[28] It appears the Bureau of Political Policies is supplanting the Presidium. It is an amendment of the constitution by practice instead of by law.

far as her former boundaries are concerned, for a long time under a dictatorship—not communism. How far she would have advanced under free enterprise as conceived by our Forefathers cannot be demonstrated. However, the original thirteen States, faced with handicaps far more difficult than those which confronted Russia, made a much better showing than Russia has done under any of her Regimes. It is probable that it was the impact of American commercial ideas which developed Russia economically, instead of her fantastic forms of government.

What the aftermath of the war will do to Russia's present form of government cannot be anticipated now. It is more than probable that the conflicting interests in her rapidly acquired territory will force many changes; probably, compel her to become subservient to the people she tried to absorb, as many of them outrank her intellectually. Berlin would be a better capital than Moscow, under the circumstances.

Chapter V, Articles 64 to 88, relates to the so-called Executive or Administrative Organs, which are directed by the Commissars, who are appointed by the Supreme Soviet by way of the Presidium. They are supposed to be under control of the legislative body. (In practice under the Presidium.) However, they issue orders and supervise their execution. They appear to act as assistants to the Presidium in directing the economic policies of the Union—the five-year plans, credits, the monetary system, foreign and military policies, etc., as well as all policies relating to transportation, communication and industry, including agriculture. The Presidium and the Commissars are described as the highest executive authority.

This procedure apparently is intended to mix the legislative authority with the executive authority as much as possible, instead of keeping such authorities separated as much as possible as the Forefathers tried to do. But this mixing follows a world-wide trend, with the United States not in the rear.

This mixing of authority is not an arbitrary matter. It is necessary under these forms of government for administrative purposes. Politically, it acts as a blind. It makes the subjects believe that they have a form of government which is democratic—reflects the will of the majority through courts and parliaments. But it is dictatorship. Perhaps the kind of government they need, although, obviously, it is not the kind of government that Lenin and Trotsky had in mind.[29]

Terms for describing government are in such confusion that one can only bring out their proper classification by ascertaining to what extent the courts and legislators are in subjection to the Executive Branch. The phrase "bureaucratic government", seems to be the most appropriate terminology for describing the forms of government which the leading nations, including the United States, have adopted. The various descriptive names for the bureaus give the impression that there has not been too much centralization. However, the great number of Administrators, Directors, Commissioners, Bureaus, Authorities and Agencies in the United States, testify eloquently to the distance she has marched away from government by duly elected congressional representatives, and independent judges, and toward the Russian philosophy that the means of production must be in complete control of the State in order to establish security.

But Russia, on paper at least, moved a long way to the right, toward democracy, when her constitution subscribed to the capitalistic doctrine of paying workers according to their

[29] Dr. E. J. Dillon, professor in Kharkoff, Russia, said: "In the Bolshevik movement there is not a vestige of a constructive social idea."

[30] " * * * Today every correspondent knows * * * That Stalin is a great nationalist who repudiated World Communism as soon as he was free * · * * of Lenin and Trotsky." p 11 of "The Real Soviet Russia" by Dallin. Dallin does not believe that to be the case and writes a very interesting chapter along that line. However, his book shows a radical departure from the classless society that communism insists upon. For instance, his brilliant and comprehensive classification:

> Soviet society as it appears at the beginning of the Forties consisted of four principal classes: The highest class was that of state employees; about eleven million people. Workers, rural and urban, about 20 million. Peasants, nearly all collectivized, about forty million. Forced labor (government slaves) estimated at about 12 million.

[31] "Words must have no relation to actions—otherwise what kind of diplomacy is it: Words are one thing, actions another. Good words are a mask for concealment of action. Frank diplomacy is no more possible than dry water or wooden iron." Stalin. Stalin's open disregard for his 1936 Constitution indicates he practiced what he preached. Lord Bryce on p 215 of "Modern Democracy" calls attention to this practice.

ability.[30] Since 1933, not counting the war, the United States has moved in the direction from which the Russians are retreating! (See Mrs. Roosevelt's book, "This I Remember.")

The change in form of government, in both cases, must be done by subterfuge. The disposition of the people not to make changes, to cling to precedents, to venerate traditions, makes it difficult to effect changes in form of government, even when necessary. Resort to fiction and subterfuge is the usual course.[31] The use of subterfuge and fiction does not always involve lack of integrity. It may be unavoidable. The Constitutional Convention is an outstanding example. Santa Claus stories are promulgated and medicine often administered in the same spirit. But the kind we are discussing cannot be justified. It represents action intended to be harmful, or else was undertaken through poor judgment. One, of course, should not ask the people to assume constant guilty knowledge on the part of leaders, for that would shake too much the already tottering confidence in them as they try to direct organized society.

The Forefathers evidently assumed that highly centralized government was undesirable. The Constitution which they made gave little opportunity for unlimited or dictatorial power to come to one man or group of men, as political or industrial leaders. They evidently under-estimated the crafty attempts to seize power that would be made under the self-righteous spell which afflicts every "liberal" and "humanitarian", and makes him feel that the world cannot be saved unless he has unchallenged authority. *That spell makes him believe that he is a patriot or a savior, and precludes him from realizing that he is actuated by a yen for the limelight, a yen which cannot be quenched or satisfied, and which will not allow him to realize he is wrong no matter how great may be the sufferings of others because of his conduct.* Under similar influences Napoleon bled

France white and Karl Marx introduced a revolution in economic theories which laid the foundation for the brutal empires of Lenin, Mussolini, Hitler and Stalin, who also obtained their power by declaring themselves to be the liberals and humanitarians of their age. They started out with the same programs that the "Liberals" are introducing into the United States.

These recent examples should (but they do not) put intelligent persons on notice that when they abandon constitutional democracy, that is, free elections (voters not beholden to government for doles, pensions, jobs, contracts, etc.), short term of office, local government, and equal footing for the judiciary, legislative and the executive, they are heading for trouble. And, moreover, by free elections it is meant that citizens shall vote only toward the general objective of having experts direct the functions of government.

Chapters IV, VI, VII and VIII of the Russian constitution provide for the separate political divisions (local government) and authorizes for them about the same form of government that the Union has. No other kind would be possible. The separate political divisions merely look like local government. *The idea of independent local government has to be abandoned when a centralized government takes control of the commercial life of a country.* The political divisions can be no more than administrative organs—concerned only with following the plans of the central authority.

The state governments of the United States follow the Federal Government in form, but on a basis of relationship opposite of that in Russia. The Constitution which binds them together aims at giving them as much local power (sovereign power) as possible, and the Federal government as little as possible, subscribing to the safe democratic principle that if people are ruling themselves, are responsible for the matters within their territory, they will be better satisfied and get better results.

It is true that local matters under the Russian government are handled by local authority—but they have to be handled in accordance with a national plan. And can anyone deny that the United States has been swept a long way in that direction?

Chapter IX, Articles 102 to 117, outlines in a general way the jurisdiction of the courts. It places the judiciary in a very subordinate position. However, is that not in harmony with world trends, including the trends in the United States? The last elections certainly demonstrated that the people in the United States expect the President to make and interpret the laws, instead of Congress and the courts.

Judges are elected for a term of five years, through the Soviet, for the Union; and for three years by the people for the Republics. This is repudiation of the constitutional theory that the judges should not be directly under the control of the policy-making political authority, but be as independent of such influences as possible—appointed for life so that changes in administration, which it was expected would be frequent, would not affect the administration of justice in connection with litigation between citizens—ancient principles, purchased by blood, but repudiated in Russia and in governmental administration throughout the world. The repudiation, of course, does not arise because of the viciousness of the participants, *but for the simple reason that when government becomes the director of business and responsible to the citizen for his job, food, pensions, and everything else, there is no place left for independent courts and legislators as contemplated by the Forefathers.* It requires governmental machinery of the kind adopted by the Russians.

One observation is in point with respect to courts not being involved in policy or political issues. Because the Constitution specifies a definite form of government, judges are required to consider the greatest of all political questions, namely, form of government. Consequently, the courts, under proper circumstances, have a right to rule on form of government.[32] That is an unavoidable result, because a constitution is supposed to set out clearly the form of government under which the citizen is functioning instead of having it a matter of speculation, more or less, as is the case in Great Britain. That situation brings about another result as clearly pointed out by Chief Justice Marshall in the case of Marbury v. Madison. In that case he ruled that Congress was not entitled to a nearly conclusive presumption that the laws it enacts are in accordance with the law of the land, but is entitled only to a presumption that it was honest and in a position to be informed with respect to its action. The rule is now often stated in reverse, namely, that there is an almost conclusive presumption that Congress is right when interpreting the Constitution. That position represents the English rule, and is proper as applied to Parliament because Great Britain has no written constitution.

Chapter X, Articles 118 to 133, may be considered the Russian Bill of Rights. It emphasizes the obligation of the citizen to his government instead of the obligation of the government to the citizen. Moreover, the government is bound only to promises for the future. A dubious and undemocratic basis of exchange in view of the fact that the subscriber, the one who can be forced to perform, has pledged everything he has. The Russian Bill of Rights is novel too (although following the modern style) in that it makes the government, to the last degree, directly responsible for the welfare of the citizen.

[32] For instance, the Marbury case, wherein a law was declared unconstitutional because it changed the form of government specified in the Constitution.

Certainly out of harmony with the approach to government by the Forefathers; but certainly in harmony with the modern approach and certainly the most glamorous, but most fallacious, deadly and dangerous influence that has ever threatened civilization.

The first article in this chapter is of special significance. It reaffirms the principle that everybody must work and will be rewarded on the basis of production. That is the song of the capitalist under a free enterprise structure. But in Russia the singer who will determine what the citizen (subject) must do, the quality of his efforts and his reward,[33] is a person not financially responsible for his orders or his mistakes—a government official. Not only is the official not responsible (in the usual sense of the word) for his conduct, but he is in a position to impose a death penalty for disobedience.[34] And as government officials are made of the same kind of clay that industrialists are made of, and with an equal urge to magnify themselves, but with less responsibility for failure, one should not be astonished at the oppression that is experienced by those not agile enough to keep the favor of the administration.[35]

[33] Stuart Chase, in "Government in Business" p 157, says in substance, "I cannot see" referring to his proposed state agenda, "where it would thwart me or destroy my freedom."

Well, he would not be allowed to make a living criticizing government. He would have to bestir himself to praising it, no matter how much he hated it. His statements on page 155 indicate he would rather die than do that. Like Patrick Henry, if he cannot have his liberty, he prefers death. Death is what he would get if the government takes the course he suggests, or else he would be sent to a concentration camp with the State indifferent to the welfare of his family, if not actually persecuting it.

[34] They find it intolerable that almost every family has some member who is being subjected to repression at home or is confined in a concentration camp, that one's every step is watched not only by superiors but also by someone else; * * * that somewhere behind one's back, behind the wall, lists of suspects are being drawn up; that one is judged by a "fixed court" * * *. p 137 "The Real Soviet Russia".

[35] See footnote 16.

A little reflection along that line will readily explain the blood purges, and should make an intelligent mind hesitate to endorse the programs of the "Social Democrats". The purges, of course, start with the cutting off of political favors, but they end in concentration camps for the independent thinkers—individuals who insist upon free speech—*criticism of government*. That does not happen because anybody is or wants to be vicious, but simply because everything is represented by government, because everything is political in its character and relationship. Do not the $10,000 fines and prison sentences which were attached to violation of the OPA laws which prohibited citizens from doing what was often necessary to live—conduct a legitimate business—reflect that very thing? These laws have public support, consent of the majority, naturally. But that does not make them democratic. According to the Russians, government of that character is a proletariat dictatorship. However the "proletariat" aspect of their government was a fiction, a deception necessary to obtain adoption. Whether the dictatorship of Stalin would have been a benevolent one, or was in a position to become that, cannot be answered because of the war. But all history and all the records and all experience with that kind of government testify to the contrary, the outstanding testimony being the United States Constitution. That Constitution tried to make it impossible as well as unnecessary for the government to be changed into a dictatorship of the proletariat. Although the Constitution was more effective than other charters in attaining its objective, it has often been helpless with respect thereto. The constantly re-occurring declaration that the Constitution is being by-passed makes one apprehensive about its future.

Article 122 of Chapter X accords women the equal right to work—in practice, this means they will do manual labor the same as the males; not only work as hard, but also bear children, born and reared in maternity "houses." Western civilization backed away from manual labor for women, tried to avoid it; [36] could do so to a great extent because of its wealth-producing structure.[37]   However, it appears that "humanitarian" government is forcing western civilization, in the name of *democracy,* to compel its women to accept this "equal" opportunity. But not only is there a world-wide spirit that encourages women to enter the field of general labor, but the "humanitarians" are including children of tender age. At the age of eighteen they were called upon to meet and endure the hardships of battle under circumstances that were more trying, difficult and brutal than ever witnessed before.

Article 123 declares that it is *natural* law (there are no God ordained laws in Russia) that all races are equal in all spheres of economic, cultural, social and political life, and provides punishment for any individual advocating racial or national exclusiveness, or hatred or contempt for another race. However, hatred and contempt for political reasons is a governmental mandate in Russia, with the result that 15 million, according to authorities, are slaves—persons without any civil rights in any field.

Whatever one may believe along that line, matters of that character unless couched in very general language, are out of place in a statute, especially in a constitution. This is so because of enforcement difficulties arising from personal relationship, for it seems to be a natural law, a law of God (primitive or na-

---

[36] "The percentage of women workers in Russia is higher than in any other country * * * except for China. * * * Only by increasing female labor and that of minors is it possible to exist at all." "The Real Soviet Russia".

[37] The western idea was that a man would be able to support a wife and children so all members of the family could properly develop. Manual labor was not contemplated for the wife and children.

tural instinct), that people prefer their own race, and consider it tyranny to be forced to abandon their practices with respect to that matter. For instance, many of them love their own color of skin to such an extent that the remotest possibility of tainting it creates in them a terrorizing fear which drives them to extremes to avoid such a result. The fear may be a subconsious reaction to the feeling that personal appearances play a tremendous part in the economic and social areas. One may readily appreciate why it is difficult for some persons to understand that it is "democratic" to decrease the possibilities of their posterity continuing as white, or increasing the possibilities of some of them becoming other than white. It appears that laws in that field often have a tendency to intensify antagonism and may partake of tyranny. The folly of such laws become obvious in times of war when it seems necessary to teach hatred and contempt beyond all reason, for no reason at all.

Article 124 is the famous article about religion. Governments having charge of the daily life of the citizen to the extent necessary to make government ownership of the means of production successful, *cannot grant religious freedom in the general sense of that word.* That is particularly true with respect to the Christian religion because it teaches in too many situations that each person should rely upon himself, his conscience, his own conception of God, with respect to what is right and wrong. Such teachings, unavoidably and necessarily, carry important and comprehensive restrictions upon governmental authority because of the emphasizes they place on the rights of individuals. They clash, therefore, particularly with the laws of communism or totalitarianism (divine right of kings in disguise) as such laws invade every aspect of daily life, including the most sacred.

It should, therefore, be clear that when government is in charge of everything, jobs, vocations, professions, schools, occupations, food, clothes and shelter, that there is little room for an individual conscience of the kind advocated by Christians. *The Russian government, or any type of government that controls the means of production is obliged, compelled, in order to protect its policies, to supress any religion that emphasizes individualism,* teaches "The Kingdom of Heaven is *within* you," that God (conscience) is first, the State second.

The battles of the Anglo-Saxon for individual freedom in religion, property ownership and occupation or profession, manifested by his charters, bills of rights, petitions for rights and the United States Constitution, would seem to preclude any ground for hope that he can long adjust himself to such an arrangement. He responds too quickly to the cry of "Give me liberty or give me death."

But the Forefathers have been discarded. The trend is to accept, more and more, the proposition that the subject should depend directly upon his government for food and shelter, a proposition which in fact is none other than the doctrine of the divine right of the State. As the State is intangible, that doctrine always degenerates into the divine right of kings, personal government—government by a "leader" and his "cronies."

It should be observed that the Russians count their cause as a holy one because of its alleged objective—elimination of poverty and distress through a proper distribution of wealth by a government official—one not driven by the motive of profit. The objective is in accord with the church, and therefore has a great deal of indirect church support as awkwardly pointed out by a Congressional committee. But the church leaders evidently do not realize that government control of food and

[38] All the social democracies, including the United States, practice that art to a considerable extent.

[39] It is worthy of note that Great Britain was most reluctant to abandon voluntary military service, deeming it a basic democratic principle. No doubt, when it is fully realized that conscription of "bodies" for war purposes is bound to force conscription of property for all purposes, the citizen will appreciate why England considered conscription for war purposes tyranny instead of democracy as it is now described and utilized, one might say, from the cradle to the grave and without limitation as to time and place.

[40] See Article 123, discussed on p 45. The United States is embarrassed the same way, for its laws subscribe to the same doctrine. The citizen is confronted with a complex program by the "humanitarians". He must hate Japanese (his first love) and love Chinese; hate Italians and love Frenchmen; hate Germans, but love Russians; exclude quite generally Hindus and Chinese, as well as Europeans, but develop others. His affection and admiration, however, must be switched so rapidly, although he is enjoined by law not to hate any race, that he is bound to be neurotic. Government will command more respect by not committing itself on such subjects.

shelter forces repudiation, to a great extent, of the Christian doctrine that God (the conception of right and wrong) is personal. In other words, forces repudiation of the *personal* Saviour doctrine, and restores the ancient worship of the State—Church and State absolutely one, which requires the individual, generally, to rely for guidance of conscience upon a State official so far as right and wrong are concerned.

Article 125 names four freedoms: speech, press, assembly and street processions. But that declaration of a fundamental is prefaced with a statement indicating that it is only to strengthen the government. Could that be anything else than a complete blacking out of the freedom promised in beautiful and elaborate language elsewhere in this constitution?

The Constitution of the United States attempts to protect free speech from the standpoint of the citizen—the democratic way. The free speech which the Russian "enjoys" is the right to praise his government. It is the modern way of saying "the king can do no wrong." [38] *It must be borne in mind that free speech is an idle term in the absence of the right of a citizen to own property or the means of production.*

Article 126 is a subtle mandate to support the Government. Articles 127, 128, and 129 guarantee court procedure in criminal cases, protection against arbitrary search and seizure, and offer a home for political refugees—persons in sympathy with the Russian form of government.

Articles 130, 131, 132, and 133, are mandates to support the government's economic programs and suggest it is *treason* to do otherwise. Article 132 is particularly noteworthy in that it makes military service compulsory and extols it as an honorable duty. That is a unique proposition for democracy and a sad commentary on the "humanitarians." [39] It certainly is out of harmony with the idea that hate and contempt for other nations is taboo. How else shall the soldier fight? [40]

But these provisions advising citizens of their duty to their government are eloquent. They imply that a club is needed to get the support the government demands, and that trouble may be anticipated for those who oppose the government in any way. The consent of the government, apparently, is absent.

Mandates of that character are not found in the Constitution of the United States. Any attempt to include them would have brought outright rejection. Imagine what Henry and Jefferson would have said had the proposed constitution carried threats of that character!

Chapter XI, Articles 134 to 142, treats the fundamental subject of elections. Article 135 is supposed to reflect a modified spirit with respect to who shall participate in government. It goes to the extreme of giving the ballot to all those above 17 years of age. The political leaders apparently were satisfied that all property owners had been liquidated and that only workers remained to exercise the ballot privileges. But one must bear in mind that the voters only vote for deputies, and that the deputies designate the members of the Presidium and the Commissars. The present ballot privileges of the Russian therefore at their best are much narrower than those provided for in the United States Constitution. In fact, it is mere gesture, because the policy fixing officials of the government are not directly affected by the ballot.

Amending this constitution is a very simple matter. Article 146, Chapter XIII, provides that a two-thirds majority of the legislators may amend it. It departs from the traditional democratic idea that constitutions must be referred to the people and that *they should be difficult to amend, because of the generally recognized and well-established principles found in them.*

However, as the Russian Constitution contains much experimental matter, it will have to be changed frequently, too often to make it practical to submit the issues to the people. The issues also will be too complex, too full of controversy and demand too much haste to justify submission to them, although in the United States voters are called upon to solve the problems which presidents, judges and congressmen have been unable to solve.

No doubt, many amendments will be made to this constitution by subterfuge and deliberate unauthorized practice. Amendments by that method are not unusual. The United States Constitution has suffered much from that practice. For instance, the so-called liberal or social laws have transferred so much authority to the executive branch that the President is forced to usurp judicial and legislative functions as well as become the war-declaring power. These same laws have so enlarged governmental benefits that the ballot, which is overwhelmingly made up of the destitute, the desperate, the ignorant, the misinformed, the fearful and the unscrupulous, directs the policies of state. A poor foundation for economic security, and certainly not what the Forefathers had in mind. The whole program is a means of amending, indeed destroying, the Constitution. It widens the field of governmental immunity (sovereign power) far beyond what is authorized under the Constitution. It upsets the relationship of the Federal Government to the States and the citizens. Washington's admonition in his farewell address with respect to amendments by subterfuge has not been taken seriously. The Civil War amendments, the income tax amendment, and the amendment changing the method of electing Senators, are, of course, entirely out of harmony with the original Constitution, and have already revealed that they are detrimental to economic security. Amendments can be disastrous if they nullify or depart from the idea in the original charter.

Because of the easy manner in which the Russian constitution may be amended the Russians, in fact, do not have a constitution. All they have is a treatise on the obligations of citizens to their leaders, an indictment of a prior economic structure, promises of great things to come, and the fundamentals of government reduced to mere statutory law. Laws which must be constantly changed because they are experimental and detailed (a factor in statutory law) have no place in a constitution, and fundamentals lose their significance if they can be readily abrogated, especially in time of economic upheaval.

This constitution has already failed in an alleged democratic objective—short term of office. The leader holds office for life on the same principles through which Mussolini and Hitler acquired such a title, which both lost for other reasons than elections.

But in what countries are the leaders not enjoying or holding long terms of office? *Government of that character precludes changes of administration, because the leaders are tied too closely to business and every other phase of life.* It is the opposite of what the Forefathers tried to make for the United States and believed would most adequately protect freedom— a chance to make a decent living by way of merit and ability in the field of production, instead of using, as required by the "liberal" forms of government, every ounce of initiative and ability to keep governmental favor.

It seems as though Karl Marx has won. Nations have embraced, or are rapidly embracing, his philosophies of government under the titles of Fascism, Democracy, Social Democracy, Dictatorship of the Proletariat, Totalitarianism and Liberalism. They come riding on the god of war, to be followed by large standing armies and the four horsemen of oppression, ignorance, famine and fanaticism. Not forever, of course, but at least until the political world learns to respect again the individualism of man.

Key Propositions

Free enterprise is not without hardships and corruption. But if civilization cannot maintain high standards under free enterprise, it certainly cannot do so under government control, a procedure which only adds more graft and corruption to the already heavy load. Under such circumstances security is bound to vanish.

There is no yardstick by which to determine when a free enterprise structure has been converted into social democracy, a welfare (police) state or communism. However, when government is responsible to its subjects for their food and shelter to the extent recommended by the "liberals", it will be the government, in times of distress, that will have to seize their farms and their homes, reduce their salaries, cut off their opportunities, compel them to move and deny them the right to exercise their own initiative and judgment. The hate and malice directed toward government under such circumstances creates a war-breeding influence. Under it the citizen is never free from the nose of the inspector.

The new forms of government are dependent. They cannot survive unless other countries conform to their standards and practices.

(1) See letter of General Knox to George Washington.

(2) "The effects of these laws, interfering between debtors and creditors, were extensive. They destroyed public credit and confidence between man and man; injured the morals of the people, and in many instances insured and aggravated the final ruin of the unfortunate debtors for whose temporary relief they were brought forward." Ramsay "History of South Carolina", vol II p 429.

"Accordingly, in some of the States, creditors were treated at outlaws; bankrupts were armed with legal authority to be persecutors; and by the shock of all confidence and faith, society was shaken to its foundations". "Life and Works of Fishers Ames" vol. II p 76.

"By 1786, under the universal depression and want of confidence, all trade had well-nigh stopped, and political quackery, with its cheap and dirty remedies, had full control of the field * * * when we have threaded the maze of this rash legislation, we shall better understand that clause in our federal constitution which forbids the making of laws impairing the obligation of contracts." Fiske "The Critical Period" p 168.

"Money capital was * * * attacked * * * by paper money, stay laws, pine barren acts, and other devices for * * * delaying the collection of debts." Beard "Economic Interpretation of the Constitution" pp 31-32.

"The actual evils which led to the Federal Convention of 1787 are familiar to every reader of history and need no detailed description here. As is well known, they arose, in general * * * from State legislation unjust to citizens and productive of dissensions with neighboring states—the state laws particularly complained of being the staying process of the Courts, making property a tender in payment of debts, issuing paper money, interfering with foreclosure or mortgages." Warren "The Making of the Constitution" pp 5, 6.

Illuminating comment on state legislation is to be found in Chap. VI, Vol. 1, Bancroft's "History of the Formation of the Constitution of the United States" under the heading "State Laws Impairing the Obligations of Contracts" pp. 230-236. Also see MacMaster and Channing.

"Power tends to corrupt and absolute power corrupts absolutely."

"LIBERALS" AND PRIVATE INDUSTRY

CHAPTER II

Free Enterprise as the Solution

It is necessary to review some familiar back-ground in order to properly evaluate the theories of the "Liberal" with respect to private industry, business, commerce, property.

At the time of the Constitutional Convention economic distress engulfed the country. Desperation, starvation, and anarchy prevailed. Civil war broke out in Massachusetts under a program to repudiate all debts and seize property for distribution to the poor.[1] Other States on the same premises were so near to civil war that another jolt would plunge them into it. Recommendations for adjustment were mostly that the government seize everything in order to pay the private debts and satisfy the hungry. The property of the Tories, of course, was in particular danger because of sentiment that they should not be allowed to keep their property while those who had fought in the war were starving.[2] However, as things stood, anyone who had property was afraid of losing it because those without property, the great majority, were ready to take it by legislation, taxation, confiscation, riots, mob action, or civil war.

55

The destitute desired to place everything under government control. Consequently, only business men, lawyers, judges and legislators who advocated repudiation of debts and seizure of property had popular favor. Many of the politicians, therefore, were keyed in that direction.[3] There was little sentiment among the destitute for representative government from the standpoint of protection for private industry—free enterprise. In those days, too, the destitute (and who could blame them) were clamoring for governmental distribution of wealth in the name of democracy, and, of course, also without realizing that such procedure would result in an economic structure in which subjects look (in vain) to government for jobs, food, homes, clothes, pensions, etc.

Also among the upper class there was not much sentiment for representative government, except from the standpoint of protection of title to property. The clamor and agitation for debt repudiation and seizure of property for government relief programs frightened the owners of property. Naturally, those with property were advocating the minimum of government control.

With the tremendous pressure on one side for debt repudiation and seizure of private property for relief of the destitute, and on the other the demand for protection of private property, it was a miracle that representative government, the right to vote and own property, as contemplated by the Constitution, came as the result of the 1787 Convention. It also was a miracle that complete government control of the means of

[3] Of course, politicians are prone to believe that citizens must rely upon government for food and shelter. What makes a better nest for them than a host of citizens dependent upon government for such things. And as in the case of the capitalist, the more absolute and abject their dependence, the greater the security for the politician. The danger is that like the capitalist he will overplay his hand and make civil war inevitable, as occurred in Italy, Germany and Russia.

production did not develop, as it developed in Russia from 1917 to about 1921.

The Objective of the Forefathers

The Forefathers, therefore, were in a position to realize that unless they took drastic action against the current proposals, economic security would permanently perish. They, particularly, were in a position to realize that a chance to be financially independent, independent of government favoritism, dole and charity, vanished completely when a substantial number of voting citizens became dependent on government, looked to it, for their food, shelter, jobs, wages and hours of work. They, therefore, turned to the theory of the right of the private citizen (under the checks of competition and ballot restrictions) to own property in any amount, especially the means of production, as the basis for economic security.

Let us digress to say that Hamilton, who is criticized by the "Liberals" for his concern about property, and his lack of confidence in poor people, was not unique in that respect. However, he, evidently, realized more fully than his contemporaries that no matter how intelligent people are, their judgment is not trustworthy where self-interest is involved, especially if they are under the pressure imposed by distress, hunger and poverty. Those who criticize him are generally the "liberals" who are making a good living at the expense of the taxpayers, when the opportunities in private industry have broken down and the voters are in confusion. It is not unfair to say that statesmen working for sound government today are subjected to the same criticisms that Hamilton received. However, they are contending with far more powerful and vicious influences than he faced.

Of course restoration of the channels of business was the

only way to remedy the situation. Healthy business eliminated unemployment and the need for charity. Healthy business also made it possible for citizens to pay their debts, make themselves independent of government doles, and, besides, make their government strong. The Forefathers tried to bring about that result by giving citizens more freedom in property ownership—freeing commercial property from arbitrary government control. They, therefore, made their rules for voting, for elections, the courts, short term of office, legislators and enforcement officers with a view to promote and protect business.[4]

They were practical enough to realize that there would always be a substantial amount of favoritism, downright corruption and graft. They hoped to remedy that evil to some extent. Their job would be difficult for political favoritism had always waxed fat through corrupt government monopolies. It was that unsavory practice which made it possible for the merchants of England to compel the colonies to trade with the mother country, and also preclude them from manufacturing at home or contacting foreign markets. As the beneficiaries of the practice controlled the ballot there was not much chance for relief through that function. To what extent they controlled matters may be gathered from the fact that in 1872 a bill was passed disfranchising Revenue Collectors (government officials) and excluding from the House of Commons the contractors,—the five-percenters.

The Forefathers, apparently were confronted with the same problems that plague the world today and always will. For instance, the governmental favorites of the old British Empire have their counterpart today in over-protected utilities, unwholesome patronage and other favored groups, including

---

[4] Today the "Liberals" use that machinery to discourage production. Like the capitalists and labor leaders, they are always terrorized by the fear of overproduction.

labor unions, notwithstanding the recent legislation.[5] The Forefathers would consider such arrangements as contrary to the principles of what they called free enterprise under the laissez faire doctrine. And such arrangements call for different election procedure than now in use if the opportunity for a citizen to earn a decent living on his merits as a producing unit is to be properly protected.[6] (See page 60 for footnotes 5 and 6.) Henry Hazlitt's suggestion with respect to disfranchisement referred to on page 65 needs careful analysis. Indeed all economists and statesmen subscribe to his proposition. Only a dishonest politician refuses to endorse it. But if this legislation called "liberal" law forces such a change in the franchise, how can it be called constitutional? And if it is unconstitutional it probably will defeat economic security—its alleged objective.

The bitter experience that merchants had with governmental interference is reflected in the constitutional set-up to bring about free enterprise—the right of the citizens to own the means of production and to trade with other citizens anywhere in the world, without special or unwholesome protection to anyone from the government. Achievement of that goal, as already suggested, was sought through observing principles long recognized but difficult to honor, namely, the principles which relate to maintaining independent judges and legislators, free elections, short term of office and the scaredness of contracts or of private property. These principles, of course, involve the free enterprise philosophy *that the individual be responsible to himself for his economic security,* that there shall be no law-decreed limitation upon the amount of property he may acquire, that taxation shall be only for the usual functions of government, and that local matters be taken care of by communities, townships, cities, counties and states, according to their readily recognized sphere of influence.

What should be considered the functions and sphere of in-

[5] The Taft-Hartley Act still leaves in a political arm (the president) the authority to determine when an injunction shall be issued against a strike. The owner of an industry is still at the mercy of a labor union's political policy,—still in such cases without the constitutional right to apply directly to the courts to protect his property.

[6] David Lawrence in a recent issue of U. S. News, sets out that fact in a most striking manner by showing how labor union norms of work are far below a reasonable output. The ballot influence apparently is so great that the elected branch is helpless so far as a remedy is concerned.

(See page 59 for text.)

[7] If the trades worked six days a week on an honest production norm, at their present wages, an excellent six-room house could be produced at about half the present price; a price that would make home ownership possible for 10,000,000 people. However, the laborer wants short hours and high pay. The politicians dare not interfere, and the money lenders do not want to. A development of such homes would, of course, destroy the value of the mortgages on the high priced property. No one, therefore, expects relief of any significance in that field.

Charles E. Wilson, Defense Mobilizer, admits that production is the only method for defeating inflation. However, he does not dare to suggest a six-day week, especially not without extra pay! If he even hinted at such procedure, the labor leaders, in the name of Liberty and Freedom, would force his resignation within a few days. It is to be noted, however, that there is no timidity about asking teenagers to give up their educational opportunities and their jobs coupled with a substantial reduction in pay, and face battlefiled hazards! Unlike Abraham, they cannot find a substitute for the child.

fluence of government in connection with promoting business (security) constituted the real knot, still does, and always will. And one cannot fail to see that many things which had to be considered as private, local and state matters in 1789, in order to promote business (protect security) must now, for that purpose, be considered national matters, and even international, and there is nothing in the Constitution which prevents them from being handled in that way. But also it should be obvious that crop control, price control, control of hours of work, closed shop laws, subsidies, etc., can readily be pushed to a point where they adversely affect public welfare and, therefore, become unconstitutional in spirit as well as in the letter of the law. It is certain that the Fathers did not intend that the voters should be direct beneficiaries of government bounty to the extent they are today, or that government officials should play such an important part in the investment of the money of the taxpayer or the conducting of his business.

According to the "Liberals" there was no danger in the early days of overproduction, gouging the public, or retarding production, and, therefore, controls of the character they recommend were not necessary. But the laws restraining monopolies prove the contrary. And just like today, the government official was the greatest offender in gouging the public and retarding production. It seems that no matter how many persons are starving and homeless, labor leaders, government officials and industrialists always have nightmares about overproduction. Modifying the evil by better means of distribution gets little attention. When there are no more destitute it will be proper for the government to worry about overproduction and try to prevent it by food destruction, five-day weeks, high unemployment awards, a large Army and Navy, unrestrained strikes, low norms of production, slow-downs and featherbedding.[7]

[8] "Russia must overtake and surpass the most advanced capitalist countries in industry and military achievement within ten years or the capitalistic countries will annihilate us." Stalin in 1931 as quoted by Scott in "Behind the Urals" p 257.

" * * * To slacken the tempo means to fall behind. And the backward are always beaten. No, we do not want this. Incidentally the history of old Russia is the history of defeat due to backwardness. She was beaten by the Mongol khans. She was beaten by the Turkish beys. She was beaten by the Swedish barons. She was beaten by the Japanese barons * * * because she was backward * * * We are fifty to one hundred years behind advanced countries. We must cover this distance in ten years. Either we do this or they will *crush* us." Stalin, Feb. 4, 1931.

"The newest furnaces in the United States are 1000 cubic meter volume; therefore it was decided that the Magnitogorsk furnaces should have a volume of in the neighborhood of 1100 cubic meters instead of 788 cubic meters. It was likewise decided that the other units of the plant should also exceed in size the best achievements of Germany and the United States as a prerequisite to equaling and surpassing the achievements of the capitalist world in the field of technique." Scott "Behind the Urals." p 271.

However, the Forefathers were trying to create an economic structure which gave the citizen the right to acquire wealth lawfully in any amount under open competition, and thus stimulate business so there would be no necessity for governmental charity or subsidies aimed at discouraging production. They were well aware of the economic disadvantages which developed from competition, but they also realized that wealth had to be concentrated to give it the strength it had to have to produce in the quickest, cheapest and best way possible. Failure in that respect would bring the maximum of distress.[8] The problem was how to keep wealth (commercial power) and political power from merging into one place—in the government, or in a private corporation.

The Forefathers evidently were persuaded that the best way to solve the complex problems that threatened security was to keep the three branches of government on an equal footing and in their usual places; keep the right to vote within the rule of *equal responsibility, equal benefits, and equal knowledge of the subject matter;* keep public sentiment and majority rule under proper checks, and particularly observe the principles of short terms of office and control of local matters for local authority. That, apparently, in their judgment constituted representative government and the best way to promote public welfare. Their solution was not perfect. Concentrated wealth and concentrated political power continue to be a source of abuse and oppression.

The Premises of the "Liberals"

At this point it is proper to introduce the major premise of the "Liberals." They believe that the remedy for poverty and misery is to bring the means of production (property) completely, or at least more fully, under the control or management of an "elected" government official. The most obvious objections to their proposition will be discussed under: Elections, Short term of office, States, Courts, Individuals, Independent Government, and the Crux of the matter.

Effect Upon Elections

Their confidence in a government official, as a manager of business, is based upon the theory that he is elected, or represents one who was elected, and will therefore respond to the majority. (As though minorities were not entitled to consideration, or that majorities are always right.) The United States Constitution of course does not provide, by elections or otherwise, for "political managers of business." However, the Russian ballot, used by the "Liberals" as an example for their propositions regarding "elected" management, has far less significance than the ballot in the United States. The Soviet builders appreciated the danger inherent in the franchise. They, therefore, gave the Russian ballot nominal weight in connection with the election of the officials responsible for the economic life of Russia.

Of course each step that government takes toward regulating, directing or owning business, requires an increase in personnel dependent upon the government for jobs, contracts, loans, relief, pensions, food, clothes and shelter. That creates a relationship between them and their government which, when there are a great many of them, should preclude them from using the ballot, except in a very indirect manner—the Russian style. In the manner that the ballot is used in the United States it takes only a small percentage of the voters receiving government benefits to destroy the proper relation between the government and the citizen from the standpoint of protecting public welfare.[9] A person seeing an opportunity to obtain a substantial benefit, especially if he is in need, will naturally resolve everything in his favor to obtain that benefit. That he will take such a course even without need, is the implication in every contract, compact, charter, constitution or law. Voters dependent upon government for their contracts, social and political positions, business privileges, homes, shelter, food and jobs, because of self-interest, *are in a poor position to measure their responsibilities with respect to public welfare.* As it is their own act, there is only praise for the government's conduct, no matter how corrupt. And let it be repeated that under such circumstances free speech (criticism of government) automatically disappears, is completely destroyed, and in the absence of free speech there is no economic security. The leaders of social democracies, therefore, *although they deny it,* soon take the steps necessary to nullify the ballot by making it mere gesture procedure. It is not done because they are vicious. It is the only course open to them to save such security as remains. Could there be a more fantastic conception of government than the popular idea of electing "political managers" of business? But is not that the very course into which the various "deals" are driving the United States? Is not the Chief Executive, in fact, already a general director of interstate business? For instance, his authority in connection with strike procedure.

Effect Upon Short Term of Office

That the Forefathers were trying to make a constitution

[9] "The clear solution of this problem is to disfranchise the governmental officeholder." Hazlitt "A New Constitution Now" p 116.

Hazlitt suggests the same rule for farmers, corporations, or any individual or agency drawing benefits from the government, unwittingly, it appears, disclosing that our present trend of government, if persisted in, will destroy free elections. That certainly would carry with it the destruction of free speech, free courts and free legislators—the only real basis for economic security.

which would prevent government from entering, regulating or controlling daily life and business affairs along the lines now recommended and practiced, is further established by their short term of office principle, as distinguished from the present life tenures by "fixed" elections. The life tenures of past rulers made it possible for them to have lifetime business favorites, with the usual adverse affect on public welfare. No doubt, it was believed that short term of office would greatly reduce such situations—prevent powerful groups or individuals, in the name of public welfare, liberalism, etc., from getting too much control of government. With a potential change in administration every two, four or six years, it would not be practical to have elected government officials too closely related to business. To change the key-men, or the men in actual control of business by popular vote would jeopardize stability of business too much—would destroy the nation because of industrial stagnation. Under such circumstances no one would care to invest money or effort in private enterprise. *Aware of that fact the Russians introduced complete government control, a situation which eliminates private property and consequently does not require money in the true sense of the word.* They believed that such a course would eliminate worry about profit, depressions, and over-production. Incidentally private industry does not develop in Western Europe because of the threat of Russian confiscation—abolition of property, as well as money, in the conventional sense of those words.[10]

"Liberalism" has brought on a similar fear in the United States—the fear that government control will advance so far

[10] That situation made, and still makes it impossible for Russia to join or accept the world bank idea. Her money system is entirely foreign to what was contemplated at the New Hampshire Conference.

that private property loses its significance. Because of lack of confidence in investment opportunities, banks pay a very nominal return on savings, etc. Business is reluctant to expand because there is no assurance that the same men will continue in office, or that the government can proceed with its plans. An election may bring in leaders bent upon changing everything. Such a situation creates stagnation because neither the government nor the business man can determine which way to move. In the absence of "fixed" elections, making a change in key-men improbable, the only investments that keep the country alive are those underwritten by taxpayers, often without their consent, and generally of such a character that no intelligent banker would accept them. Of course, the taxpayers underwrite these investments whether they want to or not. The "peoples" government politely (tyranically?) assumes that they want to invest and that they want the government official to spend and invest their money in various ways! As suggested, the Russians solved these problems by abolishing the right to own property and discarding conventional money. The latter an unavoidable result.

The low interest on public debt is often pointed to as a benefit derived from "modified" government control. But what is gained in that way is lost three-times over in low interest on saving accounts, absence of accounts, lack of opportunity in the investment field and idle dollars, because of the threat of possible abolition of property—government assuming too much control over the means of production.

The same trends occurred in Germany. Her communistic or totalitarian social experimentations (at first called social democracy) started with "liberal" laws of the character highly

[11] On page 85 of "Government in Business" Stuart Chase in showing advancement of public business states: "We must remember that England is thirty years ahead of the United States in social security legislation. Lloyd George forced through the Old Age Pension Act in 1908. Unemployment insurance followed in 1911, compulsory health insurance in 1912. She has maintained a vast army of unemployed on the dole since the war. Between 1919-1929, she built 1,275,000 houses, one-third by lump sum subsidies from the State, * * *. In January 1939, the government launched a nation-wide housing and slum clearance measure. Whole areas in London and other big cities will be transformed. It will be a punishable offense for more than two persons to occupy a single room. The number of houses to be replaced is expected to run into hundreds of thousands. Housing is not the only measure of large scale public enterprise financed by the British government. It has nationalized the superpower network, rigidly controlling both the generation and the distribution of power. It has nationalized radio broadcasting. It has set up a series of agricultural controls more far reaching and more effective than those of the AAA. The financiers of the City carry on, as is the way with Englishmen, but business in 1935 is a very different kettle of fish from business in 1913, or in 1930."

But England was not able to pay anything on her First World War debt, and had to call on capitalistic United States in 1940 to save her from an enemy not half her size. What conclusion must one draw from that?

[12] "Before Fascism came to power in Italy, about 1921, Italian labor through its own organization had won collective bargaining, compulsory accident, old age, invalidity and unemployment insurance; reduced hours of work, and secured government supported employment agencies. The condition of Italian labor was slowly but surely being improved. Then came Fascism. All these gains won with infinite effort wiped out; hours of work lengthened, wages were reduced, and the standard of living lowered. Union headquarters, newspapers, and cooperatives were destroyed. With the stabilization of the lira in 1927 began continued and drastic wage cuts. From 1927 to 1935 day wages were reduced 37 per cent. Measured against the cost of living the purchasing power of day wages was reduced at least 15 per cent. Actual annual earnings have declined even more. Fascists organizations were given exclusive privileges of placing workers: unemployed members of the fascist party had the preference for the job. Funds which went into accident, old age and sickness and insurance have been in one form or another taken from the beneficiary because the government had increasing use for these funds as a source of credit." Pettengill. "Jefferson, the Forgotten Man" p 181.

See footnote 18 for Social Laws in Germany; footnote 31 for Russia, and footnote 26 for Ancient Rome. Also see footnote 15 of Chap. VI.

recommended by Stuart Chase,[11] and accordingly endorsed by the Newdeal. But before many years had passed, to meet her obligations she was compelled to steal the trade of smaller countries, resort to barter and exchange because of corrupted money, and eventually plunge the world into war. Nothing short of civil war could have driven Hitler from his exalted position. The short term of office principle had been completely destroyed by "fixed" elections. His life-term grip on office came by way of social reforms of the same character as those embraced by Italy, Russia, Great Britain and the United States.[12]

The NRA may be used as a further illustration of the proposition that the short-term of office principle must be abandoned if the government-in-business tendency continues. If the NRA had remained in force for several years, it certainly would have involved complete control of business by trained government officials. Changing officials so intimately connected with business under a short office term, controlled by general elections, would wreck any commercial program. A governmental set-up of that character requires an unbroken policy. It is as impracticable to change such an administration by way of elections as it would be to have military leaders elected by ballot, or industrial leaders elected every two years by the employees. The relationship to the undertaking by the responsible person is of a character which precludes relying upon voters who, no matter how noble or intelligent they are, are not in a position to grasp the issues.

That changing policies would involve too much danger was admitted during the presidential campaigns. The Republican party wanted to keep the machinery—only change the engineer. But there were too many voters who were afraid to change. That accounts for keeping an engineer who was in poor health, and certainly suggests that he had a life-time

[13] Former Secretary Wallace, who, no doubt, was the most vivid and active spokesman for the European social programs, including those recommended by Lord Keynes and Labor leader Laski, insistently proclaimed that such programs did not interfere with or preclude the forefathers' conception of constitutional government—free enterprise.

That Mr. Wallace has the same objectives that the Forefathers had may be taken for granted. However, it is believed that the Fathers would be startled if they could hear him say that his programs would be endorsed by them. It is probable he more nearly represents the governmental machinery Daniel Shays had in mind. If he said what is in his heart, he would admit that he knew his methods were altogether alien to their ideas, but that he believes his methods are much better to bring about the common objective.

[14] "The most persistent problems of American constitutional law arise from the fact that to a multiplicity of state legislatures have been assigned the most important powers of government over private rights. * * * as rights (property rights) have been nationalized so must political power, upon which rights necessarily depend, be nationalized correspondingly," Pp 90 and 91 of "Twilight of the Supreme Court" Corwin.

A subtle suggestion that state legislatures are not to be taken too seriously, although the Milk Case, 291 US 501, quoted on p 99 of Corwin's book, seems to throw back to the states the duty of protecting public welfare in somewhat the same fashion as the Slaughter House case.

The following decisions clearly demonstrate that Professor Corwin was trying to justify legislation which required abandonment of the constitutional conception of states. Not because of changes in the social structure, but because of radical changes in the philosophy of government:

Marbury v. Madison, jurisdiction of the three branches of government; Fletcher v. Peck and Dartmouth Case for constitutional protection against state laws; Martin v. Hunter's Lessee for Federal authority over state courts, and Gibbons v. Ogden for Federal authority over commerce.

tenure, the same that Hitler, Mussolini and Stalin had, and that others now enjoy. Like Roosevelt and Truman, future presidents will be confronted with the same situation.

A primary danger in these arrangements is that even under a nominal program, the leader can easily allege or introduce the emergencies which will make him the indispensable man. *If he is a normally ambitious individual, it is to be expected that he will do so.* In that respect, Mark Anthony and Caesar were not unique characters; neither were Hitler, Mussolini, or Stalin. Constitutional prohibitions are inadequate.

There is therefore in that kind of government, whether it is NRA, AAA, or OPA, the seed of perpetuity in office—the death of elections, democratic government. Under such circumstances, without any reflection upon intelligence, integrity or patriotism, elections are bound to degenerate into stampedes for governmental benefits; are bound to create a relationship between the citizen and his government that makes elections of the American type too dangerous and results under any election procedure in one-party rule, life-time office for leaders: first, by consent; but eventually by fear, fraud, graft and corruption.

Effect Upon the States

Moreover, such a type of government throws out of balance the intended constitutional relationship between states and the federal government, especially with respect to local responsibility—a fundamental democratic principle.[14] It is impossible to administer the NLRA, the Wage and Hour Act, the present agricultural acts, and the general subsidies to business and the States, including pensions and relief, and not reduce the States to administrative organs. Their citizens are obliged to look to Federal policies for their privileges and benefits. Their courts and laws are obliged to follow Federal policies. The Supreme Court's condemnation of the NRA and the AAA are pertinent.

The unavoidable consequences of these programs is to increase corruption because the responsible authority is too far away to administer effective rebukes or remove the cause.

Political divisions such as states are the usual and necessary consequences of government. The Constitution excels all other documents in defining the jurisdiction of such divisions. The doctrine of states, or local government, is based on the fact that the inhabitants in the vicinity are best qualified to determine the laws necessary for local business, charity and morals. There is always confusion as to where local government should terminate and centralized government begin. That confusion not only called into existence charters and constitutions, but caused a lot of bloodshed, including the Civil war. It is not so much that the terms in the charters are not clear. The difficulty arises because human beings, minds swayed by self-interest, are bound to interpret words so as to increase their own power. Language is not sufficient to restrain them.

The provisions in the Constitution with respect to the jurisdiction of states are of such a character that changes in the economic structure do not require alterations. The cases referred to on page 70 establish that. Justice Marshall was contending with the usual matters of government. Today the contention is about the lack of integrity of business men, their "high" integrity when they become government officials, and the new idea that the tax payers through a government official can arrange matters so that there will be no hardships. That raises new questions. How far can the Federal Government advance with the new ideas without impairing the foundation of democracy (economic security)—local government?

The lawyers tried to stop the stampede to federal control by using the Commerce Clause, the Due Process Clause and the Contract Clause. Those phrases applied to Marshall's problems, but not to the problems confronting them. They really had only one issue: These laws defeat economic security.[15]

Effect Upon the Courts

The proper relation between the government and the courts is destroyed by this kind of government, even as matters stand today. The Constitution is based upon a proposition that judges cannot be independent if too much of the litigation is between the citizen and his government.

It was the futility of pleading for relief in civil matters before the King's judges (the government owning most of the property) that caused the Forefathers to plan so carefully to have a structure under which the citizen did not have to contend with his government about property, homes, jobs and wages. Otherwise, when a judge undertakes to decide a case, he is obliged to antagonize, or at least oppose, the government's economic policies as occurred in the Newdeal cases and brought on the court "purge." That is too difficult a position for a judge. Under such circumstances he, generally, supports the administration and will abuse the citizen who is foolhardy enough to complain. The judges would have to be much more than humanitarians to justify anyone in expecting any other attitude.[15a] But, nevertheless, it is a reflection on the integrity of every judge, president and congressman, if he does not make constant protest to such a violation of democratic government. Obviously, under the form of government advocated by the

[15] That they do is obvious as they force the States to follow the Santa Claus policies of the Federal Government. What is disturbing as well as alarming is that the States want to exercise the socializing prerogatives that the Federal Government has introduced.

[15a] The 1936 Russian Constitution recognized that difficulty and therefore placed the courts in a subordinate position.

[16] See Chap. IX of the Russian Constitution.

[17] For instance the NLRA, which makes it impossible for the government to protect employees who have not joined a union, and also those who because of family expenses need more than a five-day week, or a forty-hour week, to meet the budget.

[18] On p 83 of "Government in Business" Chase tables the pre-war social structure in Germany for about 1936 in this manner:

"If he is under twenty-five, he may be ordered to turn his business over to an older man and go into the labor service or the military forces.

If he is unemployed, he may be sent to a labor camp.

If he is a farm hand, he cannot go to the city to seek work.

If he is a peasant, his farm becomes an "hereditary manor" which he cannot sell, but must hold intact for his eldest son.

If he is a shopkeeper, he is liable to arrest for raising prices, even if his costs go up. (In the United States, under OPA, he was liable to arrest for either raising or lowering prices).

If he is a manufacturer, he must employ as many workers as the state commands, whether he needs them or not. He must consult with his workers, organized into Nazi Unions, and be responsible for their welfare.

If he is a professor, artist, writer, clergyman, he must conform to Nazi dogma or lose his livelihood, if not his citizenship."

It appears from Manya Gordon's book, "Fifty Years of Russian Labor", from John Scott's book, "Beyond the Urals", and from White's "Report on Russia", that Stalin's program is far more drastic.

[19] What seems to be overlooked by the Church leaders is that the Russian government cannot function under a theory of individual rights of the character involved in Christianity.

"Liberals", the appointment of judges for life has an effect opposite to what the Forefathers aimed at. They become administrative helpers, instead of checks upon arbitrary conduct of the legislative or executive branches. Such an arrangement calls for short term of office for the judges. The Russians recognized that fact in their 1936 Constitution.[16] At least, no one has been able to suggest a way of keeping judges independent, in the true sense of the word, when government is closely tied into every phase of daily life as is now, generally, the case. Are not the numerous governmental agencies acting in a three-fold capacity evidence to that effect? The cry of the "liberal" is that ownership of private property makes the judges too subservient to private individuals. But, apparently, the government control recommended by the "liberals" only aggravates the matter complained about.

Effect on the Individual

When government assumes all the responsibilities now urged upon it and being rapidly embraced by it, it soon finds itself in a position where it cannot consider as paramount the individual's inherent rights.[17] It then in time of peace, as in war, if it continues such procedure long enough, has to assign his job, ration his food and clothes, restrict his associations, stipulate his hours of work, specify his wages [18] and either eliminate or name his God.[19] That aspect of political science seems to be difficult, for even the intelligent German did not realize that such was true until it was too late.

That kind of government is keyed to *military procedure* and has to abandon the constitutional conception of free speech, separation of church and state, protection against seizure of property, court procedure and elections. A military organization when threatened with immediate destruction cannot use

[20] Wallace denied this in his book, "Sixty Million Jobs", but he does not show how it can be avoided and apparently is satisfied that the experiences in the past, including those in Italy, Germany and Russia, are not pertinent.

Three theories have developed from this confusion. One is that government planning can avoid collapse. The other two do not accept that position. One of them believes that when a collapse does occur, that will be a good time to invest—evidently assuming that free enterprise will return to a sound basis. The other one, which seems to be the most general, is that when a collapse does occur, complete government control will result, i.e., that is an economic structure where private property will receive little, if any, consideration.

It is obvious that no human mind is comprehensive enough to anticipate what the future holds for the human race. It is sure if men are to be obliged to rely on political relations for their economic security, instead of property, that they will experience tyranny that will bring on civil war.

[21] It appears that most analyzers of communism overlook that elementary but most important fact. Dallin in his careful analysis of 1944 in "The Real Soviet Russia" in comparing Stalin's nationalism with that of Trotsky, seems to miss that point. (See his chap., "The Devil's Name is Trotsky.")

elections, or civil courts, or honor an individual's religious convictions. The advocates of these new forms of government, especially the kind Wallace represents, apparently do not realize that they are asking that wartime powers be granted in peacetime.[20]

With so many urging government to plunge or wade deeper into ownership and direction of business, it cannot be repeated too often that such a course will destroy the four freedoms for the great majority and expose them to the ravaging of the four monsters, corruption, waste, want and war. It certainly is not the road to democracy! It brought the people of Italy and Germany the terrors of tyranny. It is to be observed that these two nations were gradually led toward absolute government control of the means of production—a form of government under which the citizen does not have a real constitution, or worthwhile courts and parliaments, and is allowed ownership only in a very nominal amount of property, with the consequence that money becomes merely a token for exchange purposes, and in a very limited field at that. The Russians, it should be observed, started with the maximum of government control and are gradually working in the opposite direction!

Effect Upon Independent Government

These forms of government cannot survive unless other countries conform to the same standards.[21] Stalin and Trotsky made that proposition the basis of their campaigns. Later, Stalin shrewdly, but deceitfully, preached to the contrary. His attacks upon capitalism proved his deceitfulness. Nevertheless Americans believed his words. The Russian party members knew better. They continued to compel governments to follow their ideas, even if they had to overthrow them. It is not that they want to rule the world: *their form of government cannot function successfully unless the other nations adopt the same style of government.* And is not the United States sub-scribing to that principle in its protests against certain forms of government in Europe and Asia? It also has accepted dependent government. It cannot for long survive economically on its "slow-downs", high wages, unrestricted strike policies, short work weeks, etc., if the other nations, with adequate machinery, are on a six-day week and a low wage scale, or use, what for lack of a better term, must be called government "slave labor." The high cost of production in the United States will make impossible profitable commercial exchanges with the cheap "slave-labor" economic structures. It will force perma-nent Marshall Plans, plus war-breeding situations, as well as isolationism by way of tariffs and other means of exclusion of cheap labor commodities.[22] One might digress enough to say that labor leaders are isolationists when it comes to preventing aliens from coming to the United States.

States.

The forefathers built the Constitution on the free enterprise theory (private citizens owning the means of production) under the conviction that such a structure would produce the best in the quickest and cheapest way possible.

The Crux of the Matter

Government control or "planning", as contemplated by the "liberals", as already suggested, is based on the proposition that it will, with fewer hardships produce more cheaply, better and more quickly than free enterprise as conceived by the Forefathers, or by the present-day conservatives. Therefore, the question is which method is the most effective.

There is no yardstick to determine when government "planning" has converted a free enterprise structure into a

---

[22] The Atlantic Pact will not be able to save us. But see article of Philip Cortney of Nov. 29, 1951, in Commercial and Financial Chronicle.

social democracy, communism, or totalitarianism, or when "planning" has advanced so far that it will force complete government control of the means of production, as in Russia. But this distinction appears to be obvious:

The "planners" put their emphasis for control of the means of production upon the judgment of *government officials*. This is primarily on the ground that a government official is not under a profit urge and will be kept in line by the ballot.

However, such factors are offset by the fact that such officials are not financially responsible for their recommendations or conduct, cannot be sued, or made to keep their promises, and have at their command the Army and Navy as well as the judges and legislators. In lieu of the profit urge is the "political power" urge. Moreover, under such circumstances, the ballot becomes an accelerator of complete government control, whereupon the worker cannot acquire property such as real estate or business, including farms and banks. Under such an arrangement the ballot must be neutralized, and it becomes necessary to appeal to the workers' patriotism, or threaten them, in order to stimulate production. (Stalin, in disregard of communism, introduced "government privileges" to stimulate production.)

The advocates of free enterprise stress the judgment of individuals financially responsible for their conduct, *who have to pay for their mistakes,* who may be sued and who do not have the Army and Navy at their command, nor have direct control of the judges and the law makers. They believe that industrialists, private citizens, under the limitations referred to, notwithstanding the "profit urge" will be in the best position to direct the economic policies of a country. To stimulate production the worker is offered wages (money) with which he may acquire property in any amount, and be free from government doles, etc.

Free enterprise (not the present concoction) was chosen by the Forefathers because the past proved that when politicians, *persons not financially responsible for their conduct,* directed the economic policy, misery and poverty increased ten-fold. Such is still the result. As an illustration: The politicians try to catch up with their promises by decreeing a minimum wage. Before a decade elapses they have to double that wage, and the doubled wage will not purchase as much as the original. The twenty-five-dollar-a-week unemployment pay has shrunk in purchase value to $10, and the thirty-dollars-a-day laborer, cannot afford to buy the things he makes. The greatest injustice befalls insurance beneficiaries, pensioners and retired citizens, who paid in advance. Their life-time investments already have lost more than half their value. Obviously there has not been much progress so far as relief from distress and misery is concerned.[23] It is a difficult program. Eggs, butter, potatoes, meat, milk, cotton and wool, must be destroyed, given away or put in storage, in order to go on with the dance. If there are any benefits, they will be temporary and eventually will have to be paid for thrice over. What an opportunity for ridicule of free enterprise (capitalism) by the Russians.

Under this heading the matter of the relationship of the citizen to government in "social" democracies should be examined. It cannot avoid a system which gives a government official a prerogative of determining whether a business of any character shall start, develop or terminate. Could one conceive of a more dangerous situation, so far as public welfare is concerned?

[23] It has been suggested to the 81st Congress by a legislator that pension and retirement income be raised whenever wages are raised. That at least will defer the day of reckoning! The original Townsend plan of $100 a month is futile now. Two hundred dollars a month is inadequate. Ten years from now, unless we change our course, $300 will be inadequate.

Moreover, because he stands in the position of owner and employer, when economic distress develops there is direct conflict between the citizens and their government with respect .o jobs, food and shelter. Civil war and revolution are the inevitable result, for the government is a primary party to the controversies and the power to be blamed. The wrath against the government is sure to materialize, for it is the government that caused them to invest in the bankrupt organization, that forecloses on their mortgages, drives them from their homes, reduces their wages, abolishes their jobs and withholds their food. The hate and malice and bitterness engendered by the collapse instead of being directed against a private individual or a private corporation, as would be the case under free enterprise, is directed toward government. What else could result but civil war under such circumstances? Civil war is inevitable for there is no neutral tribunal or arbitrator. The government is a party to the controversy. The citizen therefore is confronted with a force (the government) which has no superior—from which there is no appeal, except the one to Heaven—the sword. Because the "planners" (dictators) are filled with the spirit of "humanitarianism", they are apt to be the first to draw the sword to defend their position.

It was hoped that free enterprise would avoid such unfortunate consequences. It was an attempt to create a situation that when distress overtook a nation the wrath of the disappointed would be directed against a private citizen or corporation, and the government would be in a position to act as a neutral tribunal, that is, not be a party to the controversy. How else could one expect to maintain sound government? Of course, free enterprise also involves the presumption that a person financially responsible for his conduct will use better judgment

[24] With all due respect to the Dean of Canterbury and his "Soviet Power", and "Sixty Million Jobs."

It should be clear by this time that security creating "free enterprise" does not have a Chinaman's chance under the government-supported labor union policies.

[24a] "I should not feel my freedom outraged * * * if the state guaranteed me economic security. "Government in Business" p 155. Chase. The premise is based on the assumption that the state can guarantee security to its subjects. The state deceitfully promises to do so, although as pointed out by Eric Johnston, such an economic structure intensifies war hazards. Under war, as now waged, all economic security is dissolved. That such government does stimulate war is obvious. Since world-wide Newdealism, hot and cold wars have been constant and without quarters—barbarism. Such economic structure stimulates war because under it governments (sovereignties) meet each other in disputes about economic security—rights in trade and property, etc. Under Free Enterprise the contestants are private individuals who must meet competition. That forces the objective to be that of producing cheaper, better and quicker than any other community—the only basis for economic security.

[25] *** * * there are so many ways to do things wrong, to talk out of turn, that somewhere between thirteen and fifteen million are always in prison. They put them to digging canals, or building railroads * * *. * * * A few million more * * * are * * * sentenced to keep on working at their old jobs with reduced pay. * * * others just drop out of sight * * *. * * * Usually no letters are allowed * * *. Politicals get the roughest deal * * * . They have NKVD spies in the markets and hanging around the store counters, waiting for someone to pop off. They usually get ten years chopping wood * * * Your passport has a red line through it. That means you can never get a house or a good job—you've got to keep moving. * * * If things don't look quite right, than you get a passport with letters in front of the numbers. This means you are under suspicion, and can never hold a key job. * * * For housing they dig a pit about 10 feet deep, 20 feet wide and 100 feet long. * * * The mattresses lie on the cold dirt. White. "Report on the Russians" p 229.**

and get better results when promoting business than a government official.

The position of the "Liberal" that there will be fewer depressions and a substantial reduction of hardships when government has charge of business as outlined by them has no foundation whatever.

Democracies (enterprise free from government control of the kind in question) were born as a protest to the permanent depressions which developed under government control of the kind they recommend. It is not unfair to say that the "liberals" are reluctant to make comparisons.[24] That their leaders (dictators), as distinguished from those of the past, are elected is no answer, for such elections soon degenerate into fictions, frauds and subterfuge. It must be borne in mind that systems which stimulate government control of industry or the means of production have a tendency to create war, and consequently, permanent destitution for the majority, and, of course, more hardships. [24a]

No government that has undertaken in such manner to adjust the hardships which arise in maintaining commercial supremacy has been nimble enough to avoid taking complete charge of business. When it does the subjects will find that the taskmaster they have is many times more heartless and arbitrary than the private corporation.[25] Such a result is inevitable, for the master will be a human being who may act without financial responsibility and is equipped with unlimited (sovereign) power, and who in order to be effective must have control of the courts and legislative bodies and maintain a large military and police force.

Under free enterprise, unfortunately, it also happens that unscrupulous men get too much control of governmental functions. No statesman hopes to remedy that evil completely.

[26] Wang Mang, about 2000 years ago. Wang An Shis, 1069 A.D., with particular interest regarding control of prices, loans to poor people and food distribution. Emperor Diocletion, 301 A.D., whose administration is of interest in connection with death penalties for those who charged too much or hoarded or destroyed food. (See "People of Ancient Rome" by Frank Forest Abbott.)

The following is a quotation from "The Crisis of Our Age" by Pitirim A. Sorokin: "All are regimented and controlled. For this purpose an enormous army of state officials is created. It robs and steals and aggravates the situation still more. The State needs gigantic financial means to maintain the government, with all their possessions. The State that took upon itself the satisfaction of all needs—public and private, finally comes to the necessity of complete regimentation of even private labor * * *. The empire is transformed into a huge factory where, under the supervision of the state officials, the population works for the government. Almost all industry is managed by the State. The State also distributes—very unequally—the produce. The members of the trade and labor unions are not free persons any more; they are the slaves of the State, that are supported, like the officials by the State, but very poorly and inadequately. Never was an administration as cruel and quarrelsome with the population and as inefficient and unproductive. The regime is based upon compulsion; everywhere is the hand of the State. Nowhere do private initiative and free labor exist. P 183 of the book referred to above, describing the Diocletian period.

But constitutional government was conceived as the best way to destroy such influences without resorting to civil war or causing governmental collapse, and by constitutional government (free enterprise) *is meant independent courts, independent legislative bodies, short term of office, carefully protected local jurisdiction, and an economic structure under which the citizen does not have to contend with government for the daily necessities of life, or look to it for his job, home, or food, and with the ballot directed so as to protect private property.* In other words, citizens in general dependent upon private industry for the necessities of life.

It is dangerous enough to grant "unrestricted" right of property accumulation under the limitations imposed by competition. But nothing has been more destructive to security than to combine political and commercial power in the manner advocated by the "liberals". That, therefore, is the relationship which democracies, constitutional governments, are supposed to prevent!

However, today the merging of these powers into one channel—political power, is falsely called democracy by the "liberals"; probably not with evil intent because they claim the merging of these powers will alleviate the hardships which befall man in building and maintaining a civilization. If in the past combining these powers had softened hardships beyond a very temporary period, informed persons would not be so skeptical.

Government and business were already too closely linked in 1929. It seems that men are trying to remedy the situation by a complete surrender of private enterprise to political control. They tried that in the past.[26] The futile attempts of the present are reflected in France, Italy, Germany and Russia. The frequent reoccurrence would suggest that it is a chronic malady. It always results in a relationship which makes it impossible for the employer to recognize merit by adequate wage rewards. There is already an undercurrent of feeling that because of governmental interference inefficiency reaps the best rewards.

Merit received little enough as a reward in the past. One more straw may be too much. The communists taught themselves a lesson in that field during the reign of terror from about 1918 to 1923, when they liquidated those who had been successful in business and in the professions, on the ground that their rewards had been too great. It resulted in a "minimum" wage law for everybody. They considered that it was most *unfair* to have a minimum wage law for certain groups, as in the United States.

Minimum Wage Laws Make a Vicious Circle

The minimum wage laws, of course, are attempts along the line of adjusting inequities. But some of the difficulties arising under them should be checked in connection with this chapter. Under such laws those just above the minimum wage, but who do not receive an increase, are subjected to a rise in the cost of living under circumstances which amount to a cut in wages for them—certainly a hardship. The consequence is a demand for adjustments.

Since there is nothing to show that those just above the minimum wage are overpaid, an adjustment is in order. The next group feels the same disadvantage. If justice is to be done there must follow an upward swing along the line until it reaches the top. When it does, all the groups are again in the same relative position! That makes a circle—a vicious one. Labor union policy makes the whole program futile by demanding and obtaining higher wages and shorter hours for their groups before the minimum wage laws can take effect. The

Communists, not Stalin, want to solve that problem by paying everybody the same amount—equalitarianism!

It seems that this circle affects most adversely those in the professional or academic fields as it gives to ordinary or common manual labor (in many instances improperly called "skilled") higher pay than those trained in colleges. *That is a sure result, since labor becomes a political commodity—a political commodity because it represents a substantial block of votes. It therefore, becomes the center of attraction for the "duly" elected legislators.* That there is a hidden challenge to the academic and to democracy in such a situation is obvious to all except the beneficiaries.[27] As the principal beneficiaries are labor leaders, inspectors and politicians, there is no way to break the circle.

These laws raise a problem in foreign commerce. There never develops among the wage-earners a sentiment in favor of reducing wages. That would be expecting too much of human beings. As wage-earners represent a voting majority, all Congress or the administrators can do, if they wish to hold their positions, is to accept the recommendations of the labor leaders with respect to higher wages and shorter hours. No commercial structure, even if it had world-wide support, could withstand such pressure. No Russian leader even is suggesting anything that silly. Nations with an economic structure keyed to a more practical arrangement, Russia's slave labor for instance, get a trade advantage. That leaves the alternatives for the "Social Democracies" of destroying the competing nations in order to maintain their trade, or abandoning the

[27] For instance, if driving a truck, or any occupation which does not involve the academic, pays more than work which requires it, there will be difficulty in keeping "boys" in school. It is difficult to get a teenager to understand that it is the academic which makes civilization (jobs) possible. Or, even if he did understand, he would not feel disposed to carry the burden.

[28] Hitler faced that issue in 1939, and decided on war. Roosevelt and Truman are accused by respectable authorities of creating war to avoid collapse of their social democracies. However, what is true beyond doubt, and a fearful fact, is that human beings need little evidence to believe that war is necessary, if it will give them a commercial or political advantage.

[29] "Some people argue that we cannot meet this challenge of full employment within the framework of free enterprise. They want us to believe that full employment and free enterprise cannot flower together; that full employment will force government to control our economy, bringing to an end our free enterprise system. Shorn of the jargon of reaction, the argument is that participation by government to achieve the end of the general welfare is destruction of our national safety as a free people. Wallace "Sixty Million Jobs" p 27 (paraphrased.)

If Wallace has in mind the same kind of full employment that Hitler and Mussolini advocated and Stalin is using, his language involves the maximum of deception.

The "jargon" that Wallace refers to means the statements to the effect that this country has moved so far toward absolute government control by way of NLRA, AAA, TVA, OPA, social security taxes, pensions, payroll taxes, minimum wages, maximum hours, doles, quotas, government cartels, that business (free enterprise) is functioning, as far as it does, only because the industrialists are supermen.

He also makes a big point about corporations "freezing inventions; but what are government imposed five-day weeks, six-hour days, full-employment programs, and crop retarding programs, but government for minorities? Moreover, the government indirectly endorses slow-downs, sit-downs and wage manipulations which must impose terrible hardships on the victims of such procedure.

less practical approach.[28] The record shows that war is the usually accepted alternative.

Laws of that nature eventually lead to the European idea of "full employment", which is already being introduced into the United States by way of the backdoor.[29] *Under it, however, independent courts, independent legislative bodies and free elections cannot be maintained.* That situation makes it possible to eliminate strikes or any substantial opposition to government plans and, for a temporary period, may be most effective. But eventually it increases intrastate, interstate, and international clashes as evidenced by the results in Germany and Italy, and by the imperialistic and, at the same time, isolationistic attitude of Russia. And it must be borne in mind that war creates permanent poverty.

There is another danger in this kind of legislation which cannot be side-stepped. If one can see that in the field of business men have no mercy for the weak, it should not be difficult to realize that they will also have no mercy for the weak in the field of politics. That rule applies to states. The day it becomes obvious to a group of strong states, the states which control legislation, that a certain kind of business could be transferred to them advantageously, the transfer is as good as made. A transfer can be forced by a minimum wage variation of one cent an hour. That is what makes the South apprehensive of a wage law. The FEPC carries similar possibilities for the South. (What could be more silly than a law which implies business men must be forced to employ efficient personnel?) The result is that the Federal Government becomes a party to a scheme to despoil a group of weak states. There is no way of stopping such trade paralyzing and war creating procedure, for it is always proposed in the name of humanity, unity, and public welfare; the promotors pose, of course, as de-

[30] How often the United States came near to dissolving may be gathered from the following incidents recorded by Beveridge in "The Life of John Marshall".

At one time, when it appeared the Assumption was defeated, Sidgwick of Massachusetts intimated that his section might secede. p. 26, Vol. II. Virginia was equally vigorous on the other side of that question. 1790.

* * * If, these self-created societies cannot be discountenanced, they will destroy the government of ths country. Washington to Randolph, Oct. 16, 1794. p. 29, Vol. II. (Beveridge uses several pages to show how the political philosophy regarding the French Revolution brought on threats of secession.)

The late attempt of Virginia and Kentucky to unite the State Legislatures in a direct resistance * * * actual preparation of supporting them with force * * * preparing considerable arsenals and magazines. p. 408, Vol. II. 1799.

* * * we thought best to declare openly and firmly, one and all, that the day such an act passed, the Middle States would arm, and that no such usurpation, even for a single day, should be submitted to. p. 544, Vol. II. 1801.

This threat of secession and armed resistance, already made in the Senate, was to be repeated three times in the debate in House. p. 73, Vol. III. 1802.

Forcible resistance, if the Republican assault on the Judiciary succeeded, had twice been intimated during the debate. * * * secession of the Northern and Eastern States * * * was common talk among the Federalists. p. 89, Vol. III. 1802.

At that moment began the movement that finally developed into the plan for the secession of the New England States from the Union. p. 97, Vol. III. 1802.

Soon, however, their dissatisfaction blew into flame the embers of secession which never had become cold in their bosoms. * * * I am convinced * * * that the accession of Louisiana will accelerate the division of these States * * *. p. 150, Vol. III. 1803.

* * * The legislature of Massachusetts formally declared that the continuance of the Embargo would endanger * * * the union of these States. Talk of secession was steadily growing in New England. The National Government feared open rebellion. p. 15, Vol. IV. 1808, 1809.

* * * If this bill passes (bill to admit Louisiana to the Union) the bonds of this Union are virtually dissolved. p. 27, Vol. IV. 1811.

* * * Joseph Story was profoundly alarmed and said, "I am thoroughly convinced that the leading Federalists meditate a severance of the Union. * * * Let the Union be severed. Such a severance presents no terrors * * *. p. 30, Vol. IV. (Opposition to the War of 1812.)

Through both these sets of resolutions—that on the Missouri question and that of the Bank decision—ran the intimation of forcible resistance to national authority. p. 326, Vol. IV. 1820.

I behold the father armed against the son * * * a brother's sword crimsoned with a brother's blood * * * Senator Walker of Georgia * * *. p. 341, Vol. IV. 1820.

[30a] Already the conflict over farm acreage is full of bitterness and corruption. For instance, the remarks of Congressman Andresen that Congressman Cooley is primarily interested in Southern crops and ready to "junk the rest of the States."

fenders of the Constitution (justice), and good government—democratic government. It should be obvious even to "liberals" that such legislation is prone to breed civil war because of its possible trade-discriminating and interfering character. Indulgence in that practice caused the Revolutionary War, near civil wars during the period of the Confederation, and the period prior to the Civil War [30] and the Civil War.[30a]

The principle of the Declaration of Independence that governments that are unjust (and they all are that in the eyes of those under a disadvantage) must be destroyed has never been abrogated. It lies dormant until a majority or a minority ignore it too long, too often and too much.

Persons not familiar with business do not realize how the additional cost of a few pennies a day in wages can force it into bankruptcy or oblige it to move to another location. Therefore, all that is necessary under the wage and hour law to cripple another section is to raise wages a few cents an hour. *If men, human beings, in private industry do not hesitate to destroy the industry of an associate or to abuse employees, why should one be so simple as to believe they will not do it through legislation?* Besides, it is generally not possible to demonstrate that a business is being destroyed until it is too late to remedy the matter.

The wage and hour law was not chosen for discussion because it is particularly bad, but because it lends itself readily to showing some of the difficulties that confront governments. Such laws represent the rockbottom of pessimism. *They are an open and profound admission that a great many will always be on the verge of destitution. In this case, by direction of the government.* The Communists, as stated before, recognized the consequences of such procedure and therefore tried to adjust matters by decreeing that there should be absolute uniformity with respect to wages and ownership of property—equalitarianism. That procedure eliminates money in the usual sense of that word.

The functional peculiarities of legislative assemblies should not be overlooked. They have so many close and sympathetic relationships, as well as most practical ones, among their members that it is usually futile, if not impossible, to stand up in the Chambers and say this measure is objectionable for these reasons—the real ones. Generally the only way to obtain a hearing is to utilize the "exchange" method, openly or by intuition, i.e., "you vote for my proposition and I will vote for yours." That difficulty was fully understood by the Forefathers. It is obviously one of the reasons why government cannot successfully enter business management, or, if it does undertake it, is obliged to submerge courts and legislators to the extent prevailing in these days throughout the world.

It should be repeated that the idea of three branches of government is not a new one. Government naturally has three divisions, law-making, law-interpreting and law-enforcing. The Forefathers clarified the jurisdiction of these three branches. The conflicts which rage about the matter arise because human beings resent limitations upon their political powers. And let it be emphasized again and again that free enterprise (the only sure protection against tyranny) involves the right of the citizen to acquire enough property to be free from the necessity of doles and pensions. It also involves local (state) government and depends upon maintaining three branches of government, separated as contemplated in the Constitution. The Executive Branch, of course, is in a strategic position to usurp authority and should have its powers most clearly defined. It is generally overlooked that the ballot is involved in this ancient principle because it requires determining who may vote, the matters to be voted upon, and term of office.

It must be remembered that the primary purpose of the Constitution was to impose substantial checks on the divine right of state. It did not abolish it. Governments always have areas where citizens are subject to the personal judgment and self-restraint of the ruler. And it must be remembered, also, that the checks were imposed to protect economic security for all. English history proved that whether the leader was a religious Stewart or a religious Cromwell, excessive power only brought excessive abuse for those not in the shadow of politicial favoritism.

Reasons Why Government Management is Inefficient

That the matter complained of (inefficiency) must be real is established by the general conviction, since the memory of man, that it is true. The Constitution, which tried to keep government out of business, is additional evidence that this conviction is not based on fiction.

One reason for the inefficiency is that the relationship of a government official to business, either as owner, regulator or director, is not adapted to produce good results. He can never be, generally, at a financial loss in the matter for he is not financially responsible for his mistakes. He may with impunity recommend shorter hours or higher wages, call for new equipment, a different location, a particular day or subject for bargaining; for, regardless of results, he is not confronted with the possibility of direct financial loss. It amounts to having a person who is not responsible telling the responsible person what to do! That generally is a most unwise procedure, certainly, not democratic.

Moreover, everybody likes to be popular. The employees are in the majority and are voters. That fact should make any honest person aware that the ballot has to be abandoned, or at least curtailed, when government enters business to the extent that many suggested was authorized under OPA. Most dangerous aspect of all, it puts a government official in a position, in the name of public welfare, to destroy any business that incurs the ill-will of an administration.

The relationship is conducive to carelessness from the standpoint of expense. It is not necessary to make ends meet out of profits. Deficiencies are made up through the Treasury. Bankruptcy does not confront any of these "servants of the people" as long as government is able to collect taxes for their salaries and what they recommend. Elections are no threat to their procedure, for the voter imagines he is a beneficiary.

The scope of action or authority of the government official has to be considered. Not only is he not financially responsible, but he represents sovereignty—unlimited power. What a situation! A person not financially responsible, but with unlimited power, directing the one, if there is any private business left, financially responsible, but without power to resist. No one can stay his hand, especially when he represents a totalitarian form of government, which after all is nothing more than complete government control of business and commerce— which appears to be the objective of the "liberals." But such a situation makes Hitlers and Molotovs no matter what their nationality may be.

This sovereign power makes it possible for the government

representatives, without liability, to do almost anything—things which would send a private citizen to jail. For instance, a private citizen cannot have a monopoly except under very limited circumstances. The government, however, is under no such restraint. A private concern, if the Union will tolerate it, may discharge an individual only for cause; but the government can hire and fire without limitation, and can impose a $10,000 fine, or five years in jail, upon a citizen trying to make an honest living for selling too cheap, too high, too much or not enough. Private corporations, of course, are confronted with anti-trust laws if they try to control the market for "public welfare" purposes, but not the government.

Another reason why government management of business is deficient is that it is far more difficult to check the books and records of a government agency than those of a private citizen. The plea of public interest can prevent an investigation, and, if an investigation is made, it is but one branch of the government checking on the other, in reality the government checking itself. How can one expect efficiency under such circumstances? Either there is no investigation, or the investigation degenerates into political persecution.

There is a supposition that the government official will be fairer than a business man in dealing with employees and the public because he is not under a profit urge. But profit only represents power. And certainly the power urge is intensified, for these kinds of government offer unlimited power to whoever gets on top. No doubt the ambitious "Liberal" senses that opportunity for power. *He makes himself believe that his enthusiasm for government control is born entirely out of his concern for the downtrodden!* But it is the urge for power that is the basis for the blood purges.

The communists' fear of the profit motive prompted them to

[31] "When government is boss, fear falls like a blanket over the people. No one dares do anything he thinks a bureaucrat might frown upon. The brains of Russia are today going into retirement because of fear. Everybody waits for orders from above. No one ventures along new lines. With the dead hand of bureaucracy the Revolution is strangling its own children. If in the factory a machine or assembly line breaks down, the foreman knows that he may be charged with deliberate sabotage, with Siberia or the firing squad as the penalty. After a Russian train wreck, it is hard to tell whether more get killed in the wreck or after it. Some time ago, before the recent blood purges, thirty-five employees of the Commissarist for Agriculture, many of them experts in foods, were shot without trial. Their blunder was that they failed to guess right. Under such conditions, the worker takes no chances. He plays safe. He makes no experiments. Engineers and inventors and executives refuse to go ahead until plans are approved by the party secretary, who probably knows little or nothing about the plan he approves. It is a grim game of passing the buck— to Moscow. The result is industrial chaos." Samuel P. Pettengill.

"Everywhere, in all these mines and plants, a large personnel of technicians, bookkeepers, overseers, watchmen, directors is required, in addition to the thousands of workers directly employed in production for the needs of agriculture. Other requirements include the operation of stores, with their managers and salesmen; houses or barracks for handy men and repairmen, carpenters, furniture makers, technical schools for training of workers, with their own teachers, directors, guards, and so on. This colossal apparatus turns out no greater volume of production than the peasants formerly produced almost entirely with their own labor; in general, grain crops, which had continuously increased before the revolution, have not shown a substantial increase in the past twenty years." Dallin, "The Real Soviet Russia." p 103.

[32] The same is true of the clergy. Sunday is the preacher's day of competition! The orator draws the crowd. How cruel for the preacher with a thick head or tongue. But its the law of the jungle, the survival of the fittest!

try to create a structure under which profit (money or other evidence of property) would not be such an impulse. They found, however, that money (a symbol of property over which the owner has complete control) was not only a medium of exchange but a peculiar kind of exchange which tolerated no limitations on the right of transfer or exchange for other kinds of property, and that the lethergy impulses arising in the worker because of limitations on his right to exchange his pay for property, created more hardships than profit impulses. To offset the lethergy, an appeal was made to patriotism. That appeal was not properly responded to. Penalties therefore were imposed upon persons who failed or made mistakes. But that was too dangerous for a worker's life. No matter how efficient he was, he was always in jeopardy because of some unscrupulous or too ambitious associate seeking position power (the essence of profit) without regard for public welfare. No matter which way the system was used it turned out to be cruel: more truly the law of the jungle than the profit system, and, besides, it brought stagnation.[31]

The tangents referred to are bound to develop because the human race recoils from furnishing all the sweat and blood and tears that civilization demands as the price of progress. The profit motive that is feared so much is but a branch on the tree of merit. Nothing short of all the endurance in him can make a musician; his fame is his profit.[32] In the event his talent is entirely natural, that only raises the tempo for one with less talents who wants to succeed. Ten thousand musicians have to fail (play a subordinate part) to make one master. That is the price of civilization in every vocation and walk of life, including religion, business and government.

Another factor that handicaps government in conducting business is that the attitude of the employee toward the public is not such as to stimulate further contacts. His customers have to come to him; there is no other place to go. His capacity to draw customers does not depend upon his pleasantness or his efficiency. His regulations therefore result in only one brand of corn, soup, beans, one pair of trousers, so much pork, so much beef, so much milk, no butter.

Italy, Germany and Russia had such regulations in time of peace. Tremendous influences are working to introduce, enlarge and keep them in the United States. The Social Democrats or "Liberals" believe in rationing everything—especially the poor man's portion of work. The only thing they do not want to ration is their own political power—the exact opposite of democracy or constitutional government.

Public Service agencies are held up as examples of efficiency. However, their efficiency emanates from the spirit and practice of free enterprise which surrounds them.[33] Should government assume control of everything, not an unusual recommendation in these days, the free enterprise checks of competition would disappear, and with them efficiency. The Director then is certainly not going to be astute in cutting expenses, for he is not financially responsible and often, with all the rest, will gain an advantage when office personnel is increased or contracts granted. Bribery is not being discussed—*just the normal consequences that develop between friends without anything being mentioned or deliberately planned.*

Hardships and Business

No economic structure can prevent property, liberty, freedom, position, fame (security), from being subjected to failure, fiction, trickery and chance, and the attending hard-

---

[33] That also accounts to a great extent for Russia's progress.

ships. The outcries against hardships, no doubt, represent the primitive rebelling against the veneer of civilization and against the sweat and energy involved in polishing the diamond. The hardships of poverty make it natural for the poor to hate the rich and to covet their wealth. The same relation exists between the poor and the rich with regard to talent, a hardship imposed by nature, and one that cannot be adjusted so that everybody will be satisfied. The ideas of the Russian about elimination of the profit motive, or prohibiting citizens from owning property, aim at preventing anybody from becoming economically independent through the "exploitation" or hardships of others. *But why does he fail to see that his method makes many politically "independent" through the exploitation of others?* It is a fantastic attempt to avoid the hardships that civilization imposes. If the industrialist is making his wealth produce what civilization has to have, his wealth or his profit is not the issue. The issue is, how can it be done with less hardships. The "liberals" want us to believe that government control will do a better job. But in either event there has to be concentration before there can be production.

No matter how mean the employer is, or how great his profits are, if he is producing and turning his profits back into the channels of trade, benefits will flow to the public in spite of him.[34] Fifty thousand persons under-paid and over-worked in private industry generally results in 50,000,000 getting a benefit in buying power, say cheaper automobiles. The same principle prevails when a million teenagers die on a battlefield to protect their country—commerce! If battlefield hard-

[33a] "The business man neither intends to promote the public interest nor knows how much he is promoting it. He intends only his own gain, and he is in this led by an invisible hand to promote the end which was no part of his intention." Adam Smith.

ships for teenagers are unavoidable in protecting a civilization, it is probable that equally trying hardships confront a nation in peace time for the same reason. A complaint against an industry, in order to be valid, must show that its policies are detrimental to public welfare. One may complain about the blood on the battlefield only when it darkens the ground in vain. That much blood is shed in vain is true, and equally true is it that in industry much abuse prevails which should be eliminated. However, most of the bungling that creates abuse, in war or in peace, develops because the meddlers do not realize how difficult the problems are.

Labor unions complain the most about hardships. But no groups of individuals have derived more benefits from *cheap labor* than *high-priced* union labor. That is why they keep themselves, or try to keep themselves, down to a nominal number by heavy membership fees. They also have trouble because each group selfishly, but naturally, tries to prove that its particular work is entitled to the highest pay—an economic advantage! However, although their race for higher wages and lower norms of production add much to the distress of many, these groups are not more brutal than other special privilege groups. It is the business of government to see that such groups do not overreach.

An argument for turning to a government official as a master business hand is that his lack of profit motive makes him neutral and therefore a fairer arbitrator or judge: a fundamental rule, but an improper application. A government official is not in the position of a neutral. He is serving a political master who is obliged to be more concerned with friends and favors than with the objective of making things better, more quickly and more cheaply than any other country or nation can.

That is an objective which must be accomplished for commerce *in times of peace* (if there is going to be "security") with the same urgency that military equipment has to be produced in times of war. Unfortunately, this will be done, in spite of everything to prevent it, with about the same amount of graft, hallabaloo, lying, cheating, fourflushing, injustice, hardships and mismanagement that prevails in time of war, an undertaking discharged by government officials. The god of war, after all, is but the god of commerce in disguise.

Three in One

These "New Order" governments, as readily admitted by the "liberals", force into one hand tremendous direct control of the courts, legislators and administrative officers. It is three combined in one, not three on an equal footing. There is only a dictator who in various ways is represented by agents dependent upon his will, who, in order to survive, must retain his favor. However, he is not in a position to exercise good judgment from the standpoint of developing commerce. His glamorous power (profit) draws to him too many advisers who want his favor for putting over something other than developing business. The mix-ups in the rubber industry, oil distribution, priorities, rationing, and drafting men for war should convince anybody of that tragic fact, if the past records of land-grabbing, bank-manipulating, and railroad frauds are not sufficient.

Business Needs the Halo Which Government Demands

The captains of free enterprise must be primarily concerned with promoting commerce. It is their life and fortune upon which they stake their money, reputation, happiness and existence. Their financial responsibility obliges them to be on the

[35] The hue and cry about full-employment establishes that fact. However, the advocates thereof mean by that term five-day weeks, six-hour days and a low norm of production; apparently, afraid of over-production, they try by back-door entrance to reintroduce curtailment of production—the pig destroying program in disguise!

It is an aspect of dishonesty on the part of the "Liberals" when they cry against "profit", but carefully avoid explaining that profits are poured back into business and consequently creates more jobs—more economic security. Their opinions would be entitled to more respect if they were astute in discovering how the money syphoned away from business is wasted by the government or actually used to cripple business.

[36] Strange as it may seem, the economic policies of this country are just the converse of this elementary principle. The consequences are that the budget cannot be balanced, inflation continues, and the national debt increased.

alert and qualifies them as directors. The harder they work at their objective—promoting commerce, the better it is for a civilization composed of artists, poets, preachers, doctors, lawyers, educators, judges, laborers and labor leaders. It is only when capital backs away from production that civilization is in danger.[35] It does seem to be overlooked that the happiness of people depends upon commerce, business—a chance to make a decent living. The belittling remark of a Supreme Court Justice in connection with the sacrosanctness of business suggests that even that body lost sight of that fact.

Social or economic security depends primarily upon a program that produces more cheaply, better and more quickly than any other nation, a most difficult assignment.[36] *Therefore, the proper attitude of democratic government toward business must be that the financially responsible person direct, without much interference, what should be done. If he proves inadequate, one will search in vain for a competent director.*

The government subscribes to the theory that producing more cheaply, more quickly and better is the issue when it denies monopoly rights to the private citizen, for it means by such denial that open and free competition, free enterprise, is the foundation of social security. It also subscribes to the theory that the one in charge cannot tolerate interference, for when it undertakes to run a business it demands unrestricted managing authority. It calls for manpower acts, work or fight acts, and seizure acts, hires and fires without limitation, and cuts away all opposition, even strikes. It invokes the old doctrine that government is holy and can do no wrong—must have unchallenged authority, including the right to impose the hardships of war, in order to protect public welfare—business. That is a correct and necessary principle in government; but,

[87] "To wage war successfully * * * the authority of the President must extend * * * to all phases of civilian life * * *. * * * The aggregate of the President's war powers * * * is extensive and *independent of congressional grant."* Attorney General's Brief in the Montgomery Ward case.

Because no one can foresee what situations may develop, even outside of war, sovereignty, to meet unforeseeable contingencies, must retain the principle of the right to act without reference to other authority. It was never intended that the Constitution should defeat the responsible ruler in executing his first duty—protect the nation. Any other position is an absurdity. The Constitution did not and could not modify the prerogative of sovereignty to that extent—that is, the right of an individual, or group of individuals, to act for the country bound only by their self-restraint.

But the Constitution is a chart, a guide, a compass, showing where, when and how sovereignty should function, and allowed a very narrow field where it should function under the self-restraint rule, especially as to the executive and the judges. That the application of this rule to the Ward case was not justified seems clear; but it is also clear that executives, judges and legislators must have a field where they function without limitation under what is called the self-restraint rule. That field will never be definitely described or defined.

Associate Justice Jackson (see PM of June 8, 1945) has stated that the doctrine of divine right of kings has become obsolete. But, technically, it has been only substantially modified. It is not believed that he intended to repudiate Lord Coke's position that the king is under God, and, therefore, represents finality. Under the Constitution judges and legislators are often in that position.

[88] "It is not within the functions of government * * * to compel any person * * * to accept or retain the personal service of another, * * * the right of the employee to quit * * * for whatever reason, is the same right of the employer * * * to dispense with the services of an employee. * * * In all such particulars the employer and the employee have equality of rights, and any legislation that disturbs that equality of rights, is an arbitrary interference with the liberty of contract which no government can legally justify in a free land. (Adair v. United States, 208 U.S. 161. Justice Harland. Sec. 10 of Erdman Act of 1891 declared unconstitutional)

It appears the judge was satisfied that any law which interfered with the right to "hire and fire" was adverse to public welfare and therefore unconstitutional. He brought in the constitutional aspect by camouflaging the word "liberty" in the Fifth Amendment. What he really subscribed to was Lord Coke's theory that any law that is detrimental to public welfare could not be treated as a valid law.

according to the Constitution, it should be restricted to well defined narrow fields.[37]

What is always overlooked, denied, or not realized is that the same principles have to be applied to the industrialist if he is going to be in a position to keep business going well enough to give individuals a chance, some kind of a chance at least, to make a decent living! However, his "holiness" is derived from the fact that he is financially responsible for his conduct. His field, in some respects, therefore, is broader![38]

Too Many Government Clerks Spoil the Broth

The idea that a government official is more humane and fair than a captain of industry with respect to employees and public welfare developed out of civil service practice. Civil Service employees had better wages, better hours and more job security than any other group. It was natural, therefore, to assume that if government had control of everything there would be an all around improvement.

Of course 130,000,000 tax payers can support in luxury, or on a high standard, three or four hundred thousand government clerks. However, when there are too many clerks, then there will not be enough taxes to continue the advantage. Under such circumstances, the government official will have to become as brutal and as niggardly as a captain of private industry. Indeed, he will become much more so[37] because he represents sovereignty, a power which it has to be assumed can do no wrong, as is expressed in the current phrase "My country, right or wrong." The outcry against dictatorship voices the fear of abuse of governmental authority.

[38] "In London, Labor Minister Bevin picks certain numbers from a hat. All youths whose registration cards match these numbers have to go down into the mines to dig coal." Phila. Record, Jan. 13, 1944. Samuel Grafton.

One would prefer the Russian way where at least an attempt is made to assign the workers to what they have been trained to do.

The reason why the government official becomes tyrannical, abusive, indifferent, calloused, brutal, dishonest, and drives government into bankruptcy, is that he is a human being made of the same clay as the business man, but one who, as already pointed out, has been put above courts, legislators, and public sentiment, and who is not financially responsible for his conduct. What could one expect under such circumstances but the maximum of injustice, abuse and oppression for those who failed to keep within government favor—the favor of a particular official?

It could not be otherwise, for a government official is not subject to the same checks as a private citizen. Generally, as the representative of government he cannot be sued or imprisoned, or held financially responsible for damages caused by conduct, arbitrary ruling, or disastrous legislation, and is in a position to break contracts with impunity.[39] Consequently, a government once started on these New Roads to Democracy soon degenerates, in spite of everything, into wealth-sharing programs by levying taxes for alleged social reforms which rush along so fast that they cannot be arrested until bankruptcy overwhelms the government.

The Constitution is evidence that the Forefathers saw there could be no more dangerous course to stability and prosperity than to make the government responsible to the citizen for his food, job, homes, profession wages, business, medicine, pensions and outright relief. Apparently they realized that under such a system courts and legislative bodies became useless, more room was made for the unscrupulous, and the most cruel system of all was imposed upon the poor, because it entrusted human beings, who are sure to believe they are humanitarians, with

[39] Of interest along that line are Bronson v Rodes, 7 Wall. 229; Butler v Horwitz, 7 Wall. 258; Hepburn v Griswold, 8 Wall, 603; Knox v Lee, 12 Wall 457, and Norman v Baltimore & Ohio RR 292 US 240.

the maximum of power; *that under such a system the govern-ment eventually is pitted against its subjects, being called upon to sue them, foreclose on their mortgages, evict them, reduce their wages, close their shops, discharge them from employ-ment, and be a party to strikes*—all of which would destroy the good will a government must have from its citizens to be free from the terrors of civil war and the necessity of main-taining large military forces to keep its people in subjection. Could there be better examples to establish this than are furnished by the European turmoil?

The King Can Do No Wrong

One cannot escape the fact that responsibility and power must march together, *and since government is not legally or morally responsible in many ways and fields for its mistakes, it is necessary to restrict its activities to the spheres where financial responsibility is not a prime factor.*

There is no way to make government responsible for its conduct, and thus justify a broadening of its field of action. It might be suggested that legislators be held financially re-sponsible for damages sustained by legislation. But if that course were taken it is probable there would be no legislation at all. Besides, the consequences are so great that financial responsibility is impossible. Neither the President nor the Courts could be held to such a rule. Who could pay for the damages resulting to business by reason of the code practices imposed by NRA, or the damage that business sustained when the Supreme Court declared it unconstitutional? Suppose it should be proved that a war had been declared under improper motives (not an unusual practice). The only redress the citi-zens would have for the loss of his property, his opportunities, or his sons and daughters, would be to impeach or refuse to reelect the offending person. That sure is inadequate compensation! It is the old idea: "The king can do no wrong."

As there is no way to make a government financially responsible for its mistakes or conduct, it is presumed that government will refrain from entering the fields where financial responsibility is a direct obligation. That is the field of business, and that is what the Forefathers had in mind when they used the terms laissez faire, representative government, and free trade, now called free enterprise. The Constitution sets forth the checks which if utilized will keep government in its proper sphere of action. They are not new or novel checks, but the old ones which time has demonstrated are those which can be used most effectively. The Constitution is the authority (king) in the United States which in theory can do no wrong, and which must be obeyed if security (business or commerce) is to be properly protected.

The House Divided Against Itself Must Fall

One thing is sure: an economic structure cannot endure if it has its commercial life divided in authority. It must either become a structure under which government has full control as in Russia, or be a structure wherein government is restricted to the ordinary functions prescribed by the Constitution. Such a structure, of course stands guard over the property rights of the individual by maintaining courts dedicated to the function of adjusting disputes between citizens and citizens (not government and citizen); by keeping legislation inside the field of protecting free enterprise and the executive authority restricted to enforcing what the legislators and judges prescribe.

Few persons would deny that today many opportunities to do business depends upon governmental favor, which can be obtained only by subscribing to certain governmental theories about economics. A lawyer in private practice hesitates to antagonize or disagree with the government because he meets the government on every corner. The worthwhile frontiers, are found in practice before the departments of the government. The lawyers certainly are not going to offend the power which controls the frontiers. That would be a foolish thing to do.

The person seeking work in private industry is confronted with a government directed and protected labor union.[40] His union affiliations mean more than his efficiency or his initiative! His hours of work are set and his wages predetermined. He generally gets so much a day whether he is single or married, has children, is efficient or deficient, or whatever his lot may be. The regimentation he invited finds him in an awkward position if he wants to cash in on his merit or his initiative. A new and most desirable frontier from the standpoint of remuneration—the protected position of a union official, is not open to him.

Notwithstanding the Taft-Hartley Act, the government is so vigorously back of labor unions (not laborers) that business men cannot successfully resist them. We are rapidly moving toward a structure where the only way a business man can open up a frontier is to subscribe to what the government dictates through its labor legislation regarding how many hours his employees may work, what he shall pay them, whom he shall employ, and under what circumstances they may paralyze his business by strikes. It was not, perhaps, intended to go that far, but once on the road, there was no place to stop. (The Taft-Hartley Act may for a temporary period have a modifying

---

[40] "Would to God the laborers form a Union and compel my competitor to do as I would gladly do in concert with them, but dare not do alone", a leading business man in Great Britain is alleged to have exclaimed.

The Union was formed and now the cry is, "Would to God somebody would do something for those who cannot form a Union." Apparently not even the government dares to help that group in the face of Union opposition.

effect.) Obviously, commerce is not free under such circumstances, and just as obviously government will have to take full control of the whole program or be met, because of halfway methods, with confusion and stagnation, which means starvation and destitution for three-fourths of the citizens and ultimately submission to foreign influences from a more productive economic structure—one with more sweat, blood and tears in the field of production,[41] and less of all three in the field of political purges and agitation. But more and more the frontiers, throughout the world, have to be sought in the field of governmental favoritism. That is not Democracy! It is not good business. It is not public welfare! It is the Russian way, and can only be effective for a short period of time.

And let us repeat that no economic structure can avoid the terrible hardships which arise because of wars, inventions, natural catastrophes, miscalculations of leaders and human deficiencies regarding mental capacity and personal appearance.

There is of course no constant measure for determining where governmental regulation or regimentation shall start or stop. The Constitution itself is a mighty document of regulation and regimentation on every phase of the political and economic structure under its control—no doubt, hated and resented by many for that very reason.

But it may be safely assumed that when laws and regulations impair court independence, hamstring the legislators, interfere with local administration, nullify free elections, infringe upon

[41] From 1929 to 1937 so-called capitalistic countries increased output 5 per cent over 1929, whereas Russia's output increased more than three times. Russian production flooding world markets naturally curtailed opportunity for export for other countries. Large investments in machinery and transportation became useless. It is therefore not strange that bankers and industrialists became alarmed at Russian progress, and, assuming that state ownership was the reason for her dominance in commerce, turned to state ownership in the name of the soft and charming word "Democracy."

free speech, restrict the amount of property a citizen may own, and curtail the right of industry to hire and fire, open and close, and to determine the price and quantities of its commodities, that then the Ship of State is far off its course, if it is proposed to sail to the land of economic security, liberty and freedom.

There is, of couse, as often stated, no rule to determine when government regulation has introduced so many restrictions that it defeats its purpose—economic security. But it is clear that security becomes a jest when government is out of bounds—has flooded its banks—is doing something in addition to acting as the umpire in property disputes between individuals, protecting citizens against those who do not or cannot respond to conventional moral codes, and keeping free and agreeable the relationships with other nations. Those three functions government must perform and always has performed. They are functions which cannot be successfully administered otherwise than through sovereignty. And properly so, for they represent the area of authority where financial responsibility is not primarily involved; could not be, because of the inmeasurable consequences.

Business (enterprise) is holy, sacred—first, because without the production of food, clothes and housing, civilization with its religions, cultures, arts, or anything else, must fail and disappear. Business (producing commodities) is therefore the first concern of government; not to own it; nor to regulate it; but to stimulate it.

THREATS TO
PRIVATE PROPERTY

KEY PROPOSITIONS

Without the taxing power government cannot exist; yet with it governments destroy themselves. The destruction, tragically enough, usually is through social undertakings called democratic, but which actually violently transgress rights in private property.

Ballots loaded with governmental benefits oblige government to seize private property on every side, and inevitably lead to war. To expect any other result is to ignore human nature.

The circumstances of war may oblige governments to exercise their sovereign prerogative to seize, without compensation, all property. Therefore as long as war is a possibility, the government, in theory, owns everything and the citizen nothing. Constitutions are protections and safeguards to prevent government from using wartime powers in peacetime.

The major protections for private property are found in the constitutional principle of equal footing for the three branches of government—not in the Bill of Rights.

Instinctively, deny it as he will, the politician realizes that there is no greater threat to his power than for citizens to be independent of government for their food and shelter.

The theory of sacredness of private property rests upon the ground that individuals who do not depend upon government for the necessities of life are free in their position to resist governmental tyranny or encroachments.

[1] "Wherever one looked, whether in the Communist Soviet Union or the New Deal USA., in Popular Front France, or Fascist Italy, one saw the steady decline or disappearance of property rights." I. F. Stone in Aug. 2, 1945, PM.

"The time has come to recall that property-holding is delegated governmental power." Tead "Adventures in Democracy" p 144.

Belgrade, Dec. 6. (AP) A law nationalizing all private economic enterprises, public works and industries in Yugoslavia was passed unanimously by both houses of the National Assembly under the chairmanship of Premier Marshall Tito. Phila. Bulletin 1947.

In "Government and Business", p 2, Stuart Chase vividly describes this trend: "The public interest and traditional rights of private property are locked in gigantic combat * * *. The New Deal is but a single engagement on a world-wide battle front. In Russia the forces of *private income producing property* are in disorderly retreat, but in all other industrial nations the struggle is grim and unremitting. * * * Wherever you choose to look—collectivism, with its centralized credit policies, agricultural subsidies, arbitrary control of exports and imports, public works, relief programs, surtaxes, social insurance, is cutting deeply into the cherished freedom of private business." One may add that such property now is in retreat everywhere—vanquished in many areas!

[2] Rousseau maintained that it was the rise of private property which brought strife upon mankind: an echo of St. Paul's observation about money being the root of all evil. That philosophy, of course, is the foundation of the Russian constitution, and the economic philosophy of Marx.

The philosophy that ownership of property is the basis of all evil has always had a great many exponents. It culminated in the 1917—23 communism of Russia. Government hardly could go in if to some extent values incident to property could not be diminished without paying for it." Justice Holmes. 260 US 393.

[2a] At least the forefathers' idea of the scope of the ballot has been completely abandoned under these laws for creating a social democracy, government assuming direct responsibility to its subjects—not citizens, for they cannot be called citizens when so dependent upon government.

"Make way for Liberty" he cried, "Make way for Liberty"
and died!

THREATS TO PRIVATE PROPERTY

CHAPTER III

"Liberals" and Private Property

The inherent rights and liberties protected by the Constitution may be divided as: Private Property Rights, Political Rights, and Civil Rights, including religion. In this chapter property rights will be discussed.

Because so many people have the false impression that under the Constitution their title to property is *absolutely* safe,[1] really their own, present limitations upon protection for property rights should be examined. It is particularly important to do so because of the current political philosophy (revival of an ancient one) that private property, especially ownership of the means of production, is the root of all evil, the barrier to economic security, and may, therefore, properly, be taxed out of existence.[2] That philosophy is, more or less, supported in the United States by about ten million voters in a strategic position. It is a direct attack upon the idea that men should seek security through ownership of property. It wants him to seek security through political relations. The Fifth Amendment is an outright repudiation of that philosophy, and an attempt to protect property from it.[2a]

But, not withstanding the Fifth Amendment, and outside of the dangerous philosophy referred to, there are still many

117

ways by which government can seize private property without compensation and compel the subject to rely on political favoritism for his security. Some of these ways will be discussed in this chapter, starting with General Taxation.

By General Taxation

Taxation is the most ancient and most frequent method used to seize property. It is, generally, not classified as seizure procedure because it is presumed that the citizen wants to pay his taxes, surrender a portion of his property (in the form of income) for governmental protection. But because he has to pay his taxes, *no matter how much he objects to what the government official is using his money for,* taxation involves a sufficient element of compulsion to be classed, for the purpose of this discussion, as seizure of property. And it bears repeating that it is the easiest and most common method for taking private property (money) without compensation to the owner, under the pretext of promoting public welfare.

No definite or fixed restriction can be placed upon this power. Without unlimited taxing power, the right to take as much money (property) from the citizen as the officials believe necessary, a government cannot function successfully. Yet, tragically enough, with this power, governments often defeat their major objective—promotion of public welfare.[3] It is generally brought about by adopting tax-supported under-

[3] No other statement is so pregnant with significance and contention as that the only limitation on the taxing power is that it must be for public welfare. One may say, however, that any taxing program which interferes with the constitutional form of government is unconstitutional, and that if it is adverse to public welfare, it may be resisted on the ground that anything contrary to public welfare cannot be law.

takings such as land grants, tariffs, big "defense" programs, subsidies, pensions, protected utilities, or outright relief.[4] In these present days the great danger to public welfare arises from the taxation which is necessary to support high wages, crop curtailments, and other means of reducing production, such as five-day weeks, low norms of production, unrestrained strike procedure, governmental monopolies, etc. Legislation to support such taxation can easily become the most vicious method by which to destroy property rights, including business and even professions. If it dries up business there is bound to be a property loss. Many business men lost their property under these laws.[5] And what a field for intimidation and graft! It should not be overlooked that many of the big industrialists favor these kind of laws, as such laws have a tendency to eliminate competition. They are introduced, generally, on the ground that they will prevent overproduction and distribute properly the hours of gainful employment.

Private Property Destroyed by Ballot Pressure on Taxation Policies

Governments with the minimum qualifications for voters (in which group the United States through disregard of the Constitution may now be classed) are particularly susceptible to taxing programs which impair or destroy title in property, and, consequently, economic security. *This is so because, when*

---

[4] "Taking up comment on what Shays (referring to Shays' Rebellion) would get from Santa Claus in Washington if he were here today, I should like to add that the legislation of the New Deal which has saved thousands of debtors from utter ruin was enacted, ironically enough, under the very Constitution which owed its existence in some measure to Shays' insurrection." Beard. "The Republic" p 95.

Beard seems to be suggesting that Shays' political ideology has been honored.

[5] See the Congressional reports on that subject.

⁶ * * * then gradually the transformation * * * the majority without capital eat up the minority (surplus) and the civilization steadily decays * * *. Sir Petrie "Revolutions of Civilizations." pp 123, 124.

That situation always develops because the voters usually are in a position where their needs will thwart their judgment. The Russians recognize that danger. Their election system cuts off all opportunity for the voter to exercise judgment.

⁷ Although Mrs. Roosevelt in "This I Remember" did not mention this important phase in President Roosevelt's political career, it is fair to him to assume that he intended, when he first took office, to direct the Ship of State away from the shoals of government spending.

^{7a} Lowell Mellett brings this fact out vividly (but not intentionally one may surmise) when he says in his column that the Republicans have made the dadblamedest "me too" record that anybody ever saw.

economic upheavals arise the destitute become the overwhel-
ming majority of voters. Naturally, through the ballot, they
control the taxing policies of the elected branches, and force
spend and spend programs until the economic structure col-
lapses.[6] That pressure forced President Roosevelt to abandon
his sober 1932 campaign promises.[7] Any administration confronted with it will be unable to avoid the same result. There is
no way to check the rush to bankruptcy or to more government
control under such circumstances, because only legislators and
presidential candidates who promise the most tax-born benefits
can win.[7a] Obviously, in the United States, the voting Frankenstein, born in government benefits created by taxation, is
out of control. The war was welcomed by many (not openly
of course) as a means to stop the monster. But it has only
strengthened him. Resort to novel bookkeeping, subterfuges,
fictions or more war will be of no avail. The fact that we
needed or still need NRA or OPA government is evidence of
how threatening the situation is. Incidentally OPA like NRA
was charged with a two-fold obligation—prevent inflation and
deflation (an economic crisis)—quite an assignment if free
enterprise and the present day out-of-bounds ballot are to be
maintained at the same time.

It is to be noted, and with apprehension, that although the
country is at peace, more alphabetical agencies prevail today
than during the Roosevelt war period. The situation illumi-
nates Eric Johnston's statement that Social Democracies create
war hazards. How could it be otherwise?

In connection with the taxing policy it is proper to call
attention to the three primary factors for voting: (a) the
voters must have equal or *common knowledge* of the issues;

[8] Beard in "The Republic" ignores that fundamental aspect of government. "With poll taxes and other limitations on suffrage we have not yet achieved universal democracy, but we have gone a long ways in that direction." "The Republic" p 4.

Demagogism. The average person does not have in mind the necessary limitations of the ballot such as age, residence, mental and moral deficiencies, education, property requirements, and the necessity for common (equal) interest, responsibility and knowledge.

Beard, on page 34 of "The Republic", is satisfied the election of senators was a step toward democracy. But if it gives the spend and spend philosophers too ready access to the treasury it may be that it was a step toward totalitarianism,—the small break in the dike that made the destructive flood. Of course, if the prime objective of democracy is to give everybody a vote regardless of the effect on public welfare, Beard may be right. The same point is properly raised concerning his references to the Fourteenth and Fifteenth Amendments and his suggestions with respect to poll taxes and educational requirements. He should be in favor of voters' determining whether war should be declared. That would save presidential candidates from making rash promises about not going to war.

"The phrase 'republican form of government' was bandied around in loose fashion * * *. One thing is certain it did not mean a democratic form of government, a government in which all adults have an equal voice * * *. No delegate plead that republicanism meant universal suffrage." p 139 "The Ultimate Power" Ernst.

We have here the same subtle suggestion about democracy requiring that everything be settled by the ballot. Democracy can mean no more than that the ballot shall elect experts, a very small group, whose judgment while in office shall in all matters be honored. The futile efforts at recalls and referendums should satisfy anybody that no other procedure is practical. One might conclude the word should be spelled Demo-Crazy.

[9] "Those who pay no taxes, disposing by their votes of other people's money, have every motive to be lavish and none to economize. As far as money matters are concerned, any power of voting possessed by them is a violation of the fundamental principle of free government; a severance of the power of control from the interest in its beneficial exercise. It amounts to allowing them to put their hands into other people's pockets for any purpose which they think fit to call a public one." John Stuart Mill.

Morris Ernst, on page 221 of "The Ultimate Power", seems to agree with Jefferson that the Louisiana Purchase was unconstitutional and undemocratic. It is clear that the purchase conflicts with some ideas about democracy, but to prove that the forefathers contemplated precluding the government from functioning in that field of sovereignty indeed would be difficult. If democracy precludes government from such action, one could hardly recommend it as a practical or intelligent method of government.

(b) a *common interest* therein; (c) and *common responsibility*. With any one of these factors missing the ballot is out of balance and futile if not vicious,[8] so far as protection to private property or economic security is concerned. (Balances or adjustments are made by property and educational requirements, and by the two-thirds or three-fourths majority rules.)

With the ballot out of balance, especially with respect to responsibility, which is the case when the disheartened and destitute voters make up the majority, property holders are without protection, notwithstanding Constitutions, Magna Cartas or Bills of Rights. The "liberal" politicians, liberal with promises which cannot be kept and with the distribution of money and property that does not belong to them, have the property holders at their mercy. They are hopeless under such circumstances, and are, therefore, the first victims.[9]

After all the money has been spent the leaders, in order to save face, undertake to cover the taxpayer by applying economic pressure upon other countries or by declaring war on them. It is done, of course, always, in the name of humanity, liberty, self-defense, war to end wars, etc., and with the consent of the majority of voters, no matter how ridiculous, dishonest or farfetched the justifying claims may be. That is the story of Russia under Lenin and Trotsky, Italy under Mussolini and Germany under Hitler. Each one of these leaders, like those before them, persuaded their followers to believe that they represented a democratic movement, liberalism. But their programs soon became, in spite of their best efforts, dictatorships, which obliged them to either tax their subjects into destitution (take all their property) or declare war upon a neighbor. It is obvious, therefore, that many

[10] The corporation or individual with a substantial business foundation can pull through a period of fixed rents, quotas and ceiling prices, but the weak ones are "liquidated." Obviously "big business" has an advantage. The government has "liquidated" the small competitor. A business man must really be astute, have vision, so far as public welfare is concerned, to oppose such an arrangement, or to realize that he is being pushed into government control.

The lazy proprietor enjoys government of that character, enjoys the "independence" it gives him from catering to customers. He may, so to speak, insult them with impunity. They beg him for what they need instead of being "always right." Too late he realizes that the competition has been changed from pleasing customers to pleasing a government—a master who may insult him, and, besides close his business.

[11] What right have the voters to assume that ordinary human beings will be able to resist the temptations that arise in administering the RFC, or any of the other agencies where a human being, without being financially responsible or even bonded, may allocate millions of dollars? Should one expect that the collateral of a friend of the Administration for a loan would be the same as that of a stranger or a bitter foe of the Administration? How naive are the voters? How brazen the public servant?

dangerous situations arise because of the disposition of distressed and frightened voters to follow leaders who promise by the use of taxes to create a world without hardships.

Private Property Destroyed By Favoritism

There arise, of course, a great many unethical influences under the "liberal" forms of government which have a tendency to impair the property rights necessary to maintain economic security.[10] For instance, very conspicuous ones arise from the fact that those who "know" the "Commissar" have a tremendous advantage. This makes especially eloquent epigrams such as "What is the Constitution among friends," and "Kissing goes by favor." *Bribing or other outright acts of corruption do not cause the real trouble.* It is the plain every-day personal relationship based on good appearance and presentation that does this.[11] All the key men are in a position to distribute or allocate to themselves or their friends millions of dollars, dollars drafted from the tax payers—their private property—not the funds of the dispenser or distributor. The RFC scandals, income tax scandals, war surplus scandals are only drops from the main scandal stream.

No honest man would dare to trust himself in such a position, at least not without bond for malfeasance. But these key-men are not bonded. That is so for the simple reason that it is practically impossible to prove fraud under such circumstances. Indeed, much of the distribution activities are labeled "confidential" or "top secret" so that it is impossible to check on them. Moreover, by means of propaganda through the radio, screen and press, the leaders can, and do, keep themselves in control by fictions about shortages and over-produc-

[11] There are thousands of unethical cases. Imagine the strategic position of a Reconversion Administrator, just with respect to getting the "edge" in the start of building automobiles.

[12] No one has explained why about ten percent of the population required more than 50 percent of the food supplies. The spoilage in storage certainly indicated it was not necessary. The conversion of 90,000 pounds of butter into soap is significant because it raises the presumption that a hundred times that much spoiled every year. Governments are in a position to hide any amount of waste. But even if they did disclose tremendous waste, it would have little effect on public sentiment. With government in possession of the food supply, who would be foolhardy enough to criticize that hoarder? Such individuals get into concentration camps by public consent!

Congress satisfied itself by charging bungling. But the bungling is too obvious to be entirely accidental. Could there be a better way to inrtoduce the Russian form of government, fascism or communism?

"If Congress can take over the coal mines, I don't see why it cannot take over these big packing companies." Senator Green in Oct. 1, 1946 Philadelphia Record.

[13] Technically free enterprise, private industry, or laissez faire mean the same thing. Such terms develop as a protest to government regulations. How much rgulation enterprise can absorb before it becomes government enterprise is a difficult question.

tion.[12] The means of propaganda under these "liberal" forms of government are so great that in a few weeks, as happened in Italy, Germany, and Russia, public sentiment can be created that will demand that government seize all property involving the means of production. The "free" press, screen and radio, *naturally, as well as expediently,* fall in line with the government's policies, especially when it has charge of the material needed for production. The business man, too, is "enthusiastic," for the government is in a position to make or break him. For instance, a labor leader may declare a strike, and the President, *a human being who depends on votes to keep his job,* determines whether it shall continue! That is tyranny, not democracy. An old-fashioned political campaign based on outcry against waste and corruption has little as a reform effort, because the voters are all partakers in the program.

The trend in this direction is everywhere, and as in the United States, is covered under high sounding phrases such as "full employment," "liberalism," "socialism," "social democracy," etc. The most deceptive aspect is that the attacks on communism are directed at the leaders, not at the form of government which they represent!

Free Enterprise (the kind provided for by the Forefathers) was introduced to stop the corroding favoritism that developed because of governmental control under the guildes, syndicates, and mercantilism of the earlier centuries.[13] It, of course, also has favoritism to quite a degree, but it does not stimulate it, as the dispenser thereof has to use his own money, at least much more so than a government official who uses the money he collects from the taxpayers—the poor people. Also the citizen who conducts his business (private property) under free

[13a] For instance, the Russian governmental policy which requires seizures of practically all property makes it difficult for free enterprise countries.

There is far more to Stalin's assertion that free enterprise (capitalism) and communism cannot dwell together as neighbors than the "Liberals" dare to admit. Obviously a political structure that precludes the private citizen from owning a business (the arms of production and distribution) and requires him to depend on political relations for his economic security can have little in common with an economic structure that subscribes to the very opposite of that theory. To divest citizens of the independence that ownership of property involves and keep them that way requires tyranny and military force. By no accepted definition can such a structure be called democratic. Yet the "Liberals" constantly refer to socialization of property as a democratic process.

enterprise principles does not act in the name of sovereignty as a government official does, and cannot, no matter what the situation is, exercise the same extensive degree of coercive influence or authority. He cannot levy taxes, impose prison terms, or, by governmental mandate execute his opponent in order to cover up misdeeds.

The industrialist, of course, tries to dominate government in order to obtain favors and advantages. *However, contrary to the teaching of the "humanitarians" or "liberals," his opportunities to do so increase under the New Orders.* He then, as a government official conducting business, comes dressed in sovereign authority. What chance is there under such an arrangement to protect title to private property? And who, twenty years ago, would have believed that statesmen, lawyers and judges would call such a course constitutional?

A particularly disturbing aspect of this situation is that when a strong nation follows such a course, undertakes to run business, it becomes difficult for other nations to avoid adopting a similar course. Hence the taxing policies "of the people" with its attending unethical practices and favoritism may compel other nations to resort to war as a matter of self-defense— protection of the private property of their citizens;[13a] or, may oblige them to take on the same kind of government, namely, preclude the citizens from owning property beyond a very nominal amount. Many of President Roosevelt's wartime speeches show how true that is. Inventions have intensified this danger, for they have made heretofore distant nations next-door neighbors. Such a situation should have some significance for those prone to abandon constitutional government (in the sense that the Forefathers used that phrase) in order to relieve the destitute or to spread the four freedoms.

[14] "The Provincial Administration of Brandenburg said the land decree would apply immediately and that it would affect all estates larger than 240 acres * * * no person would receive more than 12 acres * * * poor quality, only 20 to 24 acres." From Sept. 9, 1945, PM, p 11, quoting with approval, apparently, distribution of estates in Germany to peasants.

This shows how widely current and popular the conviction is that the government should divide estates,—corporeal for the present, incorporeal in the future, which would include the fortune back of PM.

There seems to be a note of regret in the article that church property was not included, as it was in Russia.

The portion of real estate assigned to the peasant, however, is much greater than that granted by the Russian Constitution.

[15] "If you approve this law * * * and a statute comes to you with * * * a tax of 20 percent upon all having an income in excess of that amount, how can you meet it?"

The highest tax now is about 90 percent of the income! There is of course nothing in the Constitution which prohibits such a law. Marshall had said the power to tax is the power to destroy. However, if such a law changes the form of government or adversely affects public welfare, the judges (also representatives of the people) are obliged to declare them void under the principle that no government official has a mandate to do wrong.

How frail the title to private property is under the policies of "the people" as directed by the "liberals"! [14]

Threats to Private Property By Special Taxation

As another illustration of attempts at seizure, without compensation, of property, the high taxes on incomes and estates may well serve. When a government needs so much money or is enthusiastic about collecting such large sums, it is a sure sign that something is wrong. However, there is a great deal of fiction about these taxes. If they were collected according to the public impression, it would not be possible to accumulate enough private capital to start any enterprise. Indeed, it would force government ownership to such an extent that money, in the correct sense of that word, would disappear as it did in Russia during her reign of terror.

However, many authorities are apprehensive that the present debt burden, if confronted with a depression, will create enough relief-taxation pressure to force government ownership (abolition of private property) in spite of the safe-guards provided for in the Constitution, and government ownership is certainly the essence of totalitarianism or of the Russian form of government.[15] That this uneasiness is deeply imbedded in the minds of persons in high position is evidenced by all the talk about four freedoms, full employment, cradle-to-the-grave security, compulsory savings, compulsory military service, compulsory 5-day weeks, etc. The Four Freedoms, of course, have no value in the absence of security for title to property, and security of title to property cannot exist where too much of the income has to be collected to pay for what is no longer in existence or has no utility.

Unbalanced budgets may constitute a threat to private property to such an extent that public welfare, democracy, is very

[16] Wallace in his testimony bearing on his nomination as Secretary of Commerce implied he was not disturbed about the debt because he believed the United States could maintain the war level of wages and production. But his concern about 60 million jobs suggests he does not believe his own testimony. If he told the truth he would say that he believes we have to follow the same "full-employment" course that Hitler adopted and Russia is using, and which has a tendency to eliminate money and create requisition government.

For a clever and subtle attempt to hide the issue, see Chap. 3 of "An Uncommon Man" by Dr. Kingdon.

Wallace on pp 76 and 77 of "Sixty Million Jobs" quotes Lord Macaulay on British debt as though Macaulay also believed government debt assured prosperity. However, England's inability to meet the first world war debt, and her need for Lend-Lease for the second world war would suggest that Macaulay and Wallace are wrong, or else the astute Lord has not been properly interpreted.

But one should be honest in these tragic days. Can we control the standards of the destroyed and debt-ridden nations so that they will not lower our wage scale to such an extent that the debt cannot be carried?

seriously jeopardized. As already suggested the present more than two hundred billion dollar debt partakes of that character. It will eventually be necessary to reduce the wage scale to meet the competition abroad. But if wages are reduced to that extent, the scale will be so low that not even the interest on the debt can be paid. Of course if wages are reduced fifty percent, the debt, relatively, is doubled, becomes $500,000,000-000.[16] It is pertinent here to note that the high cost of production made a farce of the loans we made to Great Britain,—indeed, of all our loans and gifts to the troubled nations.

Adverse Influence of Private Wealth

The political pressure for heavy taxes on estates and large incomes developed from the theory that individuals in possession of great wealth prevent enactment of legislation which aims at modifying the brutal policies involved in long hours, low pay, poor working conditions and age limitations. This theory, therefore, was introduced to impose restrictions on the accumulation of wealth, and thus destroy the influences which interfered with social legislation or the removal of hardships in connection with conducting or promoting business. However, heavy taxes eventually became necessary to support the unemployed and the aged. If the heavy taxes resulted, as many economists say, in armies of citizens becoming dependent upon government for food and shelter(which eventually results in disaster for everybody), the attempted remedy brought on a situation more brutal than that of working killing hours with minimum pay for private industry. The long-hour worker knows at least that if he is producing something there may be a chance for him or some one near him to get "from under."

This raises the issue as to whose program is the most humane: Is it the program of the "brutal" industrialist who teaches that ownership of property rights is the basis of economic security? Or, is it the program of the "kindhearted" "liberal" who teaches that ownership of private property is the root of all evil? Russia's experience is in point. Stalin, advertised sometime ago by our government as the essence of kindness, in fifteen years changed Russia from a half-starving country to one that began to dominate world markets. But Stalin built his commercial empire with a much greater degree of brutality than was ever used by the capitalists,[17] and, according to good authorities, with more disastrous results, and a great many less benefits.

However, industrial empires are won in the same manner as wars are won—with the blood, sweat and tears of the weak and innocent. The industrialist as a private individual, therefore, *to be successful in developing commerce* (business) *must have the same unrestrained authority that government has to have* to accomplish its objectives. What, therefore, can be more idle, or more deceptive than talk about the abundant life, as though it could be created without heart-rending hardships? Even Stalin has not been guilty of practicing that vicious deception. He, of course, used other methods of cheating.

War is a means of protecting commerce, public or private. It is to be anticipated, therefore, that promoting commerce calls for as many sacrifices in peace time as in times of war, no matter who is in charge, a government official or a captain of private enterprise. And it must be borne in mind that constitutional free enterprise (the private property theory) was chosen because government-controlled enterprise (mercantilism

[17] Stakhanovism, as outlined in Manya Gordon's "Fifty Years of Labor in Russia", show how the Russians were subjected to the most intense production strains and endurance tests.

"It was a great shock to us when in 1938, after I had moved to Moscow, the police made Vera and several other disfranchised minors move to Chelyabinsk on twenty-four hours notice." Scott "Behind the Urals" p 131.

or Roman diocletianism) had a record of extreme brutality without progress—in fact, was brutality and stagnation, notwithstanding its introduction as the road to democracy, humanitarianism and liberalism—public welfare. No normal person delights in imposing hardships. It is probable that the industrialist was realistic instead of deceptive, for today the trends he tried to stem are sweeping in complete government control in every corner of the world.

A big company corporation is generally used to show the "awful" results which develop from allowing private individuals too much control of property. Although it is hard to prove that the employment policies of a private corporation are detrimental to public welfare, the politicians have no difficulty in making people believe that it is true. But just as it is impossible to prove that the general who ordered a million men into battle did not serve his country properly by that act—did not promote public welfare, so it is impossible to prove that a corporation which reduces the price of a commodity has not also served its country in spite of the numbers "slain." It certainly has not been established that private wealth (regardless of the amount accumulated) concentrated in industry is always a menace to good government and therefore should be destroyed or at least curtailed to the extent that the "liberals" suggest. The reformers are too sure they are right. Their judgment is not entitled to much weight if they are the beneficiaries of the program they recommend. The "humanitarians" could have done it all much better, cheaper and quicker without concentrating wealth or demanding the maximum from employees, no doubt!

It does not appear that industry's "crime" was that it created idle money, for the governmental wrath and punishment fell upon the industries which were creating jobs and producing

[18] Stuart Chase in "Government and Business", Chap. XVI, suggests that human nature has changed for the better. On that premise "Liberals", including the historian Beard, concluded that government officials (not industrialists) could be granted power without fear of abuse or tyranny. (See Chap. VII). The Russians are more astute. They teach that a government official is a safe and proper distributing agency because he is not driven by a profit urge. All of it disregards Locke's controlling doctrine that sovereignty is an irresponsible power and, therefore, should be restricted, and, in addition, have its authority divided. In other words, a government official is not financially responsible for his conduct. He, therefore, in sound judgment, cannot be authorized to use tax money for general investment or as risk money, or for charitable purposes. The only funds available to him for disbursement are funds obtained by compulsion—the recalcitrant taxpayer is put in jail. Funds thus acquired create a most sacred trust relationship. Legislation which give an irresponsible agency wide discretionary power of the use of such funds violates legal principles, sound judgment and moral concepts. Majority voters cannot bestow such authority on a government official, legally or morally. To do so is to impair economic security. The proclaimed justification of such procedure is evidence of the unscrupulousness of the *security urge*. The fact that brilliant educators are recommending such a course is conclusive evidence that human nature has not changed. Indeed, it is more self-righteous than ever in its lying and cheating and taking advantage of the unwary to satisfy its security urge. One may say "Liberals" prefer dollars, fame and power to honesty. But security for all is dependent on honesty.

"We should, of course, have to wait a long time to achieve a democratic State if we had to change human nature." Tead in "Adventures in Democracy", p 144.

wealth. The attacks were most severe at the time when it was not engaged in "influencing" government, so that influencing government improperly was not the crime in question.

What the government intended to do with the money it forced out of legitimate production was lost sight of in the enthusiasm aroused by the slogan "soak the rich", a subtle attack upon private property. One could hardly expect laymen to understand that this slogan really meant—*give the politician more power and have title to private property decided by the ballot instead of by the courts*;[18] that ultimately it would result in machinery which would destroy the last chance anyone had of being independent of government "dole"; that it transferred power from a private citizen, one with many legal checks on his conduct, to a government official, a human being, without any such checks—one representing sovereign power.

Modern Methods for Destroying Private Property

In recent years other methods by which government can seize, destroy or interfere with title to private property have been emphasized, such as one-sided anti-strike laws,[19] price controls, minimum hours and wage laws, production controls, hidden subsidies, or government acting as investor, landlord, philanthrophist (giving tax-payer's property (money) to foreign countries); or as a parent, compelling children to save part of their wages, the parent exercising complete control or ownership over the part saved. No potentate ever had such extensive control, especially investment control, over the property of his subjects. (The taxpayer indeed is a "trusting soul" to believe that human beings can be given that much power, without financial responsibility, and not abuse it!) The Forefathers never expected such a result from their Constitution! Just how far is the United States from the condemned European governments in that respect? How much farther must we go before the "liberals" can no longer hide that they are following in the steps of Mussolini, Hitler, Lenin and Stalin?

What the "Liberals" Believe

From what has been said, it appears that the "liberals" believe that the government can be given enough control of production and distribution to assure abundance and avoid over-production and distribution difficulties. Some of the supporters of this objective frankly admit that their programs involve abandonment of the conventional ideas of private property and money because so many of the workers will be on the same basis as a soldier—necessities, food, clothes, transportation and shelter furnished on requisition. Others, the dreamers, believe that such an objective can be obtained without abandonment of the principles of the American Constitution as they relate to free enterprise or private ownership of the means of production. But all of them are dissatisfied with the distance that the United States has already traveled in that direction, and are sure that it can go much farther without any danger of being obliged to go all the way, accept Stalin's system. His system (not communism) is a form of government which objects to a citizen owning the means of production, and requires so much political supervision of daily affairs that the subject is a government (political) slave or pawn.

The "liberals" do not state how far they want to go. But, like Stalin, they minimize the government slave labor phase by teaching that *citizens should be just as willing to sacrifice their property and their lives for their country under a peace program as under a war program; that, indeed, they should be more willing, since a peace program is constructive and certainly gives the government a better right to demand the citizen's all.*

These propositions seem plausible enough. No politician has difficulty in selling them, notwithstanding the fact that they involve abandonment of the doctrine of sacredness of private property that the Forefathers subscribed to . Of course, a new and more enlightened conception of private property is announced to take the place of the old doctrine.

Such propositions are being brushed aside too lightly especially by the layman. No one can foresee what kind of government will develop upon the bursting of the bubbles blown on the pipes of spend-and-spend, governmental debt-has-no-significance, and labor's right to strike must not be abridged. But how, step by step, the whole constitutional conception of government is being discarded, and the divine-right-of-government idea introduced to direct every phase of life! We fail to recognize this as the Russian or European way because of prejudice, and because of the solemn and earnest declarations of the "Liberals" that they are leading us toward democracy, freedom from want and fear.

But let us look at some of the obvious objections and difficulties. Because of the great amount of power which accrues to one person under this kind of government, the *power* urge, instead of the *profit* urge, is bound to be so great that contentions for this power will result in blood purges terminating in civil war, stagnation and starvation. (The political pressure which made a four-term president, in fact, a life-term one, is evidence enough of the uncontrollable power urge.) The European blood purge and concentration camps are inevitable results. When that happens private property is destroyed for the great majority.

Another difficulty is that if we use their "full employment" programs honestly, the machinery in the United States can, in many instances, produce enough for most of the world. As other countries also will want to produce, in order to be independent, it is obvious that much machinery will be idle. One should bear in mind that the 60-million job boast really is no more than 60 million half-time jobs—in fact is 30 million jobs divided to give 60 million, at least, some work! These forms of government, therefore, present a world problem and involve half-time employment for the industrious and intelligent along with the lazy and the morons.[20] Equality with a real sting in it! And what about the war hazards?

Collapse for government enterprise always comes as a surprise. Hence no steps are taken to prevent it until it is too late. The unexpected element arises because the leaders dare not disclose the true state of affairs. Indeed, on the contrary, they have to deny that there is danger. If they showed they were alarmed, immediate panic and confusion would seize the country. All they can do is to deny that the danger exists and pray God that things will turn out all right. They therefore use fictions or psychology such as a mother employs for frightened children, a general for a panicky army, bankers for disturbed depositors, doctors for delicate patients.

The possibility of collapse of government enterprise is greater than for free enterprise because the government official is in a particularly good position to hide facts from inquiring minds. He can plead as the basis for not disclosing facts public necessity or "military" secret, etc., which the record indicates he does freely, frequently, unnecessarily, and often, if not generally, viciously. There is, therefore, no way to ascertain when a collapse is imminent. The first rule of Democracy with

---

[20] "A world-wide system of proper distribution geared to a maximum industrial output that will give a job to everyone who wants to work will be necessary in the post-war era, Mrs. Franklin D. Roosevelt said today." AP Washington, Apr. 24, 1944.

The First Lady apparently did not weigh the full significance of that statement.

respect to protection for public welfare and private property is therefore ignored when a government gets into a position where it has to beguile citizens with propaganda (fictions) for fear that if they had the facts their judgment would defeat government plans. Such a situation creates a relationship between the citizens and the government which destroys the protection for private property that was contemplated by the Constitution. How can one escape from realizing that these practices, starting under the guise of taxation, government investment, compulsory savings and full employment, lead to the type of government Hitler, Mussolini and Stalin represent or represented? [21]

War Powers and Private Property

One of the grave objections to the theory of the "Liberals" is that it gives the government official too much "wartime" authority during peacetime. Because the "Liberal" denies this, it is necessary to set the matter out in detail for clarification purposes.

In war, a government may find itself in a position where it must command the last dollar—ignore every restraint on seizure of property. As long, therefore, as nations *can declare war* the citizens, in theory, *owns nothing,* and the *government owns everything,* and consequently the government has no restraint on its conduct either as to taxation or direct seizure

[21] Kingdon on page 88 of "An Uncommon Man" dismisses the whole subject by implying that all persons who oppose these ideas are Hitlerite blackguards. Wallace on page 32 of "Sixty Million Jobs" delicately suggests the same thing by using the phrase "the dirty work of scoundrels."

But why should the words of individuals trying to build a commercial empire be less trustworthy than those bent on establishing a political empire or writing books which are bound to have a tremendous sale value? In a court of law they would have little standing because of obvious self-interest.

[22] "War is the *unlimited* use of men and material, all forces material and moral for the purpose of destroying the forces of the enemy and rendering him powerless to offer any further resistance." Beard. "The Republic" p 103.

It is obvious that Beard recognizes that regardless of constitutions, war may create a situation where citizens of a country are in complete subjection to the judgment of a single individual. A dangerous situation indeed. There should, therefore, be substantial sentiment to reduce war possibilities. It is not probable that the United Nations will be too helpful in that respect as it divides nations into categories of peace-loving nations and war-loving nations, a division which the record does not justify or establish. That unfortunate division, born out of a self-righteous spirit, is no doubt, the principal reason why peace movements are always frustrated and futile.

As leaders are prone to believe in their own nobleness, no amount of evidence would help them to realize the tragic consequences of their arbitrary categories.

of property, regardless of Constitutions or Bills of Rights.[22] Such instruments were never intended to obliterate the power described in such phrases as "divine right of government," "the king can do no wrong," "my country right or wrong." That power of course is to be used only when circumstances compel the government to follow such a course. Nevertheless, when necessary, government has to be in a position to take life and property without any obligation for compensation. The eminent domain proposition in the Fifth Amendment loses its significance when confronted with governmental necessity. However, it is a very valuable check on the officials who exercise the "King-can-do-no-wrong" prerogatives of sovereign power.

The king-can-do-no-wrong phrases are ways of saying that an individual is supposed to assume his government represents an informed majority and is therefore right even if its demands are to the extent of terminating life and seizing property. These phrases are unfortunate and misleading ways for describing majority rule, or the simple idea that one person with a minimum of information should not pit his judgment against the opinion of a whole nation or the opinion of a majority of the experts.

These extreme statements of governmental power no doubt grew out of the necessity to refute the equally extreme theory that a person was obliged to follow his conscience (God) no matter what other persons believe, a theory which embraced the idea of an unlimited right in property for the individual— in delicate words—the dignity of man, rugged individualism to the last degree.

The limitations which the Constitution imposed upon government were an implied protest against the abuse of the theory that government can do no wrong, a theory which certainly jeopardizes the citizen's title to his private property. The Constitution tried to correct the unsound conceptions about the authority of the king (government) and the title to property vested in an individual.

However, the theory that the government can do no wrong, the old divine right of kings theory, is being rapidly restored to its original paralyzing position under the glamour of governmental controls, benefits and ownership. It is that theory which the "liberals" have in mind when they say they are fighting a war to abolish poverty and social inequality. They are asking for war powers in times of peace! *The Constitution tried to make it impossible for government officials to exercise wartime powers during peacetime, because that would subject title to private property constantly to wartime jeopardy,* that is, practically leave it without protection and eventually, if past experience means anything, would result in permanent destitution for many and special privilege for the few—only a few to enjoy the Four Freedoms.

War, generally, is not waged to such an aggravated extent that government is justified in seizing life and property without responsibility for compensation. The citizen, therefore, generally enjoys his property as though he owned full title. *However, when government undertakes to banish poverty under the same unlimited power which it uses to conduct war, it will always be exercising the maximum of authority over property. Such a situation, of course, creates permanent insecurity for private property.* The paralyzing effect of that relationship between the government and the citizen is the primary reason why these so-called democracies make for misery and stagnation.

Property ownership, because it creates security dependent

upon the owner's judgment and integrity is, of course, one of the main driving impulses of civilization and therefore should be entitled to governmental protection. It was the serious consequences which followed inadequate protection for title to property that gave birth to the numerous world-renowned charters, petitions and constitutions, including the Constitution of the United States. Apparently the sublime faith in these documents is not justified, for astute politicians with the consent of the misguided, frightened, or greedy majorities, generally reduce them to useless scraps of paper.

Major Protection for Private Property Under the Constitution

The major protection afforded by the Constitution against the devices for seizing property, or reducing its title value, are the ancient principles therein providing for the specific jurisdiction of the different branches or divisions of government, including local sovereignty, such as city, county and state control.

Imagine the effect upon rights in property if the legislators or the President acted as judges, especially during an economic upheaval when a majority of the voters are made up of the destitute, the ignorant, the misinformed, and the discouraged, disappointed, sick, desperate and helpless. Such voters, no matter how intelligent or how honest, could hardly be expected to vote against spending money in their own behalf, regardless of its origin or the manner of collection. As an example, in the Detroit sit-down strike, a Constitution, a governor, and appointed judges were almost helpless in the task of protecting to only a nominal degree title to private property. That strike demonstrates the present weakness in title to property. The elected officials, because of the ballot pressure, were not far

[23] The Secretary of Labor seemed to think so.

[24] On p 200 of "The Republic", Beard subscribes to the proposition that under "new deal" legislation the executive becomes practically supreme, the legislature a poor second and the courts supplanted by administrative agencies. Beard apparently is satisfied with that trend.

"Our federal political machinery devised for a simple agricultural society, is not competent to resolve efficiently the issues forced upon government by the needs of our great industrial nations." "The Republic" p 246. Beard.

[25] See message to Congress in January 1944, 1945, 1946 and 1947, regarding "Economic Bill of Rights", and practically pledging the taxpayers to a program of direct social responsibility for eliminating economic distress for all.

Dr. Kingdon in Chap. 15 of "An Uncommon Man" concludes that all will be safe in the United States under governments patterned on communism, fascism or nazism, because the American people have been *trained*.

Although these kinds of government require placing the maximum of authority in the hands of one person, alleged to be the "people", he feels there is no danger from Hitlers, in spite of his declaration that the country is full of men who put dollars above people and who hated Roosevelt as they hate Wallace, because of their defense of the "common man."

And although Roosevelt was in office for life, just as Hitler and Mussolini were and Stalin is, and all such leaders have been before, he still feels that the kind of government he advocates does not tend to create prepetuity in office or a breakdown in free elections!

from conceding that private ownership of an industrial plant was a wicked fallacy and should be abandoned.[23]

Just imagine the result if the judges who are appointed for life made the laws, or the ballot's scope was enlarged under referendums, initiatives and recalls so that the voters themselves were required to settle the complex issues of government which have confused and confounded judges, statesmen, economists and presidents—individuals supposed to have special preparation for that kind of work. It is obvious, therefore, that it is the democratic principle of separate powers which protects the inherent rights to property—and, after all, very ancient and honored aspects of government. Nevertheless, politicians sincere or otherwise, have been particularly busy fooling the voters into believing that these principles should be discarded,[24] and have already forced government a long distance in that direction.[25]

One subtle way they have of fooling the people is to proclaim that everything is safe under these new forms of government because of the Bill of Rights. *That Bill, however, is futile and worthless under their systems of government because they defeat the principles involved in free speech, free elections, short terms of office, independent courts and legislators and local government (state government).* These principles of course are significant because they protect the theory of the sacredness of private property, the free enterprise system, without which social security cannot be maintained.

There is much lip-service about independence of courts,[26] the limitations on the executive and the legislators, and the free ballot. However, the numerous and constant curtailments of the rights in private property through enhanced and glamorous authority exercised over them by government officials under

[26] See footnote 25.

cradle-to-the-grave and full-employment programs, should be a clear and definite signal to anyone that all is not well.

The check on the ballot provided by the Constitution is of particular importance in the protection of property rights. An unwary person listening to the average politician talking about Democracy could well draw the conclusion that everybody from the cradle to the grave voted, and that they voted on every question. However, generally, one has to be 21 before he can vote and, besides, in many instances, he has to own property as well as have a certain amount of education, and even then he can only vote, not on governmental policies or particular laws, but merely for certain individuals to represent him, and who are supposed to use their judgment, not the voter's, with respect to governmental policies.

The Constitution does not say anything directly about age limitations, property and educational qualification of voters, but it was ordained under the assumption that the limitations then in effect would continue. There would have been an altogether different constitution had the creators thereof been confronted with the ballot as it is used today. The change in ballot restrictions makes it impossible to honor many of the fundamental principles in the Constitution.

As things stand today, the limitations on the ballot have been removed to such an extent that our present form of government has been driven so far to the left that it is not entitled to being classed as a democracy, if one means by that term protection of title to private property as contemplated by the Forefathers.

The careless as well as adroit use by prominent people of the word "democracy" has made it mean benevolent dictatorship, a form of government which cannot recognize the constitutional principle of equal footing for the three main branches of government. That is so because that principle imposes too many restraints on the seizure of property necessary to maintain such forms of government. It is probable that these countries described as democracies, which included Japan before the war, have the government which affords them the best chance to live, to promote commerce and business; but their governments in no sense of the word can be called democracies, unless one wishes to use the word to describe any type of government which appeals to him.

Laissez Faire for Business as Property

The main principles of government in the Constitution, especially the idea of equal footing for the three usually mentioned branches of government and the Fifth Amendment, seem to indicate that the Forefathers believed that social security, progress, democracy, strength in government, justice, mercy, humanitarianism, a chance to make a decent living, freedom and liberty, independence from systems of other countries, depended upon what is called the theory of unqualified title to property. This theory is now generally referred to by such words and phrases as free enterprise, capitalism,[27] no limit to the amount of property one person may accumulate by lawful means, merit is entitled to its reward—the laissez faire theory.

[27] The word "capitalism" unfortunately is subjected to the same emotional misinterpretations which are used for free enterprise, laissez faire, dictatorship, communism, etc. The dictionary is seldom used to get at their correct meaning. The true meanings are usually deliberately avoided. For instance: "Laissez faire is the successor of feudalism in occidental civilization." Boucke. "Laissez Faire and After" p 34.

Laissez faire was primarily a protest to syndicates, trade unions and government favoritism to "control without ownership." The last proposition named is now recommended as something new and valuable, although it is the main principle in corporations, and no doubt the cause of the 1929 debacle because of lack of financial liability of the directors. If that was the result under private enterprise, what must be expected under government control when the "directors" are practically immune from prosecution?

It should be observed that today this theory is only applied to the fields of medicine, science, literature, entertainment and religion.

The "liberals" recognize the laissez faire doctrine for the arts, for entertainment and for government. The forefathers, however, aimed at a liberal application of the laissez faire doctrine to business—laissez faire for business, *but not for government* because it was not responsible, in the usual sense of the word, for its conduct.

This theory, of course, involves the principles of unqualified title to property, that is, private citizens owning the means of production. They are the same principles which prevail when an artist is allowed his recognition without interference by the government, a general his glory, an inventor his credit, a poet his fame, a statesmen his honor—all without limitation as to amount regardless of the heart-break for others who try to follow, and all without interference, restriction or curbing by government on the ground that the fame or the glory will give the owner too much power. No one, so far, has suggested a law that they should be limited in their quest for achievement. However, the enthusiasm for "floors" and "ceilings", cradle-to-the-grave aid, and full-employment schemes demonstrates that there is now a world-wide spirit to have government determine, not only how much property one may acquire, but also what vocation a citizen should follow, where he should live, what he must do, how long he should work, and what he may receive as pay—a spirit certainly not in accord with that of the Constitution, and certainly striking at the very heart of security through ownership of property, and opening the flood-gates of governmental corruption and permanent distress for the greatest number of people.

Of course, under an economic structure based on the constitutional theory of courts and legislators, that is, unqualified title to property, capitalism, free enterprise, rugged individualism, or whatever it should be called, boys and girls, and men and women, because of low income and for many other reasons, have not a chance in the world of reaching their objectives; but they have a much better chance to do that under such a structure than they have under the schemes of government control proposed in the United States and in the rest of the world in the name of liberalism; but, unfortunately, not enough of such opportunity to avoid dangerous social unrest because of the rank injustice which prevails.

However, there is one important advantage under free enterprise. The wronged person (and there will be always a great many of them) seeks redress for a grievance from individuals and employers who are subject to law and court restraint, whereas under the "New Orders" his contentions are with his government, a supreme power which may disregard his grievance with impunity and often affords him no redress except by civil war.[28] This remedy, generally, is so clearly futile that the government official does not hesitate to do as did the oppressors referred to in the Bible, increase the load whenever a subject complains. Therefore there will be no complaints, and in the absence thereof the government official will boast of unity, liberty and prosperity until civil war overtakes him. Such a situation cannot develop if the ancient principles with respect to independent branches of government and short term of office are properly adhered to. The economists or politicians who complain that under capitalism or free enterprise a few people own all the property, or enough to control government, should know that such a situation is evidence that the Consti-

---

[28] " * * * at the present stage of industrialism there is little or no difference in the situation of the worker employed * * * by the * * * State or the worker employed by private enterprise." Reeves "Anatomy of Peace" p 55.

An unfortunate and dangerous premise, but generally accepted.

[29] "A state-controlled economy can build factories and produce commodities just as well as a system of free enterprise. Ownership of capital, tools and means of production does not appreciably affect either the economic or the social structure of a State." Reeves "Anatomy of Peace" p 72.

If that is correct, Lenin and our Forefathers misconceived their issues.

"But the nation-states, like feudal knights, are chaining their subjects to the soil of their homeland, refusing them that most elementary of freedoms, the freedom of movement. The interference in this field of liberty is identical. with the absolute rule of the feudal landowners over their serfs. The system of passports, visas, exit permits, immigration quotas, is incompatible with free economic exchange." Reeves in "The Anatomy of Peace" p 166.

Reeves apparently is not concerned about confiscation of money, private property and private enterprise.

[30] "It should be remembered that of the three fundamental principles which underlie government, and for which government exists, the protection of life, liberty and property, the chief of these is property; not that any amount of property is more valuable than the life or liberty of the citizen, but the history of civilization proves that, when the citizen is deprived of the free use and enjoyment of his property, anarchy and revolution follow, and life and liberty are without protection." Judge Van Orsdel in the Adkins case. 261 US 525.

[31] The politician has to keep political power away from the subject to gain his ends for the same reason that a capitalist has to keep money away from workers. In that respect both of them aim to keep their proteges destitute. One grabs political power (profit) and the other gold or commercial power (profit).

On page 139 of "Economy of Abundance" Chase states that bankers do not want people to have money. In the same sense, the bureaucrat or politician does not want people to have money—money representing independence.

tution has been ignored. They should also know that their program will only aggravate such situations because it concentrates wealth and political power absolutely in one place—the head of government, and, therefore, is bound to increase oppression and corruption ten-fold.[29] This is so because it gives a human being too much power without the proper checks, and, therefore always results in abuse.

That is the major basis of every limitation on human conduct, and is the premise for the limitations which the Constitution imposes upon judges, congressmen, presidents and voters in order to protect private property (interests), the protection of which appears to be the surest road to general economic security.[30] The limitations, of course, can be maintained only by keeping intact the principle of separated powers. Hence no provision was made for "humanitarians" who believe they can be trusted with these powers combined! Indeed, governmental restrictions are aimed particularly at that group, for their god-complex makes them imagine they cannot do, or be, wrong and stimulates their ego toward purges and schemes for seizing property in the name of public welfare. The greatness of the Forefathers is manifested by their recognition that they, like all human beings, should not be trusted with sovereign power, except in the narrow field or area provided by the Constitution. They knew they were not holy men.

In spite of loud denial, the political "humanitarians" and "liberals" realize instinctively that there are no greater threats to personal political power than divided governmental authority and citizens who own enough property or have sufficient income to be independent of political favor.[31] From that fact arises their enthusiasm for concentrated governmental authority—an attitude which they are bound to believe, because of

[31a] See Justice Harlan's opinion in the Adair case, 208 U.S. 261. (1907). That case would have had more weight if the judge had shown more clearly that any other position would only add to poverty, misery and hardships. The judge did not anticipate the political fantasies which were soon to put constitutional government to flight.

In these days one should not hang far-reaching public policy questions on the constitutional pegs of Liberty of Contract, Interstate Commerce, or Due Process. The welfare of the country is at stake. The issue should be met head-on. It is Public Welfare (economic security). Today only overwhelming evidence that the so-called social legislation is detrimental to economic security will cause a judge with a "liberal" mind to understand that the legislation is unconstitutional. The questions of today are not the ones that confronted John Marshall. The attacks today are on the philosophy of the Constitution about the rights of citizens with relation to property. The government official is saying that the citizen is responsible to see to it that no one shall starve, and that, therefore, the government official may tax him accordingly. Neither the Forefathers, nor John Marshall, nor President Jefferson, ever dreamed of such a fantastic conception of the taxpayers' obligation.

self-interest, is humanitarian, no matter how silly. Their disposition to believe that others have improper motives, should put them on guard as to the natural trend of the human mind, including their own.

Restraints on Builders of Commercial Empires

Recognition must be made of the value, weight and significance of the complaint that when a citizen has extensive property holdings, he exercises too much control over the machinery of government, and consequently too much control over the property rights of others. But if there is a remedy it is not more government regulations or ownership of a character which will result in having both wealth and political power concentrated in one place. Because of the tragic results which would follow such a course it is a primary objective of democratic government to keep these two powers separated as much as possible. The argument must be whether the principle of divided powers as expressed in the Constitution is the most effective way. This raises the old and hereto unanswered question of the checks which should be imposed on the authority of human beings in the administration of the affairs of state.

The scope of that authority must vary according to circumstances. Congested areas certainly impose restraints which would not be tolerated in rural communities. However, congested social structures do not give rise to circumstances which compel or require nullification of the principle involved in divided political authority, namely, courts and parliaments as recognized by the Constitution. That principle carries with it short term of office, a free ballot for electing representatives, a right to own property in any amount, *including the right of the employer to hire and fire in peace time or any other time to the same degree that government requires that power in wartime.* [31a]

" The function of capitalism is *not* to furnish people with things they want. Goods are supplied only for profit." Chase "The Economy of Abundance" p 138. (Paraphrased.)

The reverse is more nearly true. The author has stated the exception as the rule. One cannot explain civilization on any other basis than stimulated demand. For instance, in 15 years capitalism found a way to reduce the price of automobiles from $5000 to $500 and at the same time increase wages 50 percent. Labor Unions, unintentionally, but greedily, have interfered to the public's disadvantage.

On page 171 in "Government in Business", Chase observes that private business is not tempted to build parks, playgrounds, etc. But private enterprise furnishes the taxes, and the average business man leads his community in advocating the use of taxes for such purposes.

It is believed that it would not be disputed that the Fore-fathers were convinced that abandonment of that kind of government would soon destroy equal opportunity, or such protection for private property rights or interests in them as is necessary to make a highly civilized community possible. They apparently also accepted as truth that the soundest method to keep misery and want at low ebb, and the abundant life at high tide, was to emphasize the individual's right to property,—to be *liberal* in that respect. The tendency today is to be liberal in the opposite way—liberal with governmental power to dispense with private property. One can hardly understand how any judge can count himself in harmony with the Constitution, a true liberal, when he subscribes to that doctrine.

The Forefathers apparently believed that the right to acquire wealth to any extent, did most to promote the spirit which made possible the objective of producing cheaper, faster and better than any other country.[32] That is the objective one has to adopt in wartime, and after all building a commercial empire may be a more bitter and exacting struggle than conducting a war. The maximum of effort, without the hot blood of war to deaden the pain, is the price a citizen must pay to be free from the necessity of government relief in the form of dole, unemployment compensation, pensions, minimum wages, etc. He, generally, balks at that price because he does not realize that such relief is particularly cruel and undesirable because it eventually imposes permanent distress upon the masses, although at first it seems to spell out security. The maximum of properly directed effort is the only rule which can be followed if a nation wishes to be prosperous and free, and independent of the economic structures of other countries. The right to build commercial empires without the assistance of governmental subsidies and in the face of unrestricted competition at

[33] Stuart Chase on pp 6, 7, and 8 of "Economy of Abundance" calls attention to waste under capitalism; namely, unnecessary factories, railroads, skyscrapers, stores, warehouses, oil wells, etc.; poor location for industrial plants causing too much transportation; overproduction of food stimulated by reclamation and irrigation projects; waste in duplicate hauling, selling forces, branches, advertising and administration because of competition; shoddy construction to create replacement activity; style changes, pleasure motoring; limited use of farm machinery, tractors, etc., used only a few days a year; destruction of food and other necessities of life to create a market. He wants to remedy this situation by government control, assuming that government officials, who do not have to pay for their mistakes, will do better work. The absurdity is obvious.

The trouble, of course, lies in the fact that business men and government officials cannot anticipate all contingencies. As long as the world is not blessed with "supermen" it will experience hardships under capitalism, communism or totalitarianism. The private property theory as supported by the Constitution, so far has demonstrated, regardless of failure, that it has the "edge" and has given mankind the most benefits,—has been the most humane.

Waste resulting from duplication prompted Big Business to utilize combinations. The combinations (monopolies) strangled Free Enterprise—competition. The government thereupon enacted regulatory legislation. Such legislation brought forth "social" legislation, and continued to make matters worse. For instance the NLRA and the wage and hour laws protect Big Business and make it impossible for Little Business to survive. It is monopoly creating legislation. Big Business, the wily politicians, and labor leaders, will defend and promote such legislation; not always openly, of course. The remedies for the waste complained about have not added to economic security. They interfere too much with the Free Enterprise objective of producing cheaper, better and quicker than any other nation.

home and abroad, with the government to see to it that this competition is not choked off, was the economic atmosphere in which the Constitution was born.

The modern economist, however, is busy discarding that philosophy. He has reversed it to such an extent that he is confronted with frozen patent rights, frozen wage scales, frozen prices and frozen hours of work, with the result that business in general, also, is frozen. He is trying to create a thaw with money of the taxpayer, not realizing that the smoke he sees indicates intense cold, not heat, and that therefore he is only freezing things tighter. Whether he wants to or not, his program will compel him to do more and more freezing. Eventually, social unrest will drive him to establishing a large military force to beat his own subjects into obedience. Before long he will be facing, to keep from perishing, the same war-making necessity which confronts the communist—force the nations of the world to accept his form of government by comintern or by war. Too late he will find that his tinkering with commerce, trade or business (private property), has intensified the hardships he intended to modify.

It seems one cannot escape the uncompromising and unrelenting fact that business (commerce, private property interests), in order to be successful enough to create security, needs the same unrestrained authority in its field that government requires in time of war. The communist indicates his recognition of that fact by his frantic effort to put everything on a war basis. The sweet phrases, full-employment, war to end poverty, security from-the-cradle-to-the-grave, and government promised food, clothes and shelter, involve the same proposition.

War, however, is the primitive method of protecting business, and war methods in times of peace, like competition, are cruel, costly and often futile.[33]

[34] There is, of course, no perfect definition of communism. However, its underlying philosophy as expressed in its constitution, is that the conventional conception of ownership of private property is the cause of all economic evils. It therefore extends itself to abolish private property.

[35] **The idea was not new. Chile burned 500,000 sheep. Brazil dumped six million bags of coffee. According to the author of "Soviet Power", a carload of oranges was shoveled into the Irish sea "on a sweltering August day." The author forgot to emphasize that this was done by government mandate. He is astute enough, however, to notice that in lieu of direct destruction programs, restrictive ones (far more subtle) have been introduced; perhaps the most effective have been the restrictions on hours of work.**

That this matter is tangled and confused in the minds of many seems obvious from the fact that those who complain about cruel and ruthless business methods are the first to shout for war, or to imagine that war is necessary, and apparently they glory in its blood, sweat and tears—not realizing that it is all in the name of business—commerce; and those who are afraid of war or pretend to tremble at it, do not hesitate to play the whip on the bare back in the name of business. Both of them demand the pound of flesh nearest the heart, and both are satisfied that they are humanitarians, and neither one realizes that he is subscribing to the doctrine of private property, rugged individualism, and (paradoxically enough) recommending the maximum of regimentation.

The Swing Toward Communism—Russian Dictatorship

Our Forefathers may have been too drastic and too narrow in their premises about competition and private property. However, the tendency is to completely reverse their position. The reverse of it is communism, from which Russia under Stalin partly backed away, although, of course, under a declaration that communism was being developed. Fortunately for Stalin, the word "communism" was worshipped in Russia without the worshipers calling for a definition.[34]

According to not a few, by an adroit use of the word "democracy" the United States is being rushed toward the kind of government Russia had or has. The similarity may not be obvious to some because the United States government aimed, in the first instance, at control of food supplies (property) by reducing output,[35] while Russia, in order to get control was obliged to aim at increased output because her subjects were starving. However, scarcity makes it much easier to justify government control. Governments have learned to use scarcity as the basis for government control, scarcity by way of fictions.

[36] Most of the alleged shortages were fictions which imposed great hardships on the public. The false scarcity was necessary to maintain government control. This scarcity is created in such a manner that the responsible authority dare not disclose the facts or take the necessary action to remove it. However, Mayor LaGuardia used bold words in PM on Oct. 6, 1946, in connection with an alleged beef scarcity: "Now let no one try to start a scare on * * * Argentine meat. * * * Our fighting men have eaten Argentine meat in many sections of the world. A *Fictional* quarantine * * * may be all right in normal times to protect our cattlemen. But when the entire country is suffering * * * it is * * * time to be *honest.*"

These programs are presented as a proposition that they will give everybody a fair share. But the unending shortages do not justify faith in them. They suggest that the real objective is not disclosed. Could it be anything else than a try for "permanent" control? Incidentally, viciousness has not been removed. It has simply been transferred from commercial profit to political corruption.

To an extent, business or free enterprise is based on *scarcity* in order to make money—profit. The Russians, therefore, concluded that elimination of money was the solution for economic security. They prohibited individuals from having money as with it one could acquire property (business) and become an exploiter. That an individual armed in that area with sovereign authority would be a far more vicious exploiter escaped their attention. The "Liberals" also disregard that fundamental aspect of government.

[37] "If ploughing in 10 million acres of cotton and destroying 5 million pigs will bring national prosperity, then I have wasted 'my life. The thing is monstrous. An age of science has given place to an age when science is frustrated. In no sense is our economic order (sponsored by government) scientific." "Soviet Power" p 3.

The author should have realized that the destruction was necessary in order to give government control! It is the only way in which the kind of government the author is enthusiastic about can be made effective. Chase stated it clearly: "It is so much easier to deal with an industry haggard with losses than one proud with profits." "Government in Business" p 285.

The fictions may give the "planners" their first real chance for permanent government control. The arguments in the fight for retention of OPA justify that conclusion. They all boil down to instigating hate, fear and suspicion of the "vicious" groups who are seeking profit. There will never be anything but scarcity if the "planners" have their way.[36]

Secretary Wallace found his precedent for governmental curtailment of food in the practice of the Captains of Industry, as though one evil justified another. The necessity for the curtailments of production was based on an alleged sympathy for the preservation of free enterprise, capitalism, the theory of private property!

The whole procedure suggests deception and fraud. The "planners" know that destruction of food is not the way of abundance.[37] The alleged purpose back of the destruction of pigs was to increase prices, admittedly an unusual way to create abundance. But it paved the way for government control by introducing scarcity. Natural scarcity was not available as it was and is in Russia and generally is during wartime. As the art of scarcity has been mastered, the dream of the "planners" should become a reality.[38] Anyhow could one conceive of a better way to remain in power? It is not being suggested that responsible government officials deliberately plan permanent government control, even of food. *But the leaders of such programs are the beneficiaries of power, prestige and office. Could they, under such circumstances, be expected to form an unbiased opinion with respect to the necessity for continuation of the program?* Is not that phase of it alone sufficient to make one apprehensive?

It must be remembered, too, that many industrialists realize

[38] Senator Moore of Oklahoma in a recent speech in the Senate declared this to be the case. There are too many statesmen who believe the same way to justify brushing the matter aside as hysteria.

that the OPA principle of government is useful in promoting shortages. So long as there are shortages, there is no danger of the depressions which arise from what is termed over-production. They prefer OPA scarcity to over-production. It will be remembered that NRA sent people to jail for not charging enough, whereas OPA sent people to jail for charging too much. However "overproduction" is the plague of free enterprise. *It is the Frankenstein that terrifies the business man into accepting NRA, AAA, NLRA, or OPA government.*

But if these programs are going to be really successful, something more than political footballs, it will be necessary to accept the principles of totalitarianism as practiced in Russia.[39] The present subsidies and privileges are enough to compel the adoption of that course. Can anyone stop this flight of the Magic Carpet? But, under such circumstances, the heart of democracy stops beating because it becomes impossible to keep judges, legislators and executives functioning in their proper spheres, and consequently free courts, free elections, free legislators, free religion and free education disappear. They dissolve automatically because of the corruption in government. And with them, of course, goes protection to private property and security.

Free Speech and Private Property

It has always been recognized that free speech (criticism of government), because it involves directly or indirectly all the other freedoms, is the principal fortification for protecting title to private property and promoting general public welfare. *But it cannot function when the subjects are directly dependent upon their government for food and other essentials of daily life.* That creates a relationship which discourages too much,

[39] See footnote 12 of Chap. II.

if not altogether, the right kind of criticism. The fact that government represents sovereignty is enough to destroy all ground for assuming that the relationship of a government official to private property is one that entitles him to much authority. It is sovereign authority which develops the greatest fear of all—the fear of the wrath of government. Therefore, when government has control of the necessities of life, a relationship between the government and its subjects arises which precludes any basis for assuming that the subjects, at least the smart ones, will indulge in criticism that will be helpful to public welfare.

Tribute must be paid to the judges and statesmen who emphasize the fact that free speech is destroyed when citizens become dependent upon government for their food and shelter For an individual, naturally, does not criticize, a benefactor, and is ready to destroy, generally, anyone who does, regardless of fair play or justice. The German atrocities are good examples. Private property protection under such circumstances simply cannot exist, neither can progress continue nor social security flourish.

The theory that private property is sacred rests upon the ground that only an individual who does not have to depend directly upon government for his food and shelter is free and therefore in a position to place proper checks upon political power. Such checks, of course, annoy the politician and is adequate basis for motive on his part to keep citizens in want and dependent upon government. Under such circumstances the citizen (subject) is indeed clay ready for the potter's cunning hand!

THREATS TO
POLITICAL RIGHTS

KEY PROPOSITIONS

Under "Social Democracy" a government official is the employer, an employer who commands the Army and the Navy and may disregard courts and legislators. As he will be made of the same kind of clay that the captain of industry is made of, it should not be difficult to anticipate the abuse in store for the employee who gets out of favor.

The new-order idea of government developed from a presumption that human beings will be satisfied if all have the same amount—let it be enough. The truth is their pleasure comes from having more than others in wages, power, property, fame or glory. Any other spirit would result in stagnation.

Governments are prone to have too many beneficiaries; generally so many that criticism is very dangerous as well as futile. That is why free speech (criticism of government) is so strongly fortified in the Constitution.

Free speech requires that the citizen maintain a relationship toward his government which will in nowise blind his eyes to its sins and faults—and that is impossible when too many of the citizens are governmental beneficiaries or hopeless or hopeful dependents in the form of clerks, creditors, debtors, contractors or pensioners. It is in the first instance surrendered by consent; after that because of fear; by consent due to benefits; by fear because of dependence on government for the necessities of life.

THREATS TO POLITICAL RIGHTS

CHAPTER IV

Political Rights

Political rights and property rights are closely tied together. Indeed, if one is not able to acquire enough property to be independent of government dole, work, food or shelter, political rights become worthless.[1] Such rights as voting, holding office, and having courts and parliaments, are therefore insisted upon by the citizen because he has to have them to protect himself against governmental tyranny (generally burdensome taxes for alleged welfare purposes) with respect to property, jobs, business or profession—matters which represent his life, home and children.

Basis of Paralyzing Fear of Government

Apparently, he does not realize how much he impairs or jeopardizes such rights when he assigns to government, as he does quite generally today, the authority to direct how long he may work, what his wages shall be, the price he shall pay for commodities and what crops he shall raise. Although it has never been done before, he, nevertheless, seems to feel that such assignments can now be made without creating a situation which requires government officials to tell him the kind of work he shall perform, where he shall live, what he may have, or what profession or business he must follow, or in what

---

[1] Without political rights all forms of representation will continue to be fraud. The proletariat will remain as heretofore in prison. Lenin. 1905.

Lenin's definition contemplates that voters shall be without conventional property rights. His definition, therefore, represents the maximum of deception and fraud.

concentration camp he must suffer—the Russian style.[2] However, that he is greatly mistaken about the matter should be readily appreciated because a government official represents sovereignty—a power under which that official may disregard promises with impunity and can cover misdeeds and bungling under false public-necessity claims or military-secret bunk. And as he is a human being, no one has a right to expect that he will not abuse such power.

It is hard to understand why the citizen does not see that under such assignments he impairs the political rights he needs to protect himself against government-decreed destitution; that under such circumstances the political rights such as free speech, courts, and parliaments, as well as the ballot, are impaired to such an extent that they are readily reduced to futile gestures, eliminated or turned against him as instruments of oppression. This is so because he is giving to one individual or one branch of government such tremendous power that it naturally *frightens away criticism,* invites blind obedience, and demands unmerited praise to such an extent that all protection for individual economic independence (security) is swept away. Germany, Italy and Russia are present-day examples.

The political rights of the citizen, therefore, represent the restrictions which he must impose upon persons acting as government officials. *They carry the implication that one generally should not place too much of the affairs of his life in the hands of another, especially if that other is a government official*—a human being exercising unlimited power—sovereignty.

---

[2] Laws dealing with full employment, minimum wages, maximum hours, fair prices, etc., in order to be effective, require the extreme position that Fascism, Nazism, Communism and Stalinism demand. The leaders of these philosophies all believed they could stop where the "Liberals" think they will be able to stop.

As we have already seen, the tendency today is to reverse
that implication on the ground that a public official is not
under a profit *urge,* or is a humanitarian and, therefore, will
not abuse power; or, that a way has been found (by use of the
ballot) to drive unlimited political power in the right direction
in spite of the frailty or viciousness of human nature; or, the
most foolish of all, that human nature has changed. The white
race instinctively recognizes the danger in these theories.
Its fear or hostile attitude toward governmental authority is
pointedly expressed in Patrick Henry's cry of "Give me liberty,
or give me death." A human being exercising governmental
authority is in a particularly strategic position to mete out
death in the name of humanity to anyone interfering with his
"highly important programs". And he will do so whether his
name be Hitler, Roosevelt, Stalin, Wallace, Lenin, Willkie,
Dewey or Truman.

It, therefore, is not fantastic, but truly reasonable, to state
that these types of so-called democracy which force so many
matters of daily life into the hands of government officials
(human beings representing sovereignty), will force us to
another Declaration of Independence because of the crucifixion
of the Four Freedoms and the introduction of government
"slavery"—government telling subjects how much they shall
earn, how long they shall work, for whom they shall work,
what they shall wear, and what their political faith shall be.
Government "slavery" is distinguished from other forms of
"slavery" in that the Master (a government official) is dressed
in the robes of sovereignty. The master and his henchmen, of
course, will be fanatically enthusiastic about the matter.

No Basis for Confidence in the "New Type Democracies"

The demands for the so-called democracies arise because
capitalism (rugged individualism, free enterprise, constitutional

government) so often is unable to prevent near starvation and other hardships. As already suggested, the unbounded confidence in them springs from the idea *that a government official is in a better position than a private individual to remedy the obvious evils. Consequently, the apostles of the "New Orders" feel that the way to eliminate the hardships which overtake citizens in building a civilization* (a commercial empire) *is to increase the authority of the government officials over the means of production, and to decrease the power of the private citizen in that field.* That, of course, is the Russian idea or philosophy of government. The "Liberal" claims, of course, that he does not want to go as far as the Russians have gone. However, he started with statements that he intended to go only a little farther than the Constitution provides. But now he feels that the Constitution is horse and buggy stuff. Apparently, he does not understand himself because he considers that all his opponents are "blackguards."

The increased governmental authority is represented as an enlargement of political rights by which the "down-trodden" will have a better chance to live decently. But the reverse must be true, for the citizen has to surrender his right of economic independence (ownership of property) in proportion that he enlarges such governmental authority.

For instance, under collective bargaining (an alleged enlargement of political rights) which involves increasing governmental authority, the better qualified individual loses to a great extent personal contact with his employer. He surrenders that right of contact to a leader who is supposed to represent all employees, including the least qualified. That arrangement enhances the opportunity of the latter, but reduces the chances of the efficient worker to receive what he is entitled to. Such "equalization" procedure, of course, eventually destroys the economic security of all, for it penalizes efficiency and merit too much. Moreover, the individual, no matter how much he needs a few extra pennies, surrenders to the judgment of another, his right to determine when he shall work overtime, accept extra wages, or buy in free markets. For an imaginary political right the worker may have surrendered the only rights (protection) he needs to make his political rights worthwhile.

The farmer under "collective" farming is obliged to use the judgment of experts who represent a political regime. However, even under the present modified programs, he soon finds himself confronted with more speculations and uncertainties than he would have met with had he used his own judgment. That result is inevitable because he has made it too easy for a government official, in the name of public welfare, to "collect" his crops.[3] At present he is enjoying subsidy benefits. But his subsidies will eventually force Russian collectivism because the taxpayer cannot carry the load.[3a]

Collective bargaining and "collective" farming programs are, of course, the direct and necessary results which develop from control of prices, wages, hours of work and subsidies. And one must be simple or "grinding an ax" if he does not realize how difficult it will be to keep such procedure from stampeding his leader into complete government control. Moreover, the leader is a human being who will receive un-

[3] "Agriculture, manufacturing, commerce and navigation, the four pillars of prosperity, are then most thriving when left most free to individual enterprise." Jefferson.

"Were we to be directed from Washington when to sow and when to reap, we should soon want bread. Our country is too large to have all of its affairs directed by a single government." Jefferson.

Jefferson, no doubt, was familiar with the story of Joseph, the oldest government food-hoarding story, and with its tragic consequences.

[3a] Senator Lucas, Democratic Leader, was realistic when he said "effective controls over both planting and marketing are necessary to continue government price supports."

limited, or, at least, more power. Would not good judgment suggest that he will be tempted to make the disturbance that will start the stampede?

The Soviet leaders were honest about the matter. Accordingly, under their constitution the Russian was told that he would be allowed just enough property to exist,[4] and no title (in the usual sense of the word) to business, farms, or other real estate. He was induced or compelled to exchange his right to hold property—to be economically independent—for a political power or function which promised to make him economically secure. But it reduced him to government-decreed destitution, and sent him to a concentration camp if he failed to be enthusiastic about the distress his government imposed upon him. The benefits he gained were swept away in the reign of terror which soon followed.[5] Stalin's subsequent dictatorship restored a semblance of order by its recognition of a few of the old fundamental principles of government set forth in the United States Constitution.[6]

But it is obvious than an enlargement of political rights or a more democratic structure did not result from these efforts. They brought the exact opposite, for democracy is a political structure with the maximum of individual rights in private property and the minimum of governmental authority in that field. And it is generally understood that such a structure can be maintained only by *keeping the three main branches of government on equal footing, by insisting on short terms of office and a properly restricted ballot, and, of course, by upholding*

[4] "Every household * * * has for its personal use a small plot of land, * * * a dwelling house, livestock, poultry and minor agricultural implements * * *." Article VII of the 1936 Russian Constitution.

[5] Famine and pestilence swept Russia in the twenties and early thirties.

[6] "In the U.S.S.R. work is a duty and a matter of honor for every able-bodied citizen, in accordance with the principle: 'He who does not work, neither shall he eat'." Article XII of Chap. 1 of the Russian Constitution.

the doctrine that majority rule means that elected experts shall use their own judgment in making the laws, and independent judges (experts) shall do the same in interpreting them; after all, the major principles of the Constitution—in economic terms, free enterprise, open competition, rugged individualism, no arbitrary limits to the amount of private property a citizen may have, or who he shall hire or fire in the conduct of business; payment according to value of work performed and not according to needs—the merit rule.

The merit rule as here suggested is a hard rule. Nevertheless its enforcement, as everybody knows, is the very essence of democracy, if by that word one means the maximum of security for the common people. As progress and prosperity (security) depend upon that rule, it is the objective of all governments to protect and enforce it. The communists tried to repeal it by decreeing that persons should be paid according to their *needs*. The "liberals" call it the law of the jungle. Much of their legislation for the last two decades is colored with this anti-merit philosophy. Justices Stone, Cardoza and Brandeis, unintentionally, or unwittingly, perhaps, followed that lead to a great extent in their reasoning in the Tipaldo case, 298 U.S. 587.[7] However, they used the merit rule, without any modification, to attain their honorable positions, we hope.

Cruel as this rule may seem to be, it is the only one which stimulates production enough so that civilization can be maintained, and, consequently, offers the maximum of political rights which bear fruit. It is the only rule under which public welfare can be protected, although it does not sound as sweet as the rule sponsored by communism, that one shall receive what he needs regardless of what he earns. The latter rule, no matter what the administrator thereof may be trying to do,

[7] See footnote 12 in chapter on Russian Constitution.

[8] "I am convinced that governmental bureaucracy, from the standpoint of honesty, efficiency and fairness compares very favorably with corporation bureaucracy. There is less nepotism, less of arbitrary and unfair action, and a more continuous consideration of general welfare. This is not because human beings in government are so much finer as individuals than human beings in corporation bureaucracies, but because continuous public scrutiny requires a higher standard." Wallace in "The American Choice."

Kingdon on page 90 of "An Uncommon Man" sums this up by saying that no matter how much power the government official has it will be properly restrained as such power will be in the "hands of the people."

The Constitution, however, tried to put government into the hands of experts. The government of Russia was in the hands of the people from 1917 to 1923. That period represents the reign of terror for Russia as 1793 represents the reign of terror for France.

"They want us to believe that full employment and free enterprise cannot flower together." Wallace in "Sixty Million Jobs." p. 27.

"They say that we have to choose liberty or security. We cannot have both." Kingdon in "An Uncommon Man." p 88.

What Wallace and Kingdon want us to believe is that the "Liberals" only want government to take up the *slack*. However, what they recommend places a government official, the executive, in a position where he can use tax money for whatever he may *imagine* is public welfare. It boils down to an endorsement of the ancient, but never dying idea, that poverty can be removed by legislative distribution of private property. It ignores the fact that the only money a government official has for distribution is that which has been forced, by threat of extreme penalty, from the citizens—mostly the under-privileged. The money, therefore, represents a most sacred trust-fund relationship. Without express authority an official has no legal or moral right to use such funds for charitable purposes or as investments for the citizens. When he has been given such authority disastrous results have been the consequence. This is bound to be so because of his relationship to the fund. He is not bonded for malfeasance or for misfeasance. When he spends such funds it falsely appears he is an honorable benefactor. If he is a human being the lack of financial responsibility, coupled with an honor (one he is not entitled to), will create in him an irresistible impulse to spend, especially for his friends and political aspirations. He will have no difficulty, no matter how silly or far-fetched the proposition may be, to convince his conscience that the spending is necessary for national defense, war or other emergency. He is in a position to create the emergency! The records reveal he has always done so whether he was a religious, military, or political leader.

176

hamstrings the strong and results in a situation where no one can get what he needs, including the political rights necessary to protect himself against corruption and tyranny as well as governmental decreed poverty.

The merit rule is often in a position where it can have no mercy for the deficient. Moreover, under it government assumes no obligation to the effect that no one shall starve or fail to get what he needs, *an obligation which the Communists, the Stalinists and "Liberals" want to charge to government— the taxpayers. But, obviously so long as wars are waged, no government set-up can fulfill a promise of that character; least of all the economic structures based on the political philosophy that a government official is best qualified to decide what one must pay his employees,* what his profit shall be, how much property he may have, or where one shall work, how and when, or that the government must own and control the means of production—the hidden propositions in what is often called "Liberalism".[8] Such a course involves dictatorship, the reverse of democracy, and is bound to stimulate war, and war breeds abject poverty—not economic security. And what could do more to stimulate a war spirit than a government spending taxpayers' money abroad to interfere with the political programs of another country?

The disputes between John Lewis and the government may be used to further illustrate aspects of the "merit" rule as it touches production and hardships. If the government is going to run the mines *effectively,* make them produce coal the quickest, the cheapest and the best way possible, it cannot accept the checks that Lewis, in order to keep his job, must impose to protect the inefficient, inadequate or unnecessary workers. If Lewis is going to run the mines effectively, he requires the same arbitrary power the government needs; that is, the right

[9] "It is not within the functions of government * * * to compel any person * * * to accept or retain the personal service of another, or to compel any person against his will, to perform personal service for another. * * * the right of the employee to quit * * * for whatever reason, is the same as the right of the employer * * * to dispense with the services of an employee. * * * In all such particulars the employer and the employee have equality of rights, and any legislation that disturbs that equality is an arbitrary interference with the liberty of contract which no government can legally justify in a free land. (Justice Harlan declaring unconstitutional Sec. 10 of the 1898 Erdman Act. 208 US 161, Adair v United States.)

It appears the judge was satisfied that any law which interfered with the right to "hire and fire" was adverse to public welfare and therefore unconstitutional. He brought in the constitutional aspect by camouflaging the word liberty in the Fifth Amendment. What he really subscribed to was Lord Coke's theory that any law that was detrimental to public welfare could not be treated as a valid law. It was the obligation of the opponents of the law to show its adverse influence upon public welfare.

[10] "The difference between them is that the conservative considers that the first duty of these institutions is to preserve the rights of property, while the liberal considers that the first duty of these institutions is to conserve the rights of human beings." Kingdon "An Uncommon Man" p 94.

One would gather from that statement that the conservative is mentally and morally depraved, inhuman. A paralyzing thought for there are a great many of them! The truth is, and everybody knows it, that there is no security anywhere outside of granting the individual an unqualified title to property. Brother Kingdon is playing with words. It's a profitable occupation.

to hire and fire and determine wages and hours according to the circumstances. That responsibility, however, would require altogether different rules than those he has to use to continue as a dominating leader.[9] Whoever takes the responsibility for doing the work, whether it be the government, the Union or a private owner, will have to be equally "brutal" in the execution thereof if it has to be done under an emergency or at high speed. *The government official, however, as he represents sovereign power, is in the best position to be "brutal" or arbitrary!* He can really get things done because he can mete out death for infraction of rules!

It is that terrorizing fact which causes charters and constitutions to spring up in an effort to curtail government power, particularly as it relates to control and ownership of property and the means of production. What other reason could there be for placing limitations upon government? The extensive governmental authority advocated by the "liberals" or social democrats, in spite of that simple truth, suggest that they are blinded by personal ambition and ready to use fiction, or anything else, to accomplish what they claim to believe is public welfare,[10] but in reality is their welfare, their advantage or security.

The three-headed way of conducting business—a government official, a labor leader and an employer (the employer, the one who has to pay, being almost a silent partner) eventually leads to making the basis of compensation "need" instead of merit. The "need" proposition developed from an assumption that human beings enjoyed work, would do the menial labor voluntarily, would be satisfied if they all had the same amount —let it be enough. But the truth is that human beings derive their major pleasure from having more than someone else in wages, power, property, fame or glory. The excess represents their security, especially from doing menial labor, or being in subjection to the arbitrary will of others. However, any other spirit or attitude would result in stagnation. But that spirit must die, especially so far as production is concerned, when government, sovereign power, takes charge of wages, hours of work, etc., to the extent now generally recommended by the "liberals." That brings the discussion back to the political philosophy of constitutional government—that government as sovereign power cannot be made financially responsible for its conduct ("cannot do wrong") *and, therefore, must be restricted in its functions to fields where financial responsibility for conduct is not the issue.* With just those elementary principles in mind, it should be obvious that the "social" democracies do not lead to economic security or political freedom, liberty, prosperity or happiness. It will clarify the issue if it is kept in mind that it is the obligation or duty of industrialists to produce as cheaply and quickly as possible and that the burden of that objective falls upon the worker, and that it is the duty and objective of labor to protect itself against long hours and poor pay. These two interests clash and are often at variance with public welfare—what is best for all. It is the function of government to stand between those two clashing interests to see to it that production (public welfare) is not interfered with improperly.[10a]

Forced Changes in Political Rights

In the Federal Government political rights generally do not extend beyond voting for representatives in national affairs, and being elected or appointed to office. However, cities, counties

---

[10a] If legislation protecting strikes is creating a situation adverse to public welfare, then such legislation is probably unconstitutional, or at least unjust, and therefore not entitled to enforcement. The Taft-Hartley Act seems to recognize that principle, but fails to be specific in regard thereto.

and states provide many local political rights. To preserve these, the Federal Courts, Congress and the Executive had their power limited to certain fields. The full faith and credit provisions, the requirement that the geographical territory of a state should not be changed without its consent, the limitations on the Federal Courts, on Congress, and the guaranty to each state of a republican form of government, show the attention given to local political rights.[11]

The Forefathers were keenly alive to the necessity of having local matters taken care of by local authority, a principle which everybody subscribes to. The difficulty arises in the application thereof. Changes forced by commercial developments make it difficult to determine when a local matter has become an issue of national concern. For instance, improvements in transportation forced the administration of many laws to be transferred from local to national, and even to international jurisdiction. Federal legislation, therefore, developed in many fields, in spite of efforts to keep control in the States. This legislation compelled new political arrangements with respect to jurisdiction of courts, legislators and executives. Transportation improvements have forced so many changes in jurisdiction that the Supreme Court decisions relating to commerce look like high-water marks of confusion and contradiction, even to the members of the bench, the legislators, and presidents.[12]

From that situation sprang the strange, if not fantastic, doctrine about sit-down strikes which the Supreme Court could partly adjust because of the switch in public sentiment after the Detroit automobile "war" which perplexed Governor Mur-

[11] The Supreme Court has often backed away from its responsibility in determining form of government. (See 223 US 118. Pacific States Tel. Co. v Ore.)

[12] Gibbons v Ogden, 9 Wheaton 1, and the controversies which developed with respect to slaves, drugs, intoxicating liquors, white-slave traffic, child labor, labor unions and corporations.

[13] Compare this with the humble approach of Washington, Jefferson and Lincoln.

Right here it is pertinent to state that Patrick Henry opposed ratification of the proposed Constitution because the form of government it represented would, in his judgment, usurp local authority to such an extent that it would adversely affect public welfare (the humanitarian approach). He foresaw dictatorship, that is, centralization of governmental authority as prevailed in Great Britain; authority too far away from base to furnish good administration. It is not unfair to say that if Henry were here today he would shout out: What I prophesied (dictatorship) is being fulfilled in your generation. However, the dictatorship aspect arises not because of power vested by the Constitution in the Federal Government, but because of a wilful disregard for its mandates.

It is contended, of course, that the changes were forced by circumstances arising from industrialism and threats of war. But the drying up of frontiers, the far-reaching effects of invention, over-crowding of population and threats of war, were not novel features. The Constitution was made in the presence of such situations. It was made by persons who had been driven from England. They did not make it for a rural people. They believed that they were creating a form of government which would function under the conditions from which they had fled.

phy. But the controversy, of course, left unanswered the question of how far government can assume responsibility to its citizens for food, clothes and jobs without destroying local administration and causing government to collapse because of political corruption.

Perhaps unemployment and governmental debt increased because the leaders were sure they could cure all evils by giving government officials more power. The confident and triumphant attitudes of "I can fix anything" [13] which prevailed during the Roosevelt administration, and still manifests itself in the "liberals" may be a necessary practice of psychology to give assurance that everything will be all right. If these attitudes are not born in the high tension of conceit, or the full measure of ignorance, or are not a part of planning for changing the form of government so that the political leaders could enjoy more power, they may represent an effort to stop a stampede for governmental favors.

But are these political philosophers concerned with the normal changes in local law, the changes in jurisidiction from state to federal because of developments in commerce? Their demands that government assume permanently direct responsibility in so many instances to the individual for his job, food and shelter, causes many persons to believe that they are hoping that the economic confusion which generally follows war will give them their great chance.

It is silly to assume that Wallace, and those backing him, did not know that the killing of the "little pigs" would result in the things the opponents complained about. The objective of the scarcity programs *was to obtain and establish political control of the food supply.* They expected that such control would eventually create abundance. They believed it had been

[14] Stakhanovism, as outlined in Manya Gordon's "Fifty Years of Labor in Russia", shows how the Russians were subjected to the most intense production strains and endurance tests.

"It was a great shock to us when in 1938, after I had moved to Moscow, the police made Vera and several other disfranchised minors move to Chelyabinsk on twenty-four hour notice." Scott "Behind the Urals" p 131.

[15] Governments have to use fiction. The enemy must be misled. One cannot tell a dangerous enemy facts, generally. But it is hard to understand how it helped the war to make the enemy believe there was a food shortage!

[15a] The ancient six-day week (the sabbath), the old syndicates and guilds, as well as the modern, tariffs, subsidies, cartels, patents, union norms of production, five-day weeks, minimum hours, restrictions on immigration, etc., represent "planned" economy, restrictions on enterprise; and all of them were introduced under declarations of making it freer.

Without challenging the necessity, many prices are maintained today by shipping material to distressed countries. It is done at the expense of the tax-payer, perhaps without his consent or knowledge, but with the enthusiastic consent of the private citizen or the corporation enjoying a profit.

[16] See foonote 35 in chapter on Private Industry.

[17] "In England or in the United States, if a member of the government disagrees with policy he can object, appeal, protest, resign. He can then take the matter to the voters, and theoretically, at least, has a chance of coming back after elections with a majority on his side, and putting through his ideas. This opposition function is recognized as an important feature of government. But in the Bolshevik Party there is no appeal after a decision has been reached. There is no protesting, no resigning. The only chance of the opposition, after they have been voted down, is conspiracy. This method of dealing with opposition sowed the seeds of purges." John Scott "Behind the Urals" p 189.

successful in Russia. As the United States had many advantages over Russia, they hoped for much better results in the United States, with a great deal less of agony.[14]

The policies of the OPA, and kindred bureaus, were based upon the same reasoning. Therefore, many of the shortages were deliberately made, and were often just plain fictions.[15] There is no other way by which government can keep up controls. Is it any wonder that "planning" never creates abundance?[15a] Have we a right in good judgment to expect any other result from human beings, even though they believe they are humanitarians?

Tendency in New-Type Democracies to Destroy Important Political Rights

As has often been pointed out, but apparently, futilely, the government control recommended by the "liberals" are bound to result in disaster because they force too many features of daily life to become government policy, that is, matters beyond the scope of a court [16] or the judgment of the citizens. Under the controls they recommend such matters must be decided by a three-headed government official, judge, lawmaker and law-enforcer (three in one)—a bureaucrat.[17] That certainly is not democracy!

Under such circumstances, it may appear that government by the people really is brought about, that a whole new set of political rights have been developed to protect the individual, but in practice it eliminates political rights and the basic property rights upon which the average citizen has to depend for his security. It makes the government the general employer, an employer who can call upon the police, the Army or the Navy for help whenever he wants to, and who may disregard courts, legislators and laws with impunity since he represents

[18] "All become slaves with respect to the government, and wolves with respect to one another." Steinberg. Also see Colton "X-Y-Z of Communism" p 15.

[19] Lord Macaulay seemed to understand that fact.

[20] " * * * Under this doctrine (restricting a corporation to control of one railway system) the sum of property to be acquired by individuals or by corporations, the contracts which they make, would be within the regulating power of Congress. If it were judged by Congress that a farmer in sowing his crops should be limited to a certain production because over-production would give power to affect commerce, Congress could regulate that subject. The result of such a principle would be not only to destroy the State and Federal governments, but by the implication of authority from which the destruction would be brought about, there would be erected upon the ruins of both, a government endowed with arbitrary power to disregard the great guaranty of life, liberty and property and every other safeguard upon which organized society depends." From dissenting opinion of Chief Justice White in 193 US 197, 1904.

The judge did not realize he was prophesying.

sovereignty. Such procedure may be necessary, but it is tyranny, not democracy.[18]

The "liberals" say that this is all nonsense because they will see to it that government control will not go that far. But why trust them? They are human beings who will receive more power as government control develops.

It should not be hard to understand that when government has reduced its citizens to economic dependence, the political rights with respect to voting and the theory of short term of office, independent courts, etc., are also reduced to outright shams, and may, with a few touches, become the Frankenstein which will destroy the benefactor as well as the beneficiary.[19]

The repercussions in Europe should make it clear that government control as recommended by the "liberals" will force into discard the local political rights which are enjoyed under state, city and county subdivisions, and particularly that aspect of the constitutional trinity which involves independent courts.

As the principle of independent judges is one of the most important democratic aspects of government for protection of political rights, their forced subordinate position under social democracies will be discussed in the next few paragraphs, and more particularly in the next chapter.

The judges during the Roosevelt administration knew that much of the Newdeal social legislation was out of harmony with the Constitution.[20] But the public-sentiment pressure for temporary governmental benefits was so great that they may have believed that resistance would be more harmful than acquiescence. The courts, therefore, were in a most difficult position and were certainly pushed a long way from their true relationship to citizens and government. They were obliged to concur in administration policies and did so on some plausible basis which allowed them to escape, to some extent, from

[21] The general excuses are that the matter is a policy matter, a political question, or that the courts are not concerned with public welfare, only with the technical or legal aspect of the case.

[22] "The criterion of constitutionality is not whether we believe the law to be for the public good." Adkins v. Children's Hospital, 261 US 525.

"I felt that measures otherwise unconstitutional might become lawful (according to the Constitution) by becoming indispensable to the preservation of the nation." Lincoln.

A subtle way of saying that either his opponents had misconstrued the Constitution, or else thought that the Constitution was more important than the nation. The Newdealers took the same position, and apparently, their opponents were unable to make satisfactory rebuttal.

[23] See 301 US 1, Big Steel case. Here the attorneys tried to argue that the commerce clause required declaring NLRA unconstitutional. The evidence presented allowed the judges to side-step the real issue—interference with business to such an extent that it had an adverse affect on public welfare.

the conviction and condemnation of their conscience that they had disregarded their oaths to defend the Constitution—had properly protected public welfare.[21]

But under such circumstances almost everything is administrative policy and, therefore, under the control of bureaus and protected by laws which are declared to be righteous and constitutional. What else can the courts do but follow? Any other course would find them bickering with their creator, or biting the hand that feeds them.

This awkward position of the courts upset lawyers and statesmen so much that they "kindly" *overlooked the elementary proposition that if a law promotes public welfare there is a presumption that it is constitutional; and that if it is contrary to public welfare, there is a presumption that it is unconstitutional.*

The courts were brought into line by accusing them of making the Constitution more important than public welfare,[22] a ridiculous and embarrassing situation for the judges. The lawyers who defend free enterprise in the new-deal days, instead of showing that these laws would be detrimental to public welfare (after all, the only issue, but a very difficult one) spent their breath on the commerce clause.[23] No doubt, political entanglements, in many cases, prompted such action.

Self-interest obliged the legislators to feel and claim that these laws were remedies. But their hasty passage was not so great a reflection upon statesmen as were the reflections on the lawyers for the hasty arguments against them, after these laws had been in force and had furnished positive or conclusive evidence that they worked against public welfare—were indeed, self-confessed unconstitutional laws. Surely, with revolution threatened as a consequence if the laws were declared

[24] "An act contrary to the first great principles cannot be considered as rightful exercise of legislative authority." Calder v Bull, 3 Dal. 386.

"In the last analysis it is for us to determine what is arbitrary or oppressive upon consideration of the natural and inherent principles of practical justice which lie at the base of our traditional jurisprudence and inspirit our Constitution. A legislative declaration of reasonableness is not conclusive; no more so is popular approval—otherwise constitutional inhibitions would be futile. Dissenting opinion of Justice McReynolds in the Employers Liability Law. 250 US 400.

"This Court has the power to prevent experiment. We may strike down the statute on the ground that, in our opinion, the measure is arbitrary, capricious or unreasonable." Dissenting opinion of Justice Brandeis in the New State Ice Co. 285 US 262.

"It is clear that there is no closed class or category of business affected with public interest, and the functions of courts in the application of the Fifth or Fourteenth Amendments is to determine in each case whether circumstances vindicate the challenged regulation as a reasonable extension of governmental authority or condemn it as arbitrary or discriminating." Justice Roberts in Nebbia v New York, 291 US 502.

"The courts are generally the last making the decision. It results to them, by refusing or not refusing, to execute a law, to stamp it with its final character." Madison.

It is highly improbable that the forefathers intended to cut away the ancient right of courts to refuse to execute or recognize laws which clearly violated, destroyed or ignored the natural rights of man. It must always be one of the primary functions of courts to protest such procedure in the name of the individual. The Constitution is a chart to guide legislators so that such laws will not be passed, and a protection to judges opposing such laws in the event they are enacted. Lord Coke was without that protection and Parliament without that guide.

unconstitutional, the cases were entitled to argument on other grounds then the ambiguous commerce clause.

That the regulation by government (which means political regulation) of prices of commodities, wages, hours, labor, control of crops and distribution of benefits as practiced by the "liberals" was not in the minds of the Forefathers when they wrote the commerce clause should be obvious. To maintain that these things come within the scope of that clause implies that every aspect of daily life is embraced within it and makes that clause more important than the Constitution itself. It has been worked to death in connection with matters that are clearly governmental policy. The same is true of the so-called liberty, contract and due process clauses.

Moreover, one can hardly expect a judge who must be an expert in judicial problems to be an expert also in determining whether a certain law will protect public welfare from a purely economic standpoint. Laws which require judges to become economic experts are probably unconstitutional because they force judges out of their intended field of authority. The enactment of such laws is a reflection upon legislators and presidents, and if they are harmful or detrimental to public welfare, *then Lord Coke, Associate Justices Chase, McReynolds, Brandeis and Roberts were right when they said courts should nullify them.*[24]

Under constitutional government, laws relating to policy, of course, may come before the court to be declared unconstitutional on the ground that they impair, upset, interfere with or destroy the proper relationship to each other of the courts, states, legislators, voters and the executive, as pointed out by Chief Justice Marshall in the Marbury case. And, if they do that, who should honor them or fail to resist them? And if they do not, *but they are nevertheless obnoxious, then they*

[25] The power to tax is the power to destroy,—unlimited power. It must be left to Congress to determine how heavy taxes shall be. But if they are unreasonable, capricious or arbitrary, clearly against public policy, it appears the courts may be called upon to declare them void, if not upon technical constitutional grounds, then on the ground that it is the spirit of the Constitution to protect public welfare, or else under the unwritten constitution that laws which conflict with justice are not laws.

So far as unwritten constitutions are concerned, every nation has one—fundamental laws and principles which are sacred but too broad and numerous to specify. For instance, the principle that a law must be just, must not contravene public welfare, must not destroy inherent rights, is a fundamental principle, not necessary to mention in constitutions, but which must be recognized by the judges because of their relationship to the individual.

Constitutions certainly are not made to cut off the right of a citizen to appeal to the courts on the ground that he cannot comply with the law, or that it is capricious, arbitrary and unreasonable. How else can it be proved that a law violates public welfare—the law of God?

[26] "Under such conditions treachery, espionage and accusation cannot but abound. No one dare speak against the dictatorship, but all loathe it." Nittl. "Bolshevism, Fascism and Democracy" p 91.

must be tested on the ground of public welfare, outside of the written Constitution, and repealed through the good sense of the legislators or nullified by court interpretation under the unwritten constitution because of the resistance to them by the citizens in the courts, or otherwise.[25]

Destruction or Impairment of Free Speech

Free speech, of course, is the main political right which every citizen in office as well as out of office should protect. And by free speech one must mean that the citizen maintain a relationship toward his government which will in nowise blind his eyes to its sins and faults—*and that is impossible where there are too many in the position of governmental beneficiaries* as government clerks, mortgagors, creditors, debtors, contractors, pensioners, etc.

A hundred thousand government clerks and an equal number of outright beneficiaries in a population of one hundred million might not adversely affect free speech (criticism of government), but when one-fifth of the population is directly associated with the government through jobs, pensions, relief, contracts, loans and obligations, *the whole political structure of the government is changed,* changed to such an extent that constitutional government as contemplated by the Forefathers must be abandoned. Under such circumstances, there will be no one who will dare to criticize government, or if he has good judgment care to do so, or will be strong enough to be effective if he does.[26] The position is trying, for should he complain he would probably be attacking friends, cutting away their benefits, or obligating himself to support them. The only criticism under such circumstances that is tolerated is that the government is not giving enough. That is the reason why benevolent dictatorships, or what are now called democracies, force or push a country into bankruptcy and permanent destitution, poverty and distress, as well as into wars to cover up mistakes. The main check—free speech, criticism of corruption in government, is dead.

Voters and politicians are human beings with the same objective, namely, accumulate as much as possible in order to add to their security, and consequently if the door is ajar they will probably founder themselves; not because they are vicious, but because if there is an opportunity to gain benefits their need or ambition will lead their judgment astray, and their utilization of the ballot, a phase of free speech, will result in their destruction.

The presumption that human beings (no matter how honest they are) will over-reach is the foundation for the contracts, laws and penalties found in civilization, and the restriction on ballots expressed in constitutions and general legislation.

There is plenty of misery for people living under government built on the principle of private property, free enterprise, capitalism, open competition, etc., *but such a form of government is the only form under which free speech from a political standpoint can exist.* And under that, generally, about one-third of the people are poorly provided for, and of such one-third, many absolutely destitute. But the types of government which the world, including the United States, is embracing today in the name of humanitarianism and liberalism, *no matter how kind and intelligent the leaders may be,* eventually will have about three-fourths of the citizens not only poorly provided for but permanently destitute, for the simple reason, and it cannot be repeated too often, that when government becomes a benefactor to too many people, free speech in the real and proper sense of the word dies and corruption and privilege for the few thrive. *The human mind is not astute enough to criticize properly the power which has direct control over its existence.* That is just as true in government as it is the family circle, the workshop, the church, between lover and sweetheart, or between employer and employee.

All government officials and especially the judges are presumed to recognize the disposition of citizens, particularly those who are beneficiaries, not to criticize the government. That is why free speech is so strongly fortified in the Constitution and why laws and courts are so liberal in allowing citizens to criticize government. Every government is prone to have too many beneficiaries; generally, so many that criticism obviously fair and constructive is very dangerous to indulge in and usually futile; often absolutely futile, until a hurricane of economic distress breaks over the land. But that situation is intensified to the maximum when the citizen, in general, looks to the government for his food, shelter, profit, or luxuries.

Free speech is never denied the citizen by a law openly stating that objective. It is usually, but of course, unwittingly, surrendered by the citizen in order to obtain benefits earned or unearned, and then lost because the citizen is paralyzed with fear because he has become dependent upon government for his existence in the form of pensions, food, clothes, homes, employment, and outright relief. The business man is in the same relationship for he has to rely on government for the material to conduct his business.

Congress, under the theory that promotion of industry helps everybody (which of course is true), started with governmental benefits to industry. That laid the foundation for benefits in other places and subsequently forced the government to give benefits, often unearned ones, to all—railroads, schools, manufacturers, labor unions, farmers, youths, the aged, the employed, the unemployed, the sick, the healthy, rich and poor.

This has developed to such an extent that no person who has any concern for his future, cares to analyze the benefits or criticize the benficiaries.[27] The beneficiaries are so well entrenched that criticism is futile *even on the part of Congressmen. It is not an exaggeration to say that the law-making body has lost much of its significance,* and the citizens accordingly, much of their political protection.

The 77th Congress was not made up of uniquely spineless men. The form of government had been changed so completely that they had no adequate chance to perform their constitutional functions.[28] They were a group of average legislators who allowed themselves to become hog-tied in a mistaken effort to aid humanity. They forgot that the Forefathers made the Constitution in the name of humanity under circumstances which compelled them to go in the right direction. Therefore, it was more than probable that procedure contrary to the Constitution would not work out to the benefit of public welfare. It was not entirely because the Executive Department had become too strong; *the ballot was out of bounds and was driving the legislative branch as well as the executive branch into paths that lead to destruction.*

As the ballot is still out of bounds, the boasts of independence in Congress will come to naught. The present swing towards independence came because of the changes forced into our economic structure by wartime conditions. When the economic collapse that always follows war overtakes the country, the same results will develop.

[27] The only safe and profitable (profit) frontier today is praising government. The most dangerous and fruitless, calling attention to its deficiencies. Under such circumstances free speech in the true sense of the word is dead.

[28] "As a general rule all reaction begins with discrediting Parliaments." Nitti "Bolshevism, Fascism and Democracy" p 168.

The reason why parliaments are the starting point is obvious.

However, this time there will be no surplus credit on which to conduct a PWA, etc. Instead of credit there will be an enormous debt. The spend and spend fever therefore will be greater: so great that many leaders will feel that the only way out will be to give government complete charge of food, clothes, and working conditions—a situation that prevailed in prewar Italy and Germany, and now prevails in Russia.

The Primary Protection For Political Rights

The primary protection for political rights is not found in the First Amendment. It is found in that part of the Constitution which proposes to keep in their proper sphere, judges, legislators, the executive, and the voters. Especially the voters, for the franchise, when dealing with government dole, is beyond doubt the most treacherous foe to good government.

So long as these branches of government are properly harnessed, the government cannot become a charitable institution or a manager of business—two functions which generally should not be undertaken by political authority, for if it does so to any substantial extent, the result is tyranny—the destruction of the political rights which are necessary to protect public welfare.

The fact that such has always been the result makes one doubt, or at least gives one ground for doubting the sincerity of the "liberals" who are insisting that government perform the functions referred to; else one must challenge their information or their judgment.

THREATS TO
INDEPENDENT COURTS

Key Propositions

If courts, so far as protecting the rights of individuals are concerned, become futile when contending with government, what must be the futility of administrative agencies whose very existence depends upon keeping the good will of their creator? It was the futility of such agencies that brought about the fight for independent judges.

In the very nature of things, government cannot be sued or be made financially responsible in the same manner as individuals. Generally, therefore, it should not be a party to litigation with citizens about property, food, jobs and shelter.

Judges, as a rule, do not interfere with administration policies. That would be the government fighting itself. However, under the "New Orders" everything becomes administrative policies. Consequently, under these orders independent judges, in the constitutional sense of the word, cannot be used. Their place must be taken by Boards and Commissions. Under such circumstances, trifles become life and death governmental policies.

Under free enterprise, judges are often the tools of powerful industrialists. But no matter in what proportion that is true, the evil is aggravated when they become the puppets of political power, which they do, no matter how honest they are, under the "New Orders."

"There is no other way under Heaven by which" we can be
saved from governmental corrosion.

THREATS TO INDEPENDENT COURTS

CHAPTER V

Civil Rights and the Courts

CIVIL RIGHTS find their major protection in courts, independent ones. The problem of keeping courts free from too
much pressure from the industrialist, the politician, or any
source, so that rich and poor, great and small, will always
receive a fair measure of justice, is still a long way from being
solved.

Destruction of Independent Courts

It has always been recognized that court independence contemplates that litigation involving the ordinary or civil affairs
of life *should be between the citizens,* and not between the
citizen and his government, at least not to the extent prevailing
today. The Forefathers no doubt believed that the Constitution would keep general litigation in its ordained field—between citizen and citizen, and thus maintain independent courts.
But with the citizen so dependent as he is today upon government for food, clothes, pensions, jobs, housing, education and
regulations of his work hours and wages, court independence
in the constitutional or democratic sense of that word has been
substantially impaired. Boards and other administrative agen-

[1] There is a great deal of talk about free enterprise, which, if it materialized, would require the usual functions of courts. The agitation about full employment is evidence that most economists do not believe that business can escape the regimenting governmental agencies which the New Deal originally planned.

Mark Sullivan, referring to the numerous phrases indicating affection for "free enterprise," quotes: "when * * * proclaims that never, never, cross-my-heart and so-help-me, shall there be government ownership, the lady doth protest too much."

J. W. Snyder, then Director of Reconversion, in supporting the full employment bill, indicated he realized there could be no employment unless there was a market. Finding a market is quite a problem, for if 60 million people go to work six days a week utilizing modern machinery, they would produce 50 percent more than any present market could consume! Wallace has not discussed that aspect of *full* employment.

cies are rapidly supplanting the courts.[1] But this is the important point: the supplanting, under such circumstances, is an unavoidable result because the relationship between the citizen and the government is such that the use of independent courts would be impracticable. Boards or other agencies have to be utilized because they are in a position to conform with administration policies. Adjustments of the disputes involved require agencies whose prime purpose is to fulfill and promote the objectives of an administration—certainly not the function of a judge. It, of course, was not contemplated under the Constitution that the citizens would use government officials to decide what their wages, hours of work, rentals and food prices would be! It is clear, therefore, that as governments move toward "social democracies," courts in the true sense of the word, must be abandoned. (Such forms of government should not be designated as liberal or democratic.)

Proper Relation of Courts to Government

Free enterprise (an economic structure where the citizen does not look directly to government for his job, food, shelter, contracts, etc.) was introduced to avoid situations of the character referred to in the preceding paragraph. But even under free enterprise the relationship of the courts to the citizen and government is a delicate one. How to keep improper governmental influences away from judges will always be, to a great extent, an unsolved problem. A few words regarding the background of that matter follow:

In earlier days the king (government) owned most of the property. Freeholds of real estate under the feudal days were obtained by direct grant from the king, and were held subject to divestment upon his judgment or whim. That resulted in a situation which put the judges under so much governmental dominance that they could not give the citizen adequate protection. Out of that improper relationship, no doubt, came one of the influences magnifying the sacredness of private property— property over which the government had no judicial control— so that when litigation developed it was, generally, concerned with citizens suing each other, and did not involve the government as an interested party to the suit.[2]

The kings or executives in the name of "public welfare" (the same technique as used today) did what they could to prevent judge control from escaping out of their hands. But even a layman should be able to realize how futile is his quest for the four freedoms when his judges, notwithstanding their robes, have to rule against the government in the disputes with respect to daily life. However, as already suggested, he does not have real judges under "social democracies." Moreover, he is obliged, generally, to contend with inspectors, bureaucrats, commissions, authorities—commissars, agencies concerned only with the administrative policies.

Judges, of course, generally should not interfere with administration policies regarding the distribution of food, wages, jobs, etc. Therefore, when government by legislation or regulations undertakes distribution or rationing of food, fuel and clothes, or designating hours of work, prices and wages, quotas and contracts, the courts should not intervene. Such a situation, of course, reduces the fields in which the courts may function. If carried far enough, courts become mere gestures, or, worse, become instruments of oppression as in Russia.

In the cases which do come before the judges in the semi-social democracies, judge bias, or lack of independence, is *substantially increased because the political and economic in-*

[2] Chafee on page 501 of his book on free speech notes that juries were introduced to offset judge bias.

*terests of so many friends of the judges depend directly upon
the survival and the promotion of the theories of the administration.* That phase of the "New Orders" is sufficient alone
to defeat the constitutional idea of independent judges and to
dry up the fountain of economic security.

The judges, under such circumstances, are confronted with
the same difficulty that confronted the legislators who in the
early days of the Newdeal were described as being spineless.
There really had been no change in the calibre of the legislators. The change was in the form of government under which
they were functioning. *The Executive Branch had become so
strong and the relief and graft ballot pressure so great that if
they tried to resist they lost.* There was no chance to win!
Even battlefield technique does not require a soldier to undertake the impossible.

Judges cannot be independent when they are constantly
called upon to rule on legislation which if declared unconstitutional brings down upon them the wrath of the legislators and
the President, the two branches of government that can destroy them. Moreover, when they declare laws unconstitutional, they not only bite the hands that "bless" them, but
also repudiate the political prestige of their party. *Obviously
the economic structure which confronts them cuts away the
foundation upon which independence of the judiciary must be
built,* and, in addition, it puts them in a position which requires them to act as economic experts and social reformers.
They have to solve the problems relating to price control, hours
of work, business and management and relief distribution;
problems which vitally interest the political arm of the government.

That the judges are not prepared to do such work is evi-

[3] Holden v Hardy, 169 US 366, 1898, holding valid an eight-hour law; Lochner v New York, 198 US 45, 1905 holding invalid an eight-hour law; Oregon, 308 US 412, 1908, holding valid an eight-hour law; Bunting v Oregon, 243 US 246, 1917, sustaining hour limitations on the work-day; Settler v O'Hara, holding valid minimum wage legislation, and Adkins v Children's Hospital, 261 US 252, 1923, holding invalid a minimum wage law. Subsequently Congress approved a federal wage and hour law which the courts held valid.

Justice Roberts in Nebbia v New York said, "It is clear that there is no closed classed or category of Business affected with a public interest, and the functions of the courts in the application of the Fifth or Fourteenth Amendments (ancient principles) is to determine in each case whether circumstances vindicate the challenged regulation (law) as a reasonable extension of governmental authority or condemn it as arbitrary or discriminating." That is the same theory that Lord Coke subscribed to with respect to limitations on parliaments.

Mr. Ernst in Chap. 23, p 268 "The Ultimate Power" under a caption of "The Weasel Words of the Constitution" sets out "brilliantly" the inconsistency in Supreme Court rulings on social problems. However, Mr. Ernst is not free from inconsistencies. He breaks his heart over oppression of negroes, lack of child-labor laws, sweat-shops, etc. Still he takes it for granted that wage earners outside of labor unions should suffer; that 18 years is old enough for battlefield hardships, and that children made destitute by the liquor industry is not a matter of much concern, etc. One might say "weasel disposition."

[5] The Communists understand that principle. Their judges are all under a short term limitation.

[6] According to F. B. Myers and Ernst Sutherland Bates, many of the decisions of the corporation lawyers on the Supreme Court interfered with social progress. (See "Story of Supreme Court," p. 144, Bates.)

Myers wrote his book "History of the Supreme Court" to discredit that Court. Unintentionally, however, he proved the underlying presumption of the Constitution, namely, that no matter how honest or intelligent men are, they must be hedged by checks to keep them from over-reaching. What right in logic had Myers to expect more of judges or of himself? His misleading book was written with an eye to making money. It amounts to fraud of a more aggravated character than of the kind he complains about. "Story of Supreme Court" by Bates falls in the same category.

[7] The cases favorable to New Deal governmental philosophy, also by corporation lawyers, have been declared good. It appears that the lawyers with broad business experience on the courts have made better decisions than those with only academic experience.

[8] See impeachment proceedings against Justice Chase.

[9] See the McCardle case, 6 Wall. 1867.

[10] See the Yerger case, 8 Wall. 85: also the Belmont Bridge case, 13 Howard. 1852.

(See text on page 209 for footnotes 5, 6, 7, 8, 9, 10.)

denced by their conflicting decisions in that field.[3] Judges are supposed to concern themselves with interpretation of laws, and should not be burdened, as has often been stated, with governmental political and economic policies.

It is true, as harped by the "liberals", that under free enterprise (constitutional government) judges often become the tools of big corporations instead of being impartial law interpreting forces. But under "social democracies" the "big corporation" is the government. As it represents sovereignty, it is, unavoidably, a far more unrelenting and dominating force than a private citizen or corporation. It is that aspect of government which causes the phrase "independent courts" to mean, in general, courts free from the influence of partisan administration. The alleged objective of the "liberals" is to free courts from the evil influences of private corporations. But the remedy is worse than the disease, for it increases political influence, the more deadly of the two evils.

For general purposes, therefore, no matter how honest and upright the judges are, it has to be assumed that they will be biased in behalf of government.

The self-righteous, of course, resent that presumption. But it can be recognized in every phase of life. For instance, a judge, especially an honest one, for fear of bias, will not try a case if he has a personal interest in it. On the same ground, the testimony of an interested witness, no matter how noble, is substantially discounted; an agent's statements about his wares are given little credit; and love is pronounced blind. The Bible subscribes to it by teaching that all men are sinners. The college man calls it self-interest.

All any form of government can do is to try to eliminate situations which will give rise to bias by keeping court functions as much as possible within a field where the judges do

not have to antagonize governmental policies. It is impossible
to fully achieve that objective. But the "New Order" governments make achievement thereof more difficult! The politician's enthusiasm for the "New Order" arises because it forces
courts to become subservient. He is well aware that independent courts constitute the greatest hinderance to acquiring
concentrated political power.

Life tenure of office, therefore, is given to judges so that they
will not be intimidated by threats to their position when arbitrary policies of government officials must be opposed. That
Congress may become afflicted with an obsession to introduce
policies of a tyrannical nature may be deduced from the obser-
vations of Justice Roberts when he said that even Hamilton
never suggested such wide powers for the Federal Government
as the legislators were endeavoring to capture for it.[4] But the
vivid eloquence of the judge did not discourage the President
nor the legislators. Their master, the voters, forced them to
disregard the judge as well as the Constitution.

The Constitution, however, clarified the boundaries within
which judges could be called upon to resist the policies of the
other branches. It stated jurisdiction in specific language. The
British judges had no written constitution which said what
Parliament could not do. They may therefore plead absence
of authority to declare that parliament has transgressed its jurisdiction. But the Constitution is clear. The President and Congress, therefore, have no excuse for usurpation. Washington
condemned such a course in his farewell address. It is obvious,
therefore, that it is a very democratic principle in government
to have a tribunal in such a position to protect economic security.

But the democratic adjustment which allows courts to overrule other agencies is completely eliminated upon the consum-
mation of the "New Orders" of the "Liberals" because so many

    [4] Justice Roberts in 297 U.S. 1.

aspects of daily life involve life and death policies of an administration. Under such circumstances an administration cannot use independent courts, but is forced to use administrative agencies. Such courts as do remain cannot resist the government without creating economic confusion. Under such conditions, life tenure in office defeats its purpose—makes it a pernicious practice in government because the judges become a prime supporting influence for the perpetuation of undemocratic policies.[5]

Under free enterprise, as already suggested, the problem of keeping judges independent or free from undue pressure from influential private citizens or big corporations is also a question as difficult as any arising in the science of government.[6 and 7]

But the evils are aggravated in proportion that government assumes control over the daily affairs of life. The litigation then brings the courts into direct conflict with the power which can really laugh at competition, has control of the Army and Navy, can collect its funds with a maximum of force, shoot its opponents under color of law, enact legislation to perpetuate itself and to justify any other conduct, remove offending judges,[8] pass laws restricting their jurisdiction[9] or nullifying their decisions.[10]

Although it is elementary, it seems to be overlooked that the reason judges are not elected is because they are supposed to be experts and in no way related to political policies. Elections are concerned with persons who represent the policing fixing programs of the government, and must be, therefore, subjected to quick removal or approval. Federal judges, because of their non-political status were recognized as superior to the judges subjected to elections. As stated above the life-time appointments now result in perpetuation of party politics.

(Footnotes 5, 6, 7, 8, 9, 10 on page 206.)

Life Tenure for the Politician

Life tenure for a judge also involves the proposition that he is an expert in law and procedure. Constant changes, therefore, would seriously jeopardize or handicap civil rights. However, under these new forms of government, the politician, due to the demands upon him to regulate and control business, also becomes a government technician and obtains a life tenure claim on office, becomes an indispensable man such as Lenin, Stalin, Mussolini, Hitler—Roosevelt, Truman, or any person who becomes the chief administrator.

He, therefore, soon acquires a position where it is practically impossible to remove him, while the judges drift into a position where they are easily removed by the appointing arm.

It seems that the "Social Democracies" reverse the rules of constitutional government: the politician in office for life and the judge in office for a short term,[11] or at least in a very subordinate or subservient position.

This has caused an anomalous situation to arise: the people readily accept the doctrine of bias for judges, but, apparently, do not care to apply that democratic principle to the political "leader." He seems to enjoy the benefit of a presumption that his judgment will not be biased by self-interest, no matter what he may receive from the office he is working so hard to secure. Indeed, he is accorded by his followers the presumption of infallibility as in the theory of "The Divine Rights of Kings." That undemocratic attitude, of course, is the result of entrusting too much power to one man; it is born in the subconscious paralyzing fear of government.[12]

[11] See provisions for judges in the 1936 Russian Constitution.
[12] Every Executive will be confronted with the same problem and be unable to solve it as long as the Federal Government maintains a parental attitude.

The deifying attitude, a world-wide disease, develops because the leaders are unrestrained dispensers of favors. However, it invariably becomes a paralyzing fear because government is in a position to withhold the necessities of life. That kind of government is restoration of the Princes of Privilege. Although a different group, nevertheless they are princes, and princes not checked by independent courts. The tremendous advantage which accrues to the politicians under a dependent court system (justice by administrative agencies) is bound to prevent them from realizing when they are over-reaching.[13] They are human beings! Every constitutional check upon the elected branches carries such an implication—not a reflection, just plain horse sense.

But, no matter what a statesman has in mind, *when he gives government officials control over daily life to the extent now generally recommended, he introduces a system of government in which law-making, law-interpreting and law-enforcement are vested too much in one body, particularly in one person, who is continued in office indefinitely because of his relationship to the economic structure.* His policies are so completely grafted onto every aspect of the commercial system that it is neither safe nor practical to remove him.[14] (The One-Term-for-President group overlook that controlling fact.)

Such arrangements must be undemocratic, in spite of what the "social democrats" say. They certainly violate the spirit

[13] No one was surer he was within his rights than President Roosevelt when he asked for his famous court reorganization plan.

Like their predecessors and contemporaries, Mussolini and Hitler, after they got into power, had no respect for courts or legislative assemblies, if their actions have any significance. The same is true of Stalin's regime.

The belittling of judges and legislators in the United States smacks of the same procedure.

[14] Willkie in his remarks about the "indispensable man" overlooked that important but controlling factor.

of the Constitution, and according to its makers, will lead to permanent distress for three-fourths of the citizens instead of one-third.[15] Nevertheless, the trend toward one-man power is world-wide, with the United States not far behind.[16] And all of this under the banner of democracy, liberalism and humanitarianism! It can only stimulate war, and war with its aftermath of ignorance, hate and poverty, will force military control, and, besides, give the morons and criminals the rewards earned by the honest and independent workers.

The Hand-Writing on the Wall

There is little enough protection for civil rights under free enterprise, but it never results in a situation where the matters of daily life, including bread and milk, *as well as trifles, become life and death governmental policies.* For instance, the clothes presser was prosecuted for charging less than what the government directed, regardless of the hardship it worked upon those who could not meet the higher price; the farmer was confronted with a prison threat if he raised more hogs, cattle, cotton, corn, or potatoes than his contract called for, no matter how many were straving; the vendor was prosecuted because he sold his chickens too cheap. Apparently we were not far from the imposition of a jail sentence upon those who worked longer hours than the law specified or did other work than that assigned to them.[17] At first the courts balked, but they eventually became submissive, even enthusiastic.

[15] "We, the people of the United States, in order to * * * promote the general welfare, * * * do ordain and establish this Constitution." If the Forefathers were living today, they would say "Security" instead of "public welfare."

[16] The termination of the war will make it appear that the trend has turned. However, Stalin's form of government swept over Europe, and has engulfed Asia, and will frighten the United States into following his form of government, may even compel that course.

[17] See footnote 18 of chap. 11.

War conditions completely reversed this trend. Under the OPA, a jail sentence confronted those who charged too much or did not do enough. But the OPA is NRA in disguise, in reverse. When the stimulants of war or its reactions cease, the first program will have to be reintroduced because of "overproduction," unless more effective means can be discovered to keep up the "shortages." War powers for government in times of peace to banish poverty, cradle to the grave security, and full (half) employment [18] programs will be very helpful in this matter.

But the all-seeing eye of the government will always be watching the subject to keep him from becoming too independent. This is an unavoidable result under OPA or Blue Eagle governments, no matter how much they are made to look like indulgent protectors. These blue-eagle systems of government have to be adopted to make the red-eagle system successful. The men who introduced them were experts and knew what they were doing. Anything short of the principles involved in an NRA, or an OPA, would defeat their objective, and make the whole proposition futile. The adverse court decisions disclosed to them that they had "jumped the gun," and taught them to introduce their programs of "liberalism" more gradually. They, apparently, were too big to be assimilated as rapidly as they were offered. The citizen had been trained too long not to depend upon the taxpayer for a living. But the legislation increasing governmental authority (in spite of all the stir about free enterprise) over every phase of daily

[18] It is probable that full-employment means a four-day week for the nominal-salaried groups, no matter how much they need six days to meet their needs. The bill puts the emphasis upon wages instead of upon production. Production, of course, raises the question of markets, and markets raise the question of world relationships. Are we to assume that Mr. Wallace is an isolationist when it comes to a question of wages, that he believes that the United States can take an independent course in that field?

life continues, and is bound to drown the Constitution and its courts in the overwhelming floods of government dole. One must be blind to the meaning of political and civil rights if he does not see the hand-writing on the wall for constitutional government as contemplated by the Forefathers,[19] and deaf if he does not hear a new eagle's piercing cry and the swish of its wings. The full-employment promises, the food-destroying subsidies, and the cradle-to-the-grave assurances suggest that the on-coming form of government is one which will put men and women in jail if they do not perform herculean tasks in the field of labor. Stakhanovism and the concentration camps in Russia are good examples.[20]

Whether the new eagle brings liberty or the reverse thereof will depend upon whether the subject is magician enough to make himself appear to be an eaglet. There will be no independent courts of the constitutional type to which he can appeal should he fail to qualify as such.

But it is necessary to say that the opponents of the new ideas about government have not been astute to show why they objected. Little worthwhile data has been presented to establish that the new policies interfered with public welfare. The opposition satisfied itself by shouting "unconstitutional," and did not even take the time to show why, beyond quoting the commerce clause or the Bill of Rights. In the absence of in-

[19] In fact, leading New Deal advocates openly recommend abandonment of constitutional government as conceived by the forefathers.

Wallace's "Sixty Million Jobs" is a cautious and indirect approach. He is advancing with his back toward his goal. He praises free enterprise and constitutional government. No one challenges his sincerity, but he is enough of an economist to know that an approximate 300 billion-dollar debt presents some unique problems in keeping up a 200-billion-dollar income scale. It will be one for the books, if destitute Europe can buy from a United States manufacturing on a five-day week and a 15-dollars-a-day wage scale.

[20] See footnote 14 of chap. IV.

formation to the contrary, one may assume that the complaints were made by outsiders trying to get in.

Government Fighting Itself

Getting back more specifically to the proposition that these "new" ideas of control make all matters governmental policies, and therefore defeat court protection of civil rights, let it be repeated that judges, no matter how brave or how intelligent they are, as a general rule do not interfere with government policies.[21] That cannot be the usual function of a judge because it would result in the government being constantly at war with itself. However, under these new forms of government (totalitarian and communistic, not democratic), activities of every nature involve governmental policies. Courts, therefore, in the true sense of the word, cannot be utilized. There is no room for them. Recourse must be had to bureaus, committees, commissions and secretaries,—all agencies which readily lend themselves to executive control. That creates a dictatorship—either a good one or a bad one.

Under such circumstances, courts as contemplated by the Constitution would not be practical. If they were independent, they would be constantly ruling against the government, and this would result in chaos. The adverse New Deal rulings made that very obvious. Moreover, a judge, to be effective would have to know all the ins and outs of business, and besides would have to have access to the confidential political information of the administration to understand its policies. A wrong decision on a chicken case might upset the administration's whole program. Even before government projected itself to a great extent along the lines in question, political influence on many occasions had too much significance in the

[21] See Marbury v Madison, 1 Cranch 137.

courts to protect public welfare.[22] But, as things stand today, expediency generally, dictates that "justice" be delivered through the channels of a bureau.

Naturally, free speech (criticism of government), a fundamental check on government, is impaired because the courts are not functioning properly.

The Forefathers will be proved wrong if a continuation of the objectionable situation does not intensify poverty and distress, and create favoritism and privilege for the few, as well as lay the foundation for war-breeding upheavals; not because the leaders want it that way, but because the load of administration becomes too heavy, the number of grafters too great, and the demand for governmental benefits too persistent, too overwhelming.

The National Labor Relations Act and the Courts

The National Labor Relations Act is an example of how legislation affects the independence of the courts. How can courts do anything else but follow the administration's policy with respect to that law? If they do not follow it, economic confusion will result. The adverse New Deal decisions in the NRA and AAA cases made it clear that the courts had to be brought into subjection. The threat of civil war—"revolution" it was called—and the other abuses the administration applied to the courts, compelled them to fall in line. Administrative abuse of the courts is not unusual.[23] It is evidence that up to that time the courts had not surrendered.

But if the courts do follow the policy of that Act, can they

[22] The Dred Scott case, 19 Howard, 1856, is a good example of unfortunate consequences because the court considered itself prepared to settle a political as well as an economic question.

[23] See Beveridge's Life of Marshall, particularly that part dealing with the Marbury case, the Yazoo fraud cases, impeachment of Justice Chase, trial of Burr, Cherokee Nations case and the Jackson administration.

avoid, eventually, telling the citizens how, when and where they shall work and for whom they must work? Such procedure is the exact opposite of democracy and certainly not within the spirit of the Constitution. The record of the administration of this Act furnishes ample evidence that courts cannot remain independent under laws of that character. Under them even Congress is by-passed. The President decides the issues. It seems to have been overlooked that the Act is charged with reducing strikes, for it was obvious then as it is now, that no economic structure can withstand for long the pressure that the unrestricted right to strike technique applies to industry. The Taft-Hartley Act has modified the NLRA, but still leaves the President, a political influence, to determine in many instances, when the courts shall take jurisdiction, if at all.

But, beyond that fact, if it is the policy of an administration to coddle unions under either one of these acts, the courts as well as the Boards have to follow—the courts to avoid chaos, the Board members to keep in office. But when it becomes necessary to turn in the other direction, then comes the time when the Board, the courts not functioning, will be the hand with which government will press a "crown of thorns on Labor's brow", denying it the protection it thought it had under the Constitution.[24] Labor then will realize that it par-

[24] "If I were in a minority of one in this convention, I would want to cast my vote so that the men of labor shall not willingly enslave themselves to governmental authority in their industrial effort for freedom." Samuel Gompers.

"Labor must suffer as much from the control over its relationship to industry that exists in a Fascist State like Italy or Germany, or by autocratic dictatorship as in Russia, as does private industry. Labor and Capital have a common cause to protest autocratic usurpation of power over their destiny by governmental agency." William Green.

No one is out of sympathy with protection for labor. However, the NLRA apparently over-emphasizes the integrity of labor leaders. They are human beings who are not in a very good position to serve public welfare. The only way they can keep in control is to promise shorter hours and higher wages, no matter what the circumstances are. The wildcat strikes are conclusive evidence of that fact.

alyzed the Constitution when it impaired the principle of independent courts and turned so exclusively to administrative agencies (outright political bodies) for relief, protection and justice.

The Nature of Courts Under the "New Orders"

Of course, there will be courts of original jurisdiction and appeal under these "liberal" forms of government. But they will not be independent courts as contemplated by the Constitution. They will be supplied with judges who will assure the people that the economic and political theories of the administration are correct, as occurred when the Federalists were "riding high." However, under the "New Orders" that will be the only course the judges can take to avoid governmental chaos or starting a civil war because of interference with policies regarding work, food, clothes, occupation and profession.

Industrialists are often not in a position to appreciate independent courts; that is, judges, who, because they have no self-interest in the matter, can see that what is so ardently sought by the industrialist would have an adverse affect on public welfare, and therefore refuse to *go along*. Under such circumstances, like the politician, the industrialist, too, will work to circumvent or intimidate the judges. He will do it of course, and perhaps sincerely and honestly, under public welfare declarations or other disguise. However, as distinguished from the politician, the industrialist, generally, has in mind a program that will create jobs, business. His motive therefore as pointed out by Adam Smith [25] is generally not properly an issue. The politician's objective generally does not involve

[25] "The business man neither intends to promote the public welfare, nor knows how much he is promoting it. He intends only his own gain, and he is in this led by an invisible hand to promote the end which was no part of his intention." Adam Smith.

creating or stimulating business—often, unavoidably, just the opposite. His motive, therefore, is a proper subject of inquiry. The particularly vicious aspects of this matter at the present time are the two-headed individuals which have developed— industrialist and member of congress. There are several of them who control judge appointments and legislation. Oil and cotton are particularly well represented, although recent additions in that field.

The Basic Proposition

The basic proposition of the "liberals" is that the Constitution does not restrict Congress or the Executive in determining what is public welfare, at least not to the extent insisted upon by the objectors. Their position has merit, *for under certain circumstances parliaments or any other body, or any person, representing sovereignty must be absolutely unfettered.* War, which often creates need for immediate action, may compel the use of this unlimited power by a military authority even of nominal rank, or even by civilian because of his strategic position.[26] Locke failed to emphasize that important fact in his penetrating discussions regarding sovereign power. (See footnote 29.)

However, their proposed application of that authority is so broad that it forces a reversion to the doctrine that the King, the Executive, is always without limitation in determining what is best for all. Unwittingly, they make the Executive so strong that judges and legislators are not properly included in that prerogative and constitutions are not sacred. Moreover, their proposition compels government in times of peace to exercise wartime control over the affairs of daily life. Their glamorous phrases of "war" to end poverty, "war" to force a

[26] See footnote 35 of chap. 2.

better distribution of property, "war" to establish the four freedoms are camouflage to beguile or "condition" the citizen into accepting war-time powers in peace time. The dangerous and objectionable aspect of the matter is that wartime powers carry the right to shoot those who dare to resist, even though it be in an effort to get something to eat. That the government official *will* shoot is evidenced by the purges which occur, no matter how kindhearted the dictator may be.[26a] *There is no appeal to a court, because the issues are all declared to be matters of government policy directed toward public welfare.* The courts, therefore, cannot take jurisdiction or interfere. Moreover, just as in war, men and women must stand ready at all times to make the supreme sacrifice—take whatever the government official sees fit to offer and obey whatever order he decrees.[27] One cannot help but realize how effective war may

[26a] It should be remembered that before the Administration disagreed with them, it described the Emperor of Japan, Mussolini, Hitler and Stalin as very desirable and democratic persons.

[27] On page 3 of "Government in Business", Stuart Chase expresses eloquently the philosophy that if the government, in order to save the country, has to run things during wartime, it should have the same unrestricted power during peacetime. He says "If collective effort was an effective way to wage wars, why not to abolish poverty?"

Mordecia Ezckiel in "Jobs for All" bases his book upon the same premises. "It does not take a very high IQ to ask why we cannot keep prosperous making plough-shares if it has been proved we can keep prosperous making swords."

But a nation cannot keep prosperous making swords. After Napoleon's conquests, France and all the rest of Europe was destitute. Where is there more waste, more brutal and unfair hardships, more disregard for life, than in war-planned industry? It repeals short hours and high wages, disregards education, upsets all private industry, and if continued long enough it will force abandonment of all social advancement because of the property it destroys, the debt it creates, and the hate and malice it engenders. It is a program of destruction, which could hardly justify confidence if the presumption about large blocs of nations' being natural war instigators is true, and will inspire still less confidence if the psychiatrist is correct in his claim that environment is responsible for the war spirit.

be in changing forms of government and, consequently, how insecure a form of government is when leaders refer to some of its fundamental principles as horse-and-buggy stuff. And it is not unfair to say that for every *substantial* move to divest government of its wartime powers two moves are made to make it impossible to discontinue them.

These forms of government are bound to have enthusiastic advocates because they offer unlimited political power, permanent in character—office for life. Every power-loving individual (the majority) therefore is enthralled by them and helps to introduce them under a "trained" conviction that he is fighting for democracy. However, as he never defines his word "democracy," as it relates to courts, ballots and parliaments, he should be on notice that his sincerity is not as deep as he thinks it is. A shadow is also cast on his sincerity because he talks about independent courts and government control in the same breath, as well as because of the sacrifice he demands of his followers. No church or priest ever asked so much of followers as did Marx, Lenin, Trotsky, Mussolini, or Hitler; and never have the sacrifices been more futile. Nevertheless the "songs" about "planning" or social democracy, constitute the most effective music for the present-day Hamlin pipers.

False tunes are also heard under capitalism, but they cannot be used so effectively because the "piper" does not have control of the Army and Navy, the Treasury, the courts and parliament. That is why free enterprise (capitalism) which insists upon equal footing for the principal branches and divisions, insists upon local administration, upon the right to own private property, upon a properly restricted ballot, and proper ballot issues, is correctly called a democracy.

The theory of unlimited government, or economic freedom

[28] E. S. Bates in the "Story of the Supreme Court" leaves the implication that leading authorities support the position that the Supreme Court can rule on any laws enacted by Congress. However it cannot, generally, rule on law reducing its personnel, laws on what its appellate jurisdiction shall be, laws governing policies such as the size of the armed forces, when war shall be declared or peace proclaimed, or how high or low tariffs and taxes shall be, etc. And no law under any circumstances can come before it unless a citizen first challenges the law. In his discussion of the matter, Bates, appears to have confused the propositions arising in the Convention as to judges acting a quasi legislators with that of reviewing law which came before the court in the process of litigation. The latter proposition was not questioned in the Convention.

Equally misleading is the trend in Smith's book "The Growth and Decadence of Constitutional Government." On page 101 is found: " * * * Every effort was made to create the impression that the Supreme Court of the United States was designed to protect the people * * * was admirably fitted to serve as * * * interpreter of their will * * *. There is probably no other instance in the whole history of constitutional development where public opinion has been so misled as to the fundamental nature of a political arrangement. * * * But the real purpose was to centralize political authority largely in the Supreme Court * * * and through the power of final interpretation make the Constitution an adequate bulwark of conservatism."

No one is advocating judicial *supremacy* except for law interpretation, in which field courts are supreme in the same sense that legislators are supreme in enacting laws. The word "conservatism" is used to suggest something absolutely adverse to public welfare. But if the Court is a political body, it became such, to the shame of the appointing power. The forefathers evidently overestimated the calibre of Presidents and Senators!

[29] Locke defines "prerogative" as the power to act according to discretion for the public good without the prescription of the law and sometimes against it. This power, according to Locke, belongs to the executive, and arises because it is impossible to foresee and so by law to provide for all accidents and necessities that may concern the public, or make such laws as will do no harm if they were executed with inflexible rigor.

"The phrase (public welfare) necessarily embraces a vast variety of particulars which are susceptible neither of specification nor definition." Hamilton in 1791 Manufactures Report.

"It is not lightly to be assumed that matters requiring national action, a power which must belong to and somewhere reside is not to be found." Justice Holmes in Missouri v Holland.

through government control, will always have its followers because of its seeming effectiveness, especially in times of emergency. No one can say exactly where government power, control or ownership must rest to promote public welfare. But the Forefathers certainly intended that the Constitution, once and for all time, should settle the questions in that field with respect to form of government. They certainly were opposed to government which precluded the courts, neutral tribunals, from telling other branches that what they proposed to do was unconstitutional and therefore conclusively presumed to be contrary to public welfare, namely, what is best for all. And they were certainly opposed to an economic structure that supplanted judges by bureaus, or put judges in a position where their decisions brought them into constant conflict with an administration's economic theories.[28] The judges seem to have lost sight of that fact.

The neutral tribunal idea contemplates a check on elected officials who represent majorities. Majorities have no respect for minorities when interests clash. Elected officials, therefore, in general do not bother with minorities. Minorities therefore seek most of their relief in the courts.

It is true, of course, that the Constitution did not attempt to set down all the rules for public welfare. Untouched by it is that field of law and legislation dealing with public welfare but not changing the form of government.[29]

If not in fact, at least in spirit, every country has an unwritten constitution, the fundamental principle of which is that any law which adversely affects public welfare is not law. The Supreme Court subscribes to that doctrine when it declares a law unconstitutional because it is capricious, arbitrary or unreasonable.[30] It surely was not the intention of the Forefathers to cut the courts off from being a haven where citizens could go to complain about oppressive laws.

Of course, judges are not perfect. Personal relations and a hundred other things will warp their judgment. A judge cannot be more than a human being, but when to all the other pressure on him there is added pressure from the authority that pays his salary, creates his job and can impeach him, and whose policies may make or break his friends, he is indeed no longer in a position to be a judge. He can be at best no more than an administrative organ, a position in which he finds himself throughout the world *in spite of Constitutions, Bills of Rights, Petitions of Rights and Magna Cartas.*

An Administrative Agency is a Broken Reed

Even the most unobserving realize that many hardships, injustices and misfortunes befall human beings in their effort to build and maintain a civilization, that many of these hardships, including war, are unnecessary and could be removed. But if courts become futile when contending with government, what must be the futility of an administrative agency whose very existence depends upon keeping the good will of its creator? It was the futility of such agencies that intensified the fight for a Constitution that would preserve independent courts by keeping litigation between citizen and citizen and avoiding litigation with government.

[30] "It is clear that there is no closed class or category of business affected with a public interest, and the function of courts in the application of the Fifth or Fourteenth Amendment (due process) is to determine in each case whether circumstances vindicate the challenged regulation as a reasonable extention of government authority or condemn it as arbitrary or discriminating." Justice Roberts in Nebbia v New York.

Lord Coke had the same idea in mind when defying a parliament which was not bothered by a written constitution.

The citizen derives benefits from these agencies so long as there is an easy appeal to regular courts. But such courts are only mirages when government undertakes to direct his daily life to the extent now generally recommended.

He may point to his Constitution, but he will find that it has been by-passed. The numerous administrative agencies, the weakness in the halls of legislation, the lack of confidence in the courts, the bought elections, the compelling obligations of business men to the government, the tendency of the press to print, the radio to broadcast, and the screen to picture what it is believed the government wants the citizen to read, hear and see, should cause him to suspect that something is wrong with the machinery of representative government.

"LIBERALS"
AND MAJORITY RULE

KEY PROPOSITIONS

Majorities rule by having small minorities act for them.

The Constitution, and all the Charters before and following it, prove how difficult it is to keep governmental power from rushing to one place or branch, and upsetting the policies under which commerce can thrive enough to keep the citizens free from the necessity of governmental charity.

The opportunity for unlimited power greatly intensifies the hallucinations in ambitious minds that they must and can fix everything. A constitution is notice that such power is not available. It, therefore, reduces the bitter contests for power which demoralize government and business.

It is fair to say that Russia developed in spite of the Czars, Marx, Lenin and Trotsky; that the introduction of American ideas of commerce saved her—not her vaunted "humanitarians."

Business structures are upset by miscalculations of strong men, by war, by new inventions and by other uncontrollable economic and social factors. But if government, because of being tied in with business, is also upset from such causes, there can result nothing but starvation and distress for three-fourths (not one-third) of the population, because business and government will be in collapse at the same time.

Even some Congressmen do not know what they mean when they say: "consent of the governed."

"LIBERALS" AND MAJORITY RULE

Chapter VI

Representative Government—Majority Rule

SUBSCRIPTION to representative government, majority rule, is based upon the presumption that the majority demand what is best for all—public welfare—justice—as determined by the "voice of God." Hence the theory that majority rule is sacred and, therefore, must be complied with, cannot be disregarded, ignored, changed or discarded. However, as most of the leaders, no matter how vicious or fantastic their programs, claim that their form of government represents justice, the "voice of God"—has majority endorsement, the meanings of such terms are in great confusion, and forms of government subjected to constant disrupting and harmful changes. This matter, therefore, should be given considerable attention.

The Constitution was introduced to dispel the confusion and to avoid the disrupting influence. It represents the dramatic "I Have Spoken" regarding the principles of government which should not be frequently altered, and particularly not to accommodate fluctuating public sentiment, even though it represents majority opinion.

It will help to understand what follows to state here that it is the limitation on changing form of government by public sentiment (improperly called majority rule) [1] that is resented by the "liberals" and impels them to discard the Constitution and swing toward one-man government—government which concentrates a great deal more power in the Executive Branch than the Forefathers thought would be wise.

The Constitution was not as effective as it was hoped that it would be. Confusion has again developed to such an extent that it is easy to introduce, even by popular elections, changes which nullify the Constitution with respect to the proper jurisdiction of the three branches of government, the relationship of the Federal Government to the States, as well as the proper restrictions on the ballot and seizure of property. We have, therefore, political movements in the United States which claim to be democratic, majority rule, liberalism, representative government, but, which in fact are totalitarian, designated as "communism" by the misguided and misinformed.

The most treacherous aspect of the matter is that these movements are always carried forward under declarations that constitutional government is being maintained, defended and promoted. But the admittedly subordinate position of the courts, the helplessness or futility of legislative bodies (because of relief-ballot pressure), the number of people dependent upon government for dole and relief, for good jobs and poor jobs, and for big loans and little ones, as well as the multitude of committees, boards, directors and authorities, plus the growing practice of government to tell citizens how to run their

[1] "It is the American people who are in the driver's seat."

On p 210 of "The Republic", Beard also seems to subscribe to the doctrine that if public sentiment favors an issue, no matter whether it is understood or not, the government is obliged to agree and conform if it wants to be democratic.

Democracy apparently is dedicated to the proposition that public sentiment, informed or misinformed, shall decide all questions. Perhaps democratic government is not supposed to move along intelligent channels. If so, it was properly condemned by Hitler.

business, what their wages shall be, and how much of their food shall be sent abroad, should make one aware that constitutional representative government is being overthrown in the United States, and a form of one-man government, called social democracy or the welfare state, substituted therefor.

That our present form of government is not representative government as contemplated by the Forefathers, especially from the standpoint of elections, should be obvious to all. That this is so, is freely admitted by many of the proponents of the new social orders.[2] They are not disturbed about it because they claim that their form of government is better. Their argument is that if it is better, it must be assumed to have constitutional sanction, as the objective of the Constitution is to bring about the best kind of government possible. But the truth is that it represents the most vicious form of government because it lends itself so readily to tyranny, oppression and corruption. That is an unavoidable result for it removes the checks which the Constitution provides. They were successful in removing these checks by propaganda that the plight of the destitute is caused by the selfishness of those who direct the commercial empires; that civilization can be maintained without hardships, and that the destitute can work out their salvation by giving to a "humanitarian" or "liberal" control, with or without the ballot, of the daily affairs of life.

It is interesting to note that many of the arguments against adopting the Constitution involved the claim that it would lead to the kind of government now practiced with respect to having so many things directed from Washington.

One-Man Government And "The Voice of God"

The leader or life-time president (dictator) of a "social" democracy is well fortified in his contention that he repre-

[2] Beard and Chase are outstanding in that respect.

sents the "Voice of God"—majority rule or representative government. He is in a position, because of his long tenure of office, to know much better than a newly elected official what the people need and how to get it for them. Indeed, in case of war, or other extreme danger, the tax-payers often consent to one man, or a small group of men, taking complete control of the political, commercial, military, and religious policies of a nation; consent, often without realizing what they are doing, to have a leader go ahead without the usual procedure for voters, courts or legislators. As he rules by consent, at least implied consent, he may claim, notwithstanding his dictatorial powers, that he represents the "voice of God", and, therefore, is entitled to implicit obedience. It should be observed that, generally, it is impossible to prove that a ruler does not have the consent of the governed.

As centralized government (dictatorship in the sense of power being concentrated in one person, or a small group of persons) is necessary in times of war to protect commerce, it should not be discarded in time of peace, when it is often more difficult to protect commerce. (The word commerce, of course, should be read as meaning liberty, freedom, the spiritual, etc.) That is the position of the "Liberal", and it commits him to the proposition that conventional elections, judges and legislative bodies (the earmarks of representative government, democracy) are too slow, inefficient and corrupt, to be qualified to represent majority rule—consent of the governed—public welfare—what is best for all.[3] That is also the underlying philosophy of the Russian political structure, expressed in Stalin's position, that the matter of *peacetime production gives the government a better claim to demand the maximum sacrifices of the subjects than the destruction of war.*

[3] "In the first four years I have been their match; in the next four years I shall be their master."

Such a position, of course, is a repudiation of constitutional government. But, as already stated, constitutional sanction is claimed for it on the ground that it is the best way to promote public welfare. However, by that manner of reasoning any kind of government could be declared constitutional, majority rule, or in accordance with the consent of the governed. Hitler and Mussolini, past examples of one-man government, claimed to be doing what the majority wanted them to do. That they had the consent of the governed is evidenced by the strength of their resistance. Nevertheless, that kind of government is a dictatorship, no matter how often it is called democratic or liberalism.

It is futile to point out that the dictator obtained consent of the governed by taking advantage of them through their fear, ignorance or greed. If majorities are so readily deceived and misled, democracy, majority rule, is destructive folly. However, when a dictator goes down, his last breath is used to proclaim that his opponents were the ones who did the lying, cheating and defrauding and by such methods destroyed his "God-ordained" government.

But one thing is sure, no matter how much one hates to admit it, these forms of government, generally, do have majority consent—consent of the governed. But they cannot be called representative government if one means by that phrase government which requires frequent elections (by voters who are not governmental beneficiaries) of the officials who make and enforce the laws; courts and legislative bodies on an equal footing with the executive; ballots restricted to election of policy officials; substantial checks on public sentiment; difficult methods for amending the fundamental laws; government that allows the citizen to own substantial property including the means of production, and to work or quit, without reference to laws which practically regulate every phase of his life.

⁴ The UN bill of rights could not specify the amount of property a citizen should own, because the Russians are not allowed to own much property, especially the means of production. Mrs. Roosevelt therefore had to accept a very general statement about property rights. If Mrs. Roosevelt had asked the members of the AYC questions along the line of property ownership, she would have discovered that not very many of those questioned by her, had a very clear idea as to what they were talking about. Evidently many members of that Congress were communists at heart without realizing it. They certainly were enthusiasts for complete government control, perhaps, beyond what Stalin recommends. Mrs. Roosevelt's definition of a communist is, generally, restricted to one who is an agent of the Russian government, and consequently she is often misunderstood when discussing the subject.

Let us digress here to say that dictatorships are not always to be condemned. They are necessary where the subjects are illiterate or too dependent upon the ruler for their food and shelter. Unfortunately, as often pointed out, such terms as dictatorship, representative government, consent of the governed, majority rule, socialism, communism, nazism, have a different meaning on every tongue. The confusion would not be so great if the citizen, when determining form of government, used as a criterion the functions performed by the courts, the scope of the ballot, the independence of the legislators, and the amount of liberty (ownership) the citizens have with respect to property, especially the means of production.[4]

The Relation of Elections to Representative Government

The dictators or leaders, no matter how disastrous or tyrannical their policies were, never admitted they had failed to respond to majority will, to protect public welfare. Those who were subjected to their vicious policies, therefore, sought means by which they could be divested of power without resorting to civil war or waiting for the whims of the Grim Reaper. Elections were introduced as a repudiation of the dictatorship theory that one person can by instinct, hunches or through assembled information determine whether the majority want him to represent them as to what is best for all.

Elections, of course, imply recognition of the principle of short term of office for the policy-making officials—the legislators, and the chief executives. The principles of electing and restricting to short term of office the persons who represent the policy-fixing power of a government are important factors in representative government because they provide a way for determining whether the policy of a leader has majority consent. But a more important consideration is that they also make it *impracticable for government to undertake direct or extensive control of business because of the possible frequent change in personnel.* They therefore prevent dictatorship, and protect and

[5] The recent presidential messages might well include all the social programs recommended by the Communists, Nazists, Fascists, etc. The general impression seems to be that these programs can be consummated without the governmental tyranny that has developed in Europe.

Lord Keynes has a very simple program according to the Sept. 9, 1945, PM. "* * * The public saves money out of income. Industry borrows these savings and invests them, creating jobs, more income and consumer spending. Depressions come when industry does not invest all the savings accumulated by the public. In such a situation, the government must assume the role of the investor, must put the idle savings to work, creating the jobs, the income and the purchasing power not provided through private investments * * *."

But why not pass a law that business men "must" invest? That would save the taxpayer.

promote free enterprise, the rockbottom of representative or democratic government.

Elections do not give an elected official the right to disregard a nation's constitution, no matter how great the majority may be that elected him, or what he proposed. When he assumes that, he has moved to a very extreme position as a dictator.

In this confusion about what constitutes representative government, it should be noted that the Russians describe their form of government as the Dictatorship of the Proletariat, and at the same time, a Union of Republics, meaning by the latter phrase, one may suppose, representative government. They do not claim that their government is Communism. It is the step by which they hope to achieve that objective.

Drift Toward Gesture Elections

The disposition of the majority to call for immediate benefits, regardless of consequences, has forced the "liberal" to become apprehensive about elections. They, therefore, generally by subterfuge try to control them so that they have no opposition significance—become gestures as was the case in Italy and Germany, and is the case in Russia, unavoidably and necessarily so.

That the United States has drifted far toward gesture elections (the first stage of election elimination) may be deduced from the fact that the two elections prior to the 1941 World War[45] brought out more statements to that effect by responsible persons than ever before in the history of this country. The number of Congressmen who had to defend themselves against charges of using relief funds (relief funds eventually force elimination of elections) was a startling proportion, especially during the Willkie-Roosevelt campaign. The numerous statements and vociferous arguments trying to prove that the election was free, and the bills, notably the Hatch Bill, all go to prove there is ground for apprehension. It is not probable that a change in administration will or can reverse the trend.[5]

⁶ These forms of government are identical in alleged objectives—government responsible to the citizen for his food and clothes, jobs, wages, hours, etc. Communism is supposed to be the most comprehensive in that respect, and, therefore, the most democratic. But the "liberals" do not want to go that far, they say.

Because of the confusion created by promoters, agitators and demagogues, about 35 percent of the electorate unintentionally vote for the opposite of what they believe in, as stated on page 240. The underlying principle that voters must have a common knowledge, common interest and equal responsibility must be carefully guarded to avoid shifting a democratic or representative form of government into a dictatorship under the guise of "social" democracy. The equal responsibility requirement is utterly disregarded when voters determine how much the taxpayer should advance to support them.

Many ridiculous situations have developed because of the violation of the common or equal knowledge rule. Voters are called upon in referendums and other ways to decide questions that statesmen, economists and judges have been unable to solve! Democratic government contemplates that the elected experts shall decide such questions.

The enormous debt alone will preclude a swing in the opposite direction.

No one can deny that there is a heavy undertow of fear about the abuse of elections. That fear, no doubt, is a substantial basis for the swing, in the name of "Liberalism", toward Fascism, Nazism, Socialism and Sovietism in the United States, at least from the standpoint of "gesture elections." [6]

Because of the intense love of representative government which has been instilled into the people, the replacement movement of course has to be carried on in a subtle way, under cover, sub-rosa. That is how it was brought about in Russia, Italy, Germany, France and Spain. In all these countries the leaders, posing as liberals, denied they were changing the form of government and claimed that such changes as were being made would lead to social security from the cradle to the grave. That they were sincere no one need doubt; but that they were prejudiced by their own personal interests should not be doubted either. What can do more to twist the ambitious mind than a chance at unlimited power, or more power than any other person ever had? That must be particularly true in the fields of job distribution, granting business privileges or determining how much food shall be raised and shipped out of the country, especially if there is to be no real accounting.

The reason such procedure is possible is because citizens do not inform themselves as to what constitutes representative government from the standpoint of elections, courts, legislators, local government and the proper relation of the government toward the citizen—what is really involved in maintaining economic security.

As an illustration: How many realize that it is ridiculous to say that an election is free when a majority, or even a substantial portion of the voters receive direct benefits from the government in the form of relief, pensions, contracts, jobs and good positions? Unwittingly about 35 per cent of the citizens plug for a form of government which they call representative, democratic, but which the dictionary describes as dictatorship, totalitarianism, fascism or communism—government in control of the means of production and, consequently, the necessities of daily life.[7] They back away from it only when such procedure becomes a disadvantage to them.

Limitations on Ballot Determines Classification of Government

That elections are the backbone of representative government cannot be denied. The difficulty in the matter is to determine who shall be allowed to vote, what shall be the matters voted upon, the proper relationship between the voters and their government, and the qualifications and functions of the representatives. The practice under those propositions determines whether a particular form of government should be called communism, totalitarian, fascist, or a dictatorship.

Newdealism has been labeled all of them. The labels were applied by men of learning, including doctors, lawyers, judges, editors and economists, and also by farmers, bricklayers, stevedores, a former paper-hanger and a former bandit. That is substantial evidence, if not conclusive evidence, that there has been a departure from the constitutional idea of representative government. Incidentally, the confusion is used to obtain excessive power for the political leader and to reduce the

[7] Supreme Court Justice Douglas estimates there are about 100,000 communists in the United States. He means, the bleary-eyed fanatics and the under-cover agents for Russia. However, the force which is driving the United States toward the Russian form of government, is the influence of the intelligent and educated individuals who are clamoring for more and more government control —the Russian type of government—government in control of the means of production.

power of the industrialist over his private property, especially the means of production.

To understand what was meant by representative government in the days when the Constitution was made, one must be familiar with the political, economic, and social life of that time. As an illustration in the political area: about one in twenty-five could vote. Generally, those who voted had to be white, citizens, property-holders, and with considerable education. Aliens, of course, were barred on the ground that they had too much foreign interest; those without property (the overwhelming majority) were barred on the presumption that they would use their power adversely to good government because they were in distress and, therefore, not in a position to exercise good judgment. Those without education were barred on the ground that governmental procedure was profoundly complex. The voter should, therefore, also be able to read and write before he could be qualified to participate in the ballot privilege.

Unjustified Criticism that Constitution Did not Provide Representative Government

The fact that only a few could vote gives color to the criticism that the Constitution did not provide representative government. However, since family and servant constituted the major portion of the social structure when the Constitution was made, the failure to provide more opportunity for exercise of the ballot did not impair representative government so much as would appear. The father qualified to represent his family and his servants. But most important was the fact that the Constitution aimed at a social and economic structure which would restore the proper relationship of the citizen to his government. It, therefore, emphasized the right to own property: the sacredness of private property, free enterprise—an economic structure under which a citizen could acquire enough property to be independent of governmental pensions or doles —free.

The Free Enterprise Revolution

Under the impact of free enterprise, more freedom in the right to own property or industry, there were soon experienced changes in the economic, social and political structure. One person in three became a voter instead of about one in twenty-five. The change was brought about without the industrialist, "liberal" or "humanitarian" having any particular part therein; perhaps, in spite of them. There were so many opportunities to make a living that the person of average intelligence and energy had a better chance to live on his own initiative than as a servant. Under that "New Order" the servant was transformed into a free man who, because of the industrial opportunities which surrounded him, worked on the basis that he could quit when he wanted to, work for whom he pleased, or go into business for himself. Of course he paid for these freedoms. He surrendered his right to look to a master for relief when in distress. But he became a responsible individual and under the rules of representative government was entitled to vote.

This wrought tremendous changes in the social, economic and political life of the nation. A revolution. But something in complete accord with constitutional government. The servant and lord relationship disappeared under the free enterprise or Laissez Faire doctrine—the doctrine that the means of production should be owned by private individuals, free from the then prevalent government controls. In its place was introduced a new relationship, employer and employee.

Servant and Lord Relationship Restored

The debacle of 1929, falsely charged to free enterprise, was used to destroy faith in that relationship. On the pessimistic premise that 75 percent of the citizens would be dependent on government for doles, pensions, jobs, homes, food and outright relief, there was re-introduced, glamorously enough, the most ancient and pernicious servant and lord relationship, that is, government functioning as the master employer, the boss, the great "benefactor."

But is makes a gloomy prospect, indeed, no matter how it is camouflaged, to assume that the majority of the citizens will be dependent upon government for jobs, pensions, food and shelter; especially when it is realized that the government is a master who may repudiate an obligation at will, and for infractions of its mandates take the life of the offender. Moreover, the record shows such a master always debauches the ballot and then moves for its elimination. The present tendency, therefore, toward having the citizen dependent upon government is not only bound to interfere with the ballot privilege,[7a] but eventually will drive the citizen back to restrictions prevailing during the colonial days—farther back than horse and buggy days. It must always be borne in mind that government control, generally, is sought to avoid overproduction!

Effect Upon the States

This relationship, fully consummated in Russia, will eventually compel the States to surrender their jurisdiction to the Federal government. It is bound to reduce them to administrative agencies, no matter what they may call themselves. These present governmental trends therefore make the constitutional

[7a] See footnote 9 of Chap. II.

aspect of state government futile as well as impossible. *The turmoil of the day is the result of a social and economic structure trying to adjust itself to an entirely different form of government from what it believes it has. It is trying to use free speech (criticism of government) free judges and legislators in an economic structure (government in control of, or drifting toward control of the means of production) which cannot function under such conditions.*

Majority Rule in Representative Government

Out of this new relationship between the citizen and government, and the confusion as to what constitutes representative government, have developed some strange doctrines as to majority rule. One is constrained, therefore, to consider that subject at some length. That the forefathers realized how difficult was the task of keeping majority rule within bounds may be inferred from the precautions in the Constitution with respect to who should vote, what was to be voted upon, who should hold office, and where more than a bare majority vote was necessary to decide an issue.

The checks suggest that they made the restriction on the ballot because of fear of agitators, not because of fear that the majority wanted to do wrong.[8] Hamilton's loose remark about not having confidence in the majority was based upon the fact that majorities can be readily led into permanent bondage because of their disposition to follow debt-making governments in the hope of escaping the usual hardships that arise in building and maintaining a civilization. Granting that he had no sympathy for the poor, his practical ability to develop business gave them a better chance to live than the methods and

[8] "The fabric of American government ought to rest on the solid basis of the consent of the people. The streams of national power ought to flow from that legitimate authority." Hamilton. Fed. 22. (paraphrased)

proposals of those who condemned him for his hardness. Politicians have always hated Hamilton's implication that they were ordinary human beings, like himself, prone to deceive themselves into believing that they were humanitarians and, consequently, in the name of humanity, ready to urge the majority to give them unlimited power on the ground that they would not abuse it, would use it only for public welfare and relinquish it as soon as possible—the maximum of demagoguery.

Majority Rule with Respect to Legislation

It is proper at this point to glance at majority rule with respect to legislation. The Constitution provides that Congress shall make the laws. That proposition repudiates the old but never-dead idea that the king or what is now called the executive branch, should make the laws. It also precludes the judges from making the laws, and repudiates, what is called improperly a democratic principle, the proposition that the voters should act as legislators by referendums, etc. It carries an implication that it requires experts to enact laws, that is persons who have ample time and opportunity to study proposals. That requirement naturally excludes, to a great extent, the presidents, the judges and the people. The people share in forming or repealing legislation by protesting in the courts when practice proves that the legislation is useless or harmful. That, of course, brings into play the courts and the executive branch.

After all, it is a democratic contribution to sound government to have laws enacted by a political branch (an elected branch) and the effectiveness or validity of the laws decided in the courts, on protest from the people, before a judge whose decisions do not, or should not, depend upon the election or

[9] "The courts are concerned only with the power to enact statutes, not with their wisdom * * *. For the removal of unwise laws * * * appeal lies not to the courts but to the ballot." Justice Stone in the AAA case, 297 U.S. 1. An unfortunate and misleading statement.

[10] Edward S. Corwin, in "the Doctrine of Judicial Review", tries to show that Lord Coke, notwithstanding his declaration that an act of Parliament contrary to common right and reason was void, nevertheless believed that Parliament was without check with respect to enacting law. He quotes Blackstone as also subscribing to that doctrine: "But if the parliament will positively enact a thing to be done which is unreasonable, I know of no power in the ordinary forms of the constitution that is vested with authority to control it; and the examples usually alleged in support of the rule do none of them prove that where the main object of the statute is unreasonable the judges are at liberty to reject it: for, that were to set the judicial power above that of the legislatures, which would be subversive to all government."

However, it would seem that Lord Coke's rule applies when it is obvious, because the law cannot be enforced, that parliament has been too arbitrary. The courts, as they too are supposed to reflect the will of the people, certainly may pronounce a law void if the people rightfully believe, and they may be in the best position to know, that a law violates common right and reason—the law of God.

In other words, there are at least some matters which oblige kings, parliaments and judges to respond to the will of the people—the "voice of God." The difficulty arises in determining when the voice is to be represented by the executive, the legislative, the judiciary or the people.

If Blackstone's words are to be taken without qualification, it would amount to divine right of parliament. However, in his division or classification of laws he specifies the laws of God, that is, laws which cannot be changed by the king, parliament or the judges, which seem to be another way of stating Lord Coke's proposition.

Of course, if the courts ruled directly on legislation—that is without having litigation before them, they might be functioning as the "supreme power." Under such circumstances, Blackstone's objection would be sustained.

party favor, and who is in the vicinity and therefore presumed to be familiar with the pertinent facts. The protests of outraged citizens in courts are often the basis for repealing laws. The possibility of having an obnoxious law repealed without such protest is not great. The Supreme Court judges who say that the citizen has in the ballot adequate protection against unfortunate or arbitrary laws certainly do not mean to modify or ignore that representative aspect of the courts.[9]

This is the justification of the old principle mentioned by Lord Coke when he remarked that laws which violate inherent or natural rights were void and might be so declared by the judges.[10] The judge, confronted with all the facts and the consequences of the law as they manifest themselves in his community, is certainly a person qualified to speak on the subject.

Upon that simple principle rests, to a great extent, what may be called the necessity for judicial review, which becomes clarified, not enlarged, perhaps restricted, *under constitutional government,* because a constitution is supposed to set out clearly the powers of the various branches. This done, it should not be necessary very often for a court to explain to the legislators or the executive the extent of their respective jurisdictions. Lord Coke was embarrassed because he had no written document like a United States Constitution by which he could measure parliament's powers and limitations. The provisions in the Constitution dealing with the courts, representative government, and majority rule, therefore add to the protection of minorities, particularly the individual. That is democracy!

The proposition generally subscribed to by the "liberals", that legislators should rely upon the wishes of the majority is a far cry from constitutional majority rule as conceived by the Forefathers. Their conception of majority rule seems to be that a majority of the people want elected experts to use their judgment in making the laws. As that is fairly safe procedure, it is to be presumed that it represents the voice of the people.

The President was given a veto power over legislation— one man in a position to overrule a majority of the legislators! Although that may appear to be a one-man-rule proposition, it is majority rule, representative government, because it has to be presumed that a majority of the people are in favor of that rule under such circumstances as the Constitution provides. One judge, also, may be in a position to overrule a majority of the legislators, the president and public sentiment, should a citizen challenge the law on the ground that it is unconstitutional.

However, these extreme cases never represent one man's judgment. For example, a private citizen does not challenge a law passed by Congress, unless there is much justification. He is usually fortified by public sentiment, arguments of trained lawyers, opinions and decisions in prior rulings of judges, and a strong minority in Congress. Nevertheless, it is a minority challenging and overruling a majority. But it occurs under such circumstances that most people see that it is a proper result. It is therefore majority rule—the voice of the people expressed in the Constitution. Another outstanding example of minority control under majority rule is the provision allowing one-fourth of the States to block an amendment.

Majority Rule in General

One would grow too weary if he undertook to point out where majority rule, as that phrase is understood, is not used in government or in daily life. The father does not use it for his children, the priest for his congregation, the doctor for his patients, the general for his soldiers, lawyers for their clients, nor merchants for their customers. In all such situations, one man because of his position, is required to substitute his judgment for that of a group. These minority guides, though they seem to be dictators, nevertheless represent majority rule because of majority satisfaction with the opinions of the experts —the majority of the experts.

The only place where a bare majority rule in connection with voting can be used is where the voters have a common knowledge (each one knowing as much about the matter as the other) and a common interest, as well as common responsibility. Such situations may prevail in clubs or other such organizations. They are presumed to prevail in general elections. Where the three requirements mentioned are not present, it is necessary to resort to balancing methods such as two-thirds or one-fourth rules. Legislative bodies, because it is assumed that the members have common knowledge, common interest and common responsibility, usually can function on a bare majority rule.

The votes cast in a legislative body bind the nation. Public sentiment should not affect the decisions of the legislators unless the public has access to as many of the facts as have the legislators. Legislation often is so complicated that experts, judges, presidents, economists and others who have studied such matters all their lives are puzzled as to what action should be taken. Such matters certainly should not depend upon public sentiment or be referred to the people for decision. The Referendum, Initiative and Recall movements failed to accomplish much because the leaders of those movements disregarded the first rules which apply to such matters.

There are a great many important features of representative government regarding which the voice of the people, public sentiment, or what a majority of the people believe, may be followed. The Forefathers put many of them in the Constitution.

They are the fundamentals of government which most people know, believe and feel are right. From that fact arises the presumption that what the Constitution provides is majority rule—representative government.

For instance, a majority of the people believe in the provisions of the Constitution that it is proper policy to have Congress make the laws, judges interpret them, and the executive branch enforce them; that policy officials, because it is hard to curb them, should be subjected to short term of office, and elected by free citizens—not citizens dependent upon government for their daily bread as is now the practice quite generally throughout the civilized world.

Most people, recognize that Congress, the legislative body, should be required to meet on specified occasions; that its convening and adjourning is not a matter over which the executive should have much control; that in time of war it is necessary to centralize power; that government must collect taxes; that there are fields in which the government must be supreme; that religion must not be made a political matter; that free speech (criticism of government) is the basic protection for social security; that cruel and unusual punishment and excessive bail are never justified, and that litigation generally, should be between citizen and citizen in properly constituted courts; not between the citizen and his government as is now so often the case, evidenced by all the commissions, boards, authorities, directors and committees taking the place of courts.[11]

Everybody knows that these principles are the fundamentals which protect the social and economic security of every country and that the Constitution contemplates that they shall not be impaired or repealed. That is why it is said that the Constitu-

[11] The frontiers throughout the world have to be sought in the field of governmental favoritism. Such a condition implies that Democracy is on the decline, if not dead.

tion provides for Representative Government—Majority Rule. And that is why people should be alarmed for their safety when such principles are abandoned for something more glamorous.

It is not only school children who are making mistakes as to what is meant by majority rule, but also a goodly number of Congressmen, presidents, columnists, text-book writers, and political orators, reformers and agitators. For instance, the theory that if a majority of the people vote for a president who is sponsoring certain reforms, the election of that president entitles him to make those reforms without regard as to whether they are constitutional; or the proposition that if a president is elected by an overwhelming majority on a novel program, he has a mandate to disregard the Constitution. That is not majority rule at all under the Constitution, or under any form of government. Nevertheless it finds hearty support as such, and its supporters do not hesitate to take advantage of a presidential suggestion that laws be enacted without reference to their constitutional character.

Critics of Constitutional Majority Rule Do not Want Majority Rule

The communists, who never had a majority or a near majority in this country, or in any country for that matter, if elected to office as Republicans, Democrats, New Dealers or Fair Dealers (which is their method of gaining power) would not hesitate to force upon this country communistic government, even though ninety per cent of the people were opposed to it. Yet the communists are loud complainers about lack of majority rule in the Constitution. Neither would they hesitate to use misleading propaganda, including downright fraud and deceit, to get control of government, in the same manner as Mussolini, Hitler or Stalin. There is no doubt that a majority of the people would be glad if Mr. Bridges would return to Australia. Russia would not take him. But instead of responding to a majority rule, which he claims he subscribes to, he resisted the government's efforts to deport him.

Labor leaders criticize the Constitution for not providing representative government—majority rule—government without special privilege. But it is to be observed that their complaints generally apply to the field of their immediate interest and not to the field of what is best for all—the true basis for representative government. They are calling and working for their programs without much consideration for the majority. With the same unholy spirit that they charge to others, they assume that the hardships which arise from their policies are unavoidable or entirely the fault of those who endure them,[12] or are caused by the opposition. The government tries to bridge the gap by food stamps—certainly a bitter portion for any person who has an ounce of independence in his soul.

Labor leaders are not unique. They are only additions to the constantly and rapidly growing groups who, in fact, resent and prevent equal and just representation because it will interfere with their special privileges, and who hide their motives behind criticism of the Constitution.

Geographical Representation
Changed to Trade Representation

The Constitution contemplated that the legislators should represent their districts, protecting all interests therein, and from the angle of what would be best for the nation. That objective becomes impossible as well as impracticable when federal legislation reaches into every vocation and undertaking of daily life. Such laws eventually compel representation by trade, profession or other occupation.

[12] What could be more unfair than the disposition of the Unions to use the NLRA for protection and still cling to an unrestricted right to strike regardless of how many people starve or how much property is destroyed!

The farmer, doctor, lawyer, preacher, business men, laborer, pensioner and reliefee is compelled to become a federal trade politician, for in the Federal Government lies his primary chance of continuing his existence. And he looks to the Executive Department, not to Congress and the courts, for his adjustments. Such a set-up certainly is not democracy. The Taft-Hartley Act has not changed that totalitarian aspect of the NLRA. The President (not the courts) determines, in practice, when a labor Union may not strike. *Under such circumstances private property has to depend upon political relations for its protection.* Could any law be more vividly unconstitutional?

The primary objection to these laws is that they involve a different principle of representation from that embraced in the fundamental law. They force representation by trade, occupation and private interests. The builders of the first communist constitution in Russia were honest enough to admit that fact. The English parliament started out under such an arrangement and still has a few touches of it in the realm of the academic.

To some persons this proposed representation by trades and professions is new and modern government. But it was one of the undesirable features of government which the Forefathers tried to eliminate, because the past showed that it carried the seeds of life and death contentions with government. And can it mean anything else to the United States. It results in one part of the country being lined up against another part on questions of important commercial advantages, fully as troublesome as those that started the Civil War.[13] Representation by trades does not make majority rule, democracy or representative government, because it tangents off on sharp issues involving minority groups instead of confining itself to those things re-

[13] See background of 14th Amendment.

garding which all have a common interest and may therefore come to a national working agreement.

When the laborer, farmer, white-collar man and professional man assign to government full charge of their occupational life, or even a substantial part thereof, they surrender their individuality in a most vital field to political control. The spirit of Patrick Henry expressed in "Give me Liberty or give me Death" burns too vigorously in the soul of the English-speaking race to justify hoping that they will consent for long to dependence upon a government official for their food, or tolerate him to direct their occupation, designate their place of dwelling, or control their opportunity to be independent; that is, own enough property so that they need not depend on government doles available only because a government official violates his obligation as a trustee of tax funds. They cannot be beaten into permanent subjection like the once independent Ukraine farmer.

Drifting Away from Liberty

Free enterprise, representative government, democracy or majority rule, or whatever it should be called, was born out of protest to that kind of government. Its implications are that public welfare, individual welfare, is most secure when each person is charged directly with responsibility for his own life and fortunes, and that if it cannot be done that way, political control will not solve the problem; that, indeed, his security is impaired if he trusts it to another, especially a government official (one who is not responsible to him financially or morally) if the course recommended crowds him into a dead-end alley of governmental regulation or forces him to accept government created bankruptcy.

It can hardly be denied that governments are rapidly drifting away from representative government, democracy. Today the popular types of government are those in which the individual is directly or substantially dependent upon government for his food, clothes, home, job, business and profession. That is the exact reverse of representative government, and if the drift continues it is bound to destroy, in spite of anything that may be done to prevent it, free elections, local government, independent courts and legislators, and introduce in their stead fascism, nazism or communism.

Many leaders, to avoid panic, prefer to deny the trend; others approach it as being a temporary matter, although nothing substantial is offered to terminate the trend. Indeed, the strongest currents are in the direction of permanency.[14] That confidence has been lost in representative government is manifested by the statements of many leaders, often amounting to disrespect, even contempt, for industrialists, legislators, judges and the ballot. According to no mean authorities, there is well-timed planning to force abandonment of many aspects of constitutional (representative) government.

The citizens, by reason of the stream of derogatory remarks about courts, legislators and industrialists, and on account of the misconduct of such leaders, have lost confidence in courts, legislators, and elections, and even in the economic structure under which they live. They are therefore in panic and confusion with respect to government and naturally turn to new forms of protection without any well-defined notion of what it should be. Under the circumstances, it can be nothing but one-man leadership, since the judges and the legislators look to the executive for guidance. However, they dare not admit it is dictatorship because of the poison in that word, but call it democracy, representative government, majority rule, or

[14] See any of the recent messages to Congress.

[15] "While consumption was drastically reduced, extraordinary measures were taken to increase the productive efforts of the population. Speeches and propaganda were supplemented by severe labor legislation. A series of decrees made it a crime to come to work more than twenty minutes late. Offenders received up to six months at forced labor. It became illegal for a worker or other employee to leave his job without the written permission of his director, while on the other hand the commissariats were empowered to send any worker to any part of the Soviet Union for as long as the interests of production demanded, whether or not he wanted to go. At the same time a decree made factory directors, departmental chiefs and chief engineers responsible before a criminal court for non-fulfillment of plan, failure of produce to come up to specifications, or jugglings of articles of poor quality. The courts were busy with public trials in which responsible administrators, indicted under above decrees, were not given a fair chance to defend themselves, and received up to eight-year prison sentences when convicted. There was no talk or at least very little of Fascist spies, insidious murderers of great literary figures, and the like, as these had been in the purge. The defendants were accused of not producing as much as the country needed to defend itself." Scott, "Behind the Urals", p. 254.

White, in "Report on the Russians", indicates that there were nearly ten million Russians in prison and labor camps.

Dallin, in "The Real Soviet Russia", shows about 10 per cent of the Russian working population as forced labor. See p. 97.

Also see Manya Gordon's "Fifty Years of Labor".

The same situation, but perhaps not quite so severe, prevailed in Germany and Italy.

whatever kind of government they feel will afford them the most protection. But, as in the days of Saul, the voice of the people is clamoring for one-man leadership—*government by men instead of by laws.*

This clamor has been intensified because people have been taught that civilization may be maintained without hardships. As they are in distress, they are ready to grasp at a straw, and consequently do not realize that the glamorous "New Orders" will double the hardships in spite of their sweet-sounding names such as Social Democracy, Dictatorship of the Proletariat, Everybody According to His Needs, Full Employment. The right name for them all is Government Slave Labor.[15]

The glamorous names are used as bait to entice the unwary to give the politician unlimited power, and to persuade them to surrender their last chance of freedom—an opportunity to own property or to use their own judgment and initiative in the field of preserving their economic independence and integrity, be free—free from the necessity of government relief or of old age pensions, etc. Of course, under the "New Orders" there will be plenty of use for judgment and initiative. *But it will have to be used to obtain food and shelter from a government official and to avoid governmental wrath.* Activities of that character do not stimulate production or business. They destroy it and consequently also destroy public welfare— social security.

But hardships are inevitable. It is highly improbable that a civilization of cities, railroads, sewers, tunnels, bridges, skyscrapers, canals, ships, airplanes, coal mines, oil wells, farms and ranches can be built *quickly without requiring at least one man in ten to forfeit* his health, ambitions, childhood, marriage, home or make other comparable sacrifices; *about the same as in war and for the same reason.* Of course, the building can be done more quickly and more cheaply with governmental "slave labor" than under free enterprise "slave labor," for the simple reason that government is a sovereign power which can deny all obligations, abolish the courts, utilize the Army and Navy, imprison or shoot a resister, send him anywhere, or starve him according to the "emergency." Perhaps Russia's economic condition justified introducing government "slave labor," and it is probable the critical commercial relations facing the United States are the basis for the "full (rationed) employment" programs which are now being presented so eloquently. But these programs, if they mean anything, will force absolute government control.[16] Such a form of government is properly classified as dictatorship—government in control of commercial affairs as well as political affairs, but it is being sold to the citizen as constitutional government. The leading salesmen, speaking without reflection upon anyone's integrity, are found in prominent places.

Under free enterprise (representative government) the employee is often at the absolute mercy of the employer, a human being, aroused to a high pitch of emotion by an objective which he believes, or pretends to believe, is so important that the individual cannot be considered is the usual way. And his objective may justify his course, as he may be in the same position the government official occupies when he orders the last man and the last dollar to the altar in wartime. But he is not in a position to be so arbitrary as a government official who

---

[16] Since the Russian Government has full control of labor, it may be considered as a nation with a National Service Act. Such an Act has been recommended for the United States because of proof that Labor Union policy tends to reduce production.

However, the government has to practice the same policies that labor unions indulge in. It was common knowledge during wartime, although the records showed 8-hour days, and no holidays, that the government was over-staffed, by about 50 percent in many cases. Just another way of effecting a "slow-down" or "sit-down" to make "full employment".

is dressed in sovereignty—the maximum of authority, and who is above responsibility.

Representative government has as its main issue the adjustment of disputes between individuals about property rights that arise because the citizen owns the means of production. Governments restricted to such an objective are not strong enough to be extremely arbitrary. Under such circumstances government is used by the individual to protect himself against the arbitrary conduct of his fellowmen—not his sovereign. To honor that principle democracy is often covered with a confusion that retards business and consequently hinders or defeats public welfare, social security.

However, with all its retardation and confusion and all its tears and sweat and blood, in the long run it serves the citizen better than the so-called "New Orders," which emphasize heavy taxes in order to provide pensions, dole, government jobs, government contracts, etc., and have always brought, notwithstanding fine promises, the maximum of confusion, retardation, war, sweat and tears, and less opportunity to make a decent living. The confusion and lack of opportunity develop because the glamorous benefits mean only more taxes and more citizens dependent upon government and eventually no funds for any pensions or benefits; mean that the law-decreed wages and hours will eventually bring the lowest possible standard of living, no matter how high the wages, to the great majority and oblige the citizen to seek opportunity in governmental favor, which can be obtained only by surrendering his own judgment and his property. In place of the hardships of free enterprise he finds the hardships of government regimentation—procedure which according to the record, is not disposed to recognize either justice or mercy. For imagined security for all, he surrenders the protection and utilization of his inherent ability, and becomes part of an economic structure in which, by order of the government, the stupidity of the moron reaps the same reward as the agile and active mind.

It may be that the principles of free enterprise and of the Constitution have been so completely twisted out of shape that the whole structure must be destroyed before representative government can be restored. The "humanitarians" and "liberals" through their "benevolent dictatorships" may be, unwittingly, under the providence of God, the instrument of destruction which will bring about that result.

Limitations of Representative Government

Representative government does not afford everybody equal opportunities. For instance, the alien is seldom admitted to the political life of the nation in which he sojourns; he does not vote, nor does he hold office. Minors, the mentally deficient and criminals, as well as paupers and wards, are excluded from that field. But they are not without a measure of justice or representation. The alien has his own country, and the deficient and unfortunate find representation and justice to some extent through parents, guardians, etc. As laws are administered by men, not gods, mercy and justice fall in a most uneven manner.

However, under governments which have charge of daily life to the extent practiced in Russia, and being embraced throughout the word, a majority of the inhabitants occupy the position of wards, unavoidably so, because of the paternalistic authority of the government official. Consequently, they are in the group that is entitled to justice and mercy, but should not participate in political functions except in a very restricted way, as in the U.S.S.R.

Because of religious or political convictions or practices, many, in every country, find themselves excluded to an extent from the political, social and economic life of the countries in which they abide. Generally such groups recognize that the discrimination is just (democratic) and, therefore do not complain about it too much.[17] Key positions, of necessity, must be accepted by those who understand the countries laws and traditions. Color often raises problems. Members of the white race in a country of different color often find themselves restricted. Some communities make it a crime for those of different color to marry. Most communities object to such marriages. Primitive instinct, no doubt, would make a law to the contrary quite futile. Interference in either direction could be tyranny notwithstanding that it had majority support. Perhaps the most difficult discriminations to defend are those which arise because of laws which exclude persons from making homes in other countries, regardless of the terrible hardships which may befall the excluded, or how noble, pure or brilliant they may be.

Government has no objective other than public welfare—what is best for all. It must choose its leaders accordingly, no matter whose pride is offended. Civilization is always under stress and strain. It is probable, therefore, that civilization's load is too heavy to enable it to make many adjustments for the deficient in mind or body or in personal appearance. It must follow the rule of directing efforts toward groups which respond most quickly. The rule becomes most conspicuous in wartime. Any other course would be too dangerous and certainly not democratic, if public welfare is the issue. Like the

[17] Because of their practices which clash with the teachings about Jesus, religious Chinese, Hindus and Hebrews sometimes have religious difficulties in Christian countries; in the same way about as the Christians have when they insist on their teachings in a foreign country.

[18] It is probable that a homely girl would make a better mother; a man without the academic, a better judge; a man with gray hair, a better executive; but, regardless, of their efficiency, they are, generally, not accepted. To force a contrary practice would intensify the suffering it is sought to avoid. Segregation, so far as the Negro is involved, is probably necessary because of the poor judgment and depravity of members of the white race in social, economic and political areas. For instance, in the social area, many of the white males do not hesitate to have relations with colored girls, if there is no danger of parental obligations. The whole matter seems to boil down to the question of whether it would for long benefit any group to make a white race other than white. However, if miscegenation is the objective of Southern segregation, it is obvious it has not been effective, except, perhaps, as a retarding method. It would be very helpful if the "Liberals" used more facts to establish that their programs do not stimulate miscegenation.

[19] U.S. v Reese, 92 US 214, voiding a law which penalized state officers who deprived anyone of his right to vote on account of race or color. (By a strained interpretation of language.)

92 US 542, squashing an indictment for depriving certain colored persons of the right of peaceable assembly. (Indictment failed to aver a particular fact.)

United States v Harris, 106 US 629, voiding a law making it a crime for two or more persons to conspire to deprive another of rights guaranteed by the Civil War Amendments on the ground that the amendments applied to only state authority.

Civil Rights Cases, 109 US 3, declaring unconstitutional laws providing equal treatment for negroes in hotels, restaurants, public conveyances and theaters.

It would be nearer the truth to say that these cases nullified, quite generally, the fantastic ideas of what the Civil War amendments contemplated. They certainly did not contemplate abrogation of the miscegenation laws, which in themselves carry some serious implications as to race superiority and associations to which a great majority of the white people subscribe. Clearly such laws would have lost all significance if the Court had upheld the contentions of the proponents.

soldier under fire, civilization often may not stop to administer relief to an unfortunate comrade. Those who are afraid to face that fact cover their weakness by a silly or a brutal attitude toward the fallen, the wounded, or handicapped.

The phrase "race superiority" is generally used emotionally—without any definite idea of what is involved. It is possible that the cannibal, the Zulu, the Eskimo or American Indian, under centuries of training might become effective in building a civilization. But at the present time they could not be classed as superior or equal in that field when compared with more advanced civilizations. Moreover, it is probable that particular groups are in such a strategic position that not to recognize them as superior (give them leadership) would result in intensifying hardships for all. It is not pertinent here to discuss how these group distinctions developed. Unnecessary abuse is probably the reason for contention about the matter. However, one is emotional if he expects that heartaches will not arise because of deficiencies in personal appearance, habits and temperaments.[18] Such problems involve too many local questions and too much fluctuating public sentiment to be made the subjects of laws or constitutions, except in a very general manner. The Supreme Court's interpretation of the 13th, 14th and 15th Amendments seem to bear out that position,[19] the recent decisions of that court, notwithstanding.

CONSTITUTIONS AND BILLS
OF RIGHTS

CONSTITUTIONS AND BILLS OF RIGHTS

CHAPTER VII

False Notions About the Protecting Power of Constitutions and Bills of Rights

BY scanning a constitution proposed in 1938 for the State of New York a conception can be gathered of what is considered constitutional material at the present time.[1]

It starts with a Bill of Rights, but does not name therein all of the inherent rights specified by the Forefathers. The free speech provisions in it refer to the law of libel and slander as it relates to private citizens, instead of to criticism about the way or manner in which government is conducted.

The Forefathers when they referred to free speech were not worrying about libel and slander as it touched private citizens. They had just experienced a war which developed because criticism of government had been a most dangerous and futile undertaking. It is probable that modern Americans will not understand the significance of free speech until they have lived under a form of government which provides an inspector for every corner, the Russian type—government which demands praise from its subjects to prove their loyalty.

Section 10 of this constitution provides for complete separation of church and state. However, it also provides that the government shall have extensive, if not complete, control over the industrial life of the people. It seems therefore that these builders have overlooked the fact that when a government

[1] See Appendix of "Constitutions of the States and the United States" by New York State Constitutional Convention Committee of 1938.

assumes control of the industrial life of a people, the only religious institution which can survive will be a State Church. The experience of the Church in Russia ought to make that clear.

This proposed constitution provides for the usual protection for legislative bodies with respect to convening, adjournment, free debates, etc. But it broadens tremendously the principle of the executive veto, and curtails legislative authority by the so-called democratic doctrines of the initiative, referendum and a legislative council. It, therefore, follows the Russian constitutional idea of mixing the executive and legislative functions, except that the Russians do it by way of a Presidium.

In defense of a council the point is made that legislators usually are amateurs and require a body of experts to direct them. But if a council is to be imposed upon legislators, men who are supposed to have ample time to study the questions and get the facts, what about the check upon the initiative and referendum—voters made up of laymen? The "duly elected" members need advice, but not the laymen? Laymen apparently are to be called upon to solve questions that the legislators and Council found too heavy and complex! See 223 U.S. 118, Pac. S. Telp. and Telg. Co. v. Ore.

The principle involved in referendum and initiative procedure has always manifested itself in some form in every well-established government, and certainly is not to be repudiated; but it certainly does not extend to the complex and involved questions of economics and other technical matters suggested in these days.[2]

With respect to courts, the provisions for the recall of judges should be expected. But that *modern* conception of "democracy" does not appear. Much space, however, is spent upon

[2] See "Popular Government." Taft.

the matter of how judges shall be appointed and court procedure conducted. Apparently the idea of the Forefathers that much of that matter should be left to the legislature was not considered good government. Jurisdiction of the courts was not considered to a great extent. A logical result, for the courts must play a very subordinate part in social democracies.

Following the *modern* idea, this constitution gives the executive branch a wide authority in the matter of making, revising, repealing, recommending and amending laws. A bold and confessed position to the effect that the Forefathers were altogether wrong in their conception as to where the authority of the executive branch should end, as well as in their efforts to give the three branches of government independent responsibility and jurisdiction over their respective fields— law interpretation for judges, law making for legislators and law enforcement for the executive branch. The whole proposition boils down to the theory that the legislative and judiciary should be subordinate to the executive. However, that is an unavoidable result, an absolute necessity, when government of the kind this constitution proposes is in effect.

Section 88 of this constitution provides that the maintenance and distribution, at reasonable rates, of a sufficient supply of food or other necessities of life, are public functions of the State, which may provide the same for inhabitants in such manner as may be determined. And are not the "Liberals" busy with that very idea?

Section 89, under the heading of Conservation of Natural Resources, is as comprehensive as Section 88.

The language in these two sections certainly does not lack much of being as broad as any found in the Russian constitution; but, nevertheless, they are called democratic! Hitler properly ridiculed the claim to democracy under such a set-up because of the pretense to preserve the theory of separate powers, free speech and private enterprise.

The principle exponent of this new constitution observes (and in the exact opposite of what the Forefathers taught, and the exact parallel of what the Russian constitution implies) that the theory of checks and balances was imposed by the fear that the nature of government is to oppress the people, and because government was viewed as a necessary evil to be kept as much as possible in a condition of inertia; but, that this fear of oppression exists no longer as now we look to government as an organ of society by which our common problems are worked out. And that conclusion is accepted in the face of the blood purges of Lenin, Mussolini, Hitler and Stalin. And could there be sweeter words for the ears of those that love to spend the taxpayers' money?

Amendment of this proposed constitution is provided for in several ways and with a bare majority vote, indicating that it is desired to depart from the old principle that only fundamentals should appear in a constitution. Fundamentals do not have to be changed very often, and if changed should be changed by more than a bare majority of the votes which decide such a matter. Too many of the voters involved in such matters generally have only a nominal degree of equal knowledge, interest and responsibility. Therefore, a bare majority vote would be inappropriate. However, when constitutions are used as vehicles to experiment with economic problems, and in addition set out details which belong to legislative authority, then the methods of amending them must be easy and quick. But such an arrangement is not entitled to the rank and dignity of a constitution, and makes a bill of rights less effective than a feather against a hurricane. *Indeed it is a subtle way of abolishing constitutions;* probably, the objective, for such instruments carry the implication that government officials, (human beings) unless they are properly checked, are prone to oppress—bound to oppress. "Liberals" resent that philosophy, and consequently, appear their efforts to impair such instruments. The pages of history give little promise that there is ground for faith that government officials will change in that respect. How could there be a change? They are human beings exercising unlimited authority (may decree life and death for trifles) without being financially responsible for their mistakes! A chance to win without the usual chance to lose! What right has civilization to expect human minds to function fairly under such circumstances? The ballot, of course, under that kind of government become the principal weapon of oppression.

The false laudation of the strength of these instruments naturally creates an impression that they constitute an unbreakable barrier against oppression. But nothing could be farther from the truth. They are futile in every respect if the general principles of government are not observed. They have value only in an economic structure of free enterprise and private property. They have no significance under "Social Democracies," except as ornaments or deceptions to be turned against the subject to confuse and oppress him instead of protecting him.[3] Our Bill of Rights, therefore, will become useless unless the form of government outlined in the Constitution is scrupulously followed. That is true of the other protections for citizens in that document. Any one of these protections is impaired by making one branch of the government stronger than the other, or not independent enough, no matter whether it is the judiciary, the legislative, the executive, or the Federal

[3] See footnote 25 of chap. II.

[4] "Our Constitution, at the time it was adopted, was far in advance of its age. Even today there could be no nobler statement * * * than the Bill of Rights. But the part of our Constitution which deals with the mere machinery of the government must now be candidly re-examined in the light of the present crisis." P. 8, of "A New Constitution Now." Hazlitt.

Hazlitt apparently feels that the ancient natural or inherent rights described in the Bill of Rights are secure regardless of the *mere* machinery of government. The Forefathers felt they had no significance or protection unless the machinery of government, the elementary principle of independnt courts and legislators, were maintained.

On page 87 of "A New Constitution Now", Hazlitt, to make the point that our constitutional government is not responsive to public sentiment writes: "Let us take as an example the Supreme Court enlargement question, raised in 1937."

The implications and ramifications of that proposition caused the President as well as many learned legislators to flounder. Yet it appears that it is desired to have such matters decided by public sentiment! Apparently there is need for a book setting forth where public sentiment can be properly used in democratic government.

[5] See discussion of Ward case in footnote 35 of Chapter II.

" * * * delegates omitted from the proposed constitution * * * right of jury trial * * * prohibition of excessive bail * * * right to bear arms, to assemble peacefully, and freedom of the press." Ernst "The Ultimate Power" p 139.

The absence in the Constitution of the rights referred to does not affect its republican or democratic aspect. To recite them is admission that government officials have a pronounced tendency to be oppressive and raises the presumption that the kind of government advocated by Mr. Ernst will prove fatal to his objective—protection of the rights mentioned in the bill he is so concerned about.

Government interfering too much with local authority—state rights.[4]

No statesman has undertaken to definitely define the particular jurisdiction of branches or political divisions of government. The authors of the Constitution made a most significant contribution in that field. But that it was not enough is demonstrated by the confusion and arguments which still confound the world regarding that matter, and the quarrels among such divisions as to their jurisdiction.

Because of the false premises built around these bills, as well as around constitutions, a summary of the limitations upon them is in order. Especially, in these days, when those seeking office are urging the citizen to help them break down rights in property and enlarge governmental authority, upon the false premise that no matter how much power the "liberal" statesman is given constitutions and bill of rights furnish adequate protection against governmental dictation, regimentation, oppression or tyranny.

An outstanding example regarding these limitations is war. War often creates a situation which requires the citizen to surrender to his government all of his rights, including his life. Constitutions and bills of rights cannot protect him against that contingency. Such instruments are not intended to interfere with war powers—hinder the war.[5] War unavoidably enlarges the executive power at the expense of the judiciary and the legislative branches. It compels them to play a nominal part in government—support the Executive, unless it is clear beyond doubt that such a course would result in great harm to the country. As it is often very difficult to determine in advance when a course will result in harm to a country, the right to resist, to take an independent course is, generally, merely an academic one. War, therefore, impairs, holds in

[6] Chafee in his "Free Speech in the United States"; is perhaps too optimistic about the proposition that only words which directly incite to acts of violation of law can be treated as words outside the scope of free speech. That is a safe rule; but it raises a conclusive presumption that the government must be right with respect to the war and the prosecution thereof. However, treaties, pacts, alliances, and checks on declaring war, constitute conclusive evidence that wars, often, if not generally, are declared for improper purposes, and therefore may be adverse to the best interests of the nation. The government therefore is not entitled to a conclusive presumption that it is right. Such a presumption conflicts too much with the thought: "I shall do much harm to the country by opposing this war; more harm, however, will result if I do not oppose it."

Chafee observes in his book that the most dangerous aspect of sedition laws is the unscrupulous way honorable men find ways to bring unpopular citizens within their terms.

He deals with all of the important free speech cases in his book.

There is a tendency to apply the term "free speech" to civil cases, such as limitation on employers criticizing unions, or individuals slandering each other, etc. Under such usage free speech could be used as the foundation for most any civil action including any restraint on making a living. The requirements of a license to drive an automobile might prevent a politician from making a speech.

abeyance, many of the usual protections arising under independent judges and legislators with respect to free speech, unqualified title to property, continuation of life, and other inherent rights. It does not abolish them; it temporarily curtails them, holds them in abeyance—requires a different application of the rules during the time that the war exists.

Free speech may be used as an example: Wartime always enlarges the power of the executive branch because of the increase in government employees, dependents, beneficiaries and government contracts. These relationships naturally put many citizens in a position where they will be reluctant to criticize government. Free speech (criticism of government) is deadened in proportion that the direct contacts with government are increased. During wartime they are increased to such an extent that criticism of government becomes futile or completely paralyzed with the result that governmental corruption and mismanagement goes unchecked.

The ballot, a symbol of free speech, naturally becomes, under such circumstances, the instrument of corruption. Moreover criticism of government, free speech, is particularly difficult during wartime, because the critic, no matter how justified his position, is readily put in the light of interfering with the war, being a traitor—helping the enemy, etc.[6] That is why there is always so much corruption during wartime, or any time when there are too many citizens closely tied to government. In wartime much corruption is tolerated because everybody realizes that everything is jammed up—in confusion, and because war is supposed to be a temporary phase. However, if it continues too long government fails notwithstanding bills of rights or constitutions; Germany, Italy and Japan being recent examples.

Governments prosecute war with declarations that they pro-

¹ "Taxes are paid in the sweat of every man who labors. If these taxes are excessive they are reflected in idle factories and tax-sold farms and in hoards of hungry people tramping the streets and seeking jobs in vain. Our workers may never see a tax bill, yet they pay it. They pay in deductions from wages, in increased cost of what they buy or (as now) in broad unemployment throughout the land * * *. Let us have the courage to stop borrowing to meet continuing deficits. Stop the deficits." President Roosevelt.

pose to use the last dollar and the last drop of blood, which is a claim to unlimited and unrestrained authority in every field, and proof that bills of rights and constitutions, at their best, are but accepted temporary curtailments of sovereignty, and such by consent of the governed.

When government officials demand wartime powers for peacetime, which they have to do to make social democracies effective, they of course, are asking, although they deny it, or do not realize it, that *bills of rights and constitutions in the conventional meaning of those words be abandoned*—thrown out of the window.

Military service even in time of peace is bound to impair for a great many persons the protective value of political instruments of the kind discussed. For instance, men under arms must surrender to a considerable extent participation in many civil liberties such as the right to marry, to work definite hours, to strike, bargain about wages, choose their clothes, or their associates—all precious privileges which these instruments are supposed to give to every citizen to the full measure. In spite of bills and constitutions, large permanent military organizations introduce into the social structure a military caste which cannot be democratic—respect civil life in the usual way, and always carry the possibility of military control of a nation should the political structure collapse.

Government debt adversely affects their protective value. Debt may attain such proportion that the citizens, because of taxation, cannot acquire property, retain prior acquired property, develop or conduct a business or profession, or purchase the necessities of life.[7] If the economic structure is such that many citizens are in debt to the government or dependent on it for food, etc., free speech is impaired, because the *debtor does not occupy a true free-speech relationship to his sovereign.*

He is under too much restraint for fear of loss or expectation of gain.

Social reforms which require the citizen to depend too directly on his government for food, occupation, employment, crops, clothes and homes, compel abrogation or abandonment of constitutions and bills or rights, although the sponsors of such reforms usually imagine they are increasing their scope and effectiveness. But such reforms can only function by reducing to the minimum the ownership rights in private property under confiscatory taxes, by imposing involuntary wage contributions, or by maintaining drastic limitations on wages and hours of employment, and by forbidding strikes; or using methods of indirect or outright seizure of private property. Governments cannot fulfill any of their promises of social security without following that course to the last ditch and not at all so long as wars and preparation for wars are indulged in. Besides in the degree that property rights are reduced there is reduced correspondingly the necessity for courts and legislators, and consequently the protective value of constitutional restraints on government.

The ballot becomes a most destructive agency with respect to such matters when it controls the political candidate to such an extent that he cannot be elected unless he promises to outdistance any spending program offered by his opponent (a general world-wide condition). Under such circumstances, it becomes the greatest threat to free speech, private property, religion and social progress and may completely nullify the protective value of a constitution or its bill of rights. Situations of that character arise from prolonged economic upheavals because they result in a majority of the voters becoming beneficiaries of government or under obligation to it, or obliged to look to it for food, clothes, jobs, credit, etc. Under such circumstances there are few who care, dare, or find it expedient to criticize government—exercise free speech, the most effective weapon against corruption, and the foundation of social progress.

It is a natural tendency not to criticize a friend, an employer, higher authority or a benefactor. That tendency, of course, is one of the reasons why graft and corruption make such tremendous headway under governmental set-ups of that character. They create a relationship between the voter and the government which is bound eventually to force the abandonment of the franchise, or reduce it to a fiction or gesture as occurred in Germany and other countries, with the result that only a few enjoy the Four Freedoms in spite of constitutions, and other instruments to protect them against governmental tyranny.

Economic upheavals may destroy the value of these instruments. For instance, the Constitution was built around the principle that the responsible tax payer should exercise the franchise. However, an economic situation may reduce the tax payers to want. Then, unless a statute divests them of the right to vote, the control of the ballot is in the hands of the discouraged, the disappointed, the destitute, the paupers, the misinformed, the ignorant, the desperate and the unscrupulous. Under such circumstances a primary governmental principle with respect to who shall vote is thrown into reverse and forces what has to be called an unauthorized amendment to the Constitution. It was not contemplated under that document that the destitute or the other classes mentioned should vote. The consequences are that the responsible tax payers, the few who are left, become a helpless minority, practically disfranchised because their votes are too few to have weight; and right or wrong, they are deprived of important protections which it was intended they should enjoy. It may be impossible to avoid these things, but when they occur the vaunted protection of the instruments under discussion disappear, at least, to a substantial degree, and always with the danger of not being restored in time to avoid collapse of government.

The possibility of restoration of these rights after the collapse is really remote. The collapse obliges the government official to accept dictatorial power which of course he will be reluctant to surrender. Indeed the advantages he enjoys by way of political power and prestige are bound to make him feel he needs more power to adjust matters. His self-interest will make logic and reason futile. *No intelligent person expects presidents or legislators to be unfriendly to a form of government which enhances their power, or to be other than fanatically hostile to movements which threaten to reduce such power.* The tendency not to relinquish power is proved by the travail which brought forth the manifold petitions and bills to restrain governmental authority. Probably the greatest difficulty in this matter lies in the fact that the associates of the dictator will not allow him to surrender his power, unless he does it to their advantage.

But even in normal times these discussed curtailments on governmental power are not as effective as alleged by the politician, for injustice abounds under all conditions. The price of civilization is blood, sweat and tears, and mostly from the innocent and helpless. Governments are conceived to modify the hardships involved in maintaining a civilization. However, no statesman ever expects to eliminate all of them.

The persistent attempts to curtail governmental power make conclusive evidence of how carelessly, readily and frequently government officials invade, nullify, disregard and destroy inherent rights in peacetime as well as in war. The Revolutionary War had to be fought to get adequate protection for inherent rights notwithstanding the fact that Great Britain had four charters to restrain government from interfering with them or destroying them.

The Bill appended to the Constitution, although it names no new rights, is the best summary of inherent rights, and like the Revolutionary War, is profound testimony that government officials are prone to destroy them. The summary is not perfect, evidenced by the controversy raging in the different branches of government, including the judiciary, as to its scope and significance.

The prime objective of these restraints of course is curtailment of governmental power. Concern in that field is always present because of the relationship of government to its subjects or citizens. It is not financially responsible to them in the usual sense of that word. It may without responsibility for damage freely experiment with tax money, although such funds constitute a trust of the most sacred character, being obtained by compulsion. Nowhere else does such power prevail. Government, therefore, can through its officials, in the name of humanity (it never is done under any other name), in spite of Bills, Petitions and Constitutions, by subterfuge and pretext (which the record shows it often does) call into play unnecessarily the Army and Navy, seize property without just compensation, quell assemblies, or cut off the right to strike, boycott or bargain, as well as cut off the right of business to protect itself against strikes. It cannot be sued as an equal, and actually can impose in many instances, any restriction it pleases, evidenced by the fact that it may call upon the citizen to surrender his life on the battlefield or as a matter of punishment.

It is because of this relationship to the citizen (the government's power to act without responsibility) that restraints must be imposed on its authority, the best way the citizen can devise.

So far Bills of Rights and Constitutions have been most effective, notwithstanding the fact that they are but self-admitted temporary (not permanent) restraints on government, and carry within themselves the seeds of modification, repeal or amendment, and may be faded out entirely if it is made to appear that they stand in the way of public welfare or social progress.

These attempts at restraint on government carry the implication that no person, no matter how intelligent, honest, righteous or kindhearted he may be, should have powers of the kind discussed without substantial limitations, and that society is only secure when these limitations are fearlessly imposed.

They aim to make the citizen free, not the government official; not only do they deny by implication that the king (government) can do wrong, or is particularly disposed to do right, but imply that he certainly will, as a human being, take advantage of his position and naturally resent and work out all kinds of schemes to overcome, avoid or defeat the restrictions it was sought to place upon him. These restraints also serve as methods to prevent private individuals from using government to oppress their fellowmen.

The Forefathers created no new branches of government. What they did was to more definitely prescribe and define the limitations, territories and fields or jurisdiction for the branches and political divisions of government.

Perhaps the time has come when these fields may be defined more clearly in order that there be not so much confusion with respect to what are the true functions of government, or what constitutes a dictatorship, a democratic, or a republican form of government.

CASES CITED

283

AUTHORITIES REFERRED TO

285